Gospel Patterns in Literature

Familiar Truths in Unexpected Places

Francis C. Rossow

Lutheran University Press
Minneapolis, Minnesota

Gospel Patterns in Literature
Familiar Truths in Unexpected Places
by Francis C. Rossow

Copyright 2008 Lutheran University Press, an imprint of 1517 Media. All rights reserved.

Library of Congress Cataloging-in-Publication Data

Rossow, Francis C., 1925-
  Gospel patterns in literature : familiar truths in unexpected places / Francis C. Rossow.
    p. cm.
  ISBN-13: 978-1-932688-31-3 (alk. paper)
  ISBN-10: 1-932688-31-5 (alk. paper)
  eISBN: 978-1-942304-55-5
 1. Religion and literature. 2. Incarnation in literature. 3. Christianity in literature. I. Title.
  PN49.R74 2008
  809'.9338226—dc22
                                  2008000018

Table of Contents

Introduction: 5

Part One: Intentional Gospel Patterns in Literature
Chapter One: *The Silver Chair* by C. S. Lewis 19
Chapter Two: *Brideshead Revisited* by Evelyn Waugh 30
Chapter Three: *The End of the Affair* by Graham Greene 37
Chapter Four: *Crime and Punishment* by Fyodor Dostoevsky 49
Chapter Five: *The Wayward Bus* by John Steinbeck 64
Chapter Six: *The Old Man and the Sea* by Ernest Hemingway 71

Part Two: Possible Gospel Patterns in Literature
Chapter Seven: Sir Gawain and the Green Knight 81
Chapter Eight: *Of Mice and Men* by John Steinbeck 90
Chapter Nine: *A Handful of Dust* by Evelyn Waugh 97
Chapter Ten: *Measure for Measure* by William Shakespeare 105
Chapter Eleven: *The Fall* by Albert Camus 114
Chapter Twelve: *The Rime of the Ancient Mariner* by Samuel Taylor
    Coleridge 123

Part Three: Unintentional Gospel Patterns in Literature
Chapter Thirteen: *The Picture of Dorian Gray* by Oscar Wilde 135
Chapter Fourteen: *The Eternal Husband* by Fyodor Dostoevsky ... 144
Chapter Fifteen: *Holes* by Louis Sachar 154
Chapter Sixteen: *The Adventures of Huckleberry Finn* by Mark Twain 165
Chapter Seventeen: *The Adventures of Tom Sawyer* by Mark Twain 174
Chapter Eighteen: Fairy Tales—An Analysis and Two Examples 180

Appendix: Gospel Themes in Other Areas 188

INTRODUCTION

How a Hunch Grew into a Thesis

Years ago when I read fairy tales to my children, I began to notice something intriguing. Again and again there appeared in these stories elements that were—or could be—reflections (often distortions of) familiar Christian truths, particularly that greatest of all Christian truths called the Gospel.

For example, so many of the fairy tales pictured the struggle between good and evil on a sub- or supra-human level. Could this, I wondered, reflect the classic conflict between God and Satan, between the kingdom of light and the kingdom of darkness? The frequent imposition in these tales of impossible tasks on ordinary mortals, tasks that could be accomplished only by supernatural aid—could this reflect that we can do all things only through Jesus Christ who strengthens us? Over and over in the fairy tales, the prince courts and marries the princess, often elevating her in rank, beauty, and/or character in the process. Might not this remind us of the marriage of Christ, the bridegroom, and his church, the bride—as well as all the glorious consequences for the bride of that marriage? Above all, there was that frequent refrain "and they lived happily ever after." Wasn't this, perhaps, a reminder of our hope that we shall live happily ever after in heaven with God, a hope that is not a fairy tale but solid truth itself? However varied or fantastic or even untrue the numerators in the fairy tales, there seemed to be these common biblical denominators. Admittedly, any one of these aspects of the fairy tales by itself was not particularly impressive. But it was their totality and their frequency that made me suspicious of the probability that the fairy tales were reflections of, distortions of, certain facets of the Gospel event.

Some years later, as a teacher of world literature, I noticed the same phenomenon in mythology. It, too, frequently echoed aspects of the Gospel event. Encountering the works of C. S. Lewis cemented this observation. For example, his novel *Till We Have Faces* suggests analogues between the Cupid-Psyche myth and Christianity. The imperfect and incomplete truth of the myth reflects—and in part distorts—the perfect, complete, and solid truth of the Christian Gospel.[1] In his more popular *Chronicles of Narnia*, Lewis juxtaposes real people from everyday life with such mythical creatures as giants, dwarfs, witches, dryads, satyrs, fauns, centaurs, and talking animals. What is so attractive about Lewis's approach is that, contrary to the usual contemporary practice, he endeavors to persuade us to believe in more rather than in less, to nudge mythology toward the level of biblical truth rather than to reduce biblical truth to the level of mythology. Instead of finding myth in the Bible, Lewis finds the Gospel in myth ("de-Gospelizing" the myth rather than demythologizing the Gospel). In short, Lewis tries to expand our faith rather than diminish it. Often he does this by standing the usual human perspective on its head, by putting the empirical, scientific approach on the defensive. There is a hilarious moment in *The Lion, the Witch and the Wardrobe* when a faun is shocked at encountering a real human being (rather than vice versa, as we might expect)—a faun, incidentally, who has in his library a book entitled *Is Man a Myth?* Whenever Lewis presents us with a fantasy world (Narnia, Malacandra, Perelandra) teeming with mythological creatures, he always depicts the ancient and classic confrontation between good and evil (God and Satan?), with God triumphing as often through acts of vicarious love and selflessness as through acts of power. Lewis's point seems to be—although the imperfect analogy is mine, not his—that where there's smoke, there's fire; that is, the frequency of mythological accounts of the struggle between good and evil argues the facticity of that struggle as depicted in the Scriptures.

The discovery excited me. I began to be on the lookout for reflections of the Gospel in many other areas. What I found changed my suspicion into a conviction. What modestly began as a hunch gradually evolved into the dignity of a thesis.

And this is the thesis: That central event of history called the Gospel event (the Son of God's incarnation, life, death, damnation, and resurrection for our salvation) has had so profound an impact on our world that it has spilled beyond the bounds chosen by God to contain it and convey it, namely divine revelation, the Holy Scriptures; that many aspects of the Gospel, such as God becoming man, the Creator sacrificing himself for the creature, the God-man dying and rising again, are in varying degrees of accuracy and completeness foreshadowed or reflected in literature.*

This book demonstrates the above thesis from the area of belletristic literature.[3]

But before embarking on that activity, I feel it necessary to acquaint the reader with both the dangers and the benefits that I see in my thesis concerning the Gospel's impact on literature.

The Dangers of the Thesis

Although my thesis is that divine revelation is not restricted to the Scriptures, we need to remind ourselves that accurate, sufficiently complete revelation is restricted to the Scriptures. Actually, this is a distinction many of us learned during childhood catechetical training under the heading, "The Natural Knowledge of God." It was pointed out then that we could learn something about God from the universe he created and from the conscience God gave to each of us. Towering mountains and galaxies of stars, for example, tell us of the majesty, power, and beauty of God. (See, for example, Psalm 19:1.) Conscience pangs tell us of God's holiness and justice. (See, for example, Romans 2:14-15.) But none of these tell us enough about God, nothing about God's disposition to save us from our sins, nothing about God's plan of salvation for us in Jesus Christ. To communicate that information, so indispensable to us, God gave us the Holy Scriptures. They—and they alone—tell us what we need to know about eternal life and what we need to know for leading God-pleasing

---

* Actually, my thesis at the time of its inception was much broader than this. It became my conviction that God's Gospel spills over into many other areas besides literature: nature, pagan religious beliefs and practices, items of human manufacture, art, music. Observations in these areas, too, played a significant role in the evolution of the thesis concerning literature stated above.

For a brief—and somewhat novel—treatment of the Gospel's impact on some of these areas, please consult the Appendix.

lives here on earth. We need to bear in mind the uniqueness of the divine revelation in the Holy Scriptures as we pursue this thesis. It is thrilling, even valuable—as I hope to demonstrate in this book—to recognize that the Gospel event has spilled over into other areas, that it surfaces in surprising places, "pops up" where it is least expected. But we will need to evaluate such echoes of the Gospel event always in terms of their correlation to and correspondence with the verbally inspired Scriptures, which alone (among writings) possess the virtue of inerrancy. "Thy word is truth" (John 17:17). And in such crucial areas as eternal salvation, sanctified Christian living, confessional purity, church union, we will need to rely exclusively on God's revelation in the Scriptures, not on such echoes of that revelation as may occur in nature, mythology, pagan religious beliefs and practices, items of human construct, music, art, and literature. While it is reassuring to the Christian to know that there are areas outside the Scriptures corroborating, in varying degrees, the presentation of the Gospel event in the Scriptures, such extra-biblical revelation, however useful it may prove to be, dare never be substituted for or made equivalent to the inspired, inerrant, wholly sufficient biblical revelation of the Gospel. At all costs the uniqueness of the Scriptures must be preserved. The purpose of my thesis is not to diminish the uniqueness and exclusivity of the Scriptures but rather to enhance our appreciation of the centrality and impact in our world of God's mighty saving acts in Christ.

There is danger, however, not merely in our stance toward Scripture. My thesis, if misunderstood or misused, can also endanger our stance toward literature. That danger, especially for a preacher, is to regard belletristic literature as little more than a source for sermon materials (especially illustrations) and to evaluate specific literary selections as good or bad depending upon the degree to which they supply such materials. We must not regard literary works as a mere mine from which we extract its theological ore and treat the rest as dross. Literature stands on its own merits and warrants our attention whether or not it meets the exigencies of the impending Sunday sermon or gratifies our theological expectations. Gospel pattern present or not, belletristic literature deserves to be read for its own sake. Even in those works where Gospel elements are clearly present, we must guard against converting art into catechism.

Another danger, for preacher and layman alike, is to become so enamored of the Gospel echo thesis that in our reading we see *only* it, rather than *also* it, thus ironically ending up with a narrowed perspective rather than a broadened one. Or, failing to see a Gospel pattern quickly or clearly enough upon a first reading, we may be tempted to force the pattern, to come up with it "by hook or by crook"—but mostly "by crook."

Faddishness is yet another danger. I am somewhat chagrined to discover that a thesis I thought relatively original at the time of its inception early in my ministry has in recent years become fashionable. Some current authors (whose names I withhold to protect the guilty) feel compelled, it seems, to insert some kind of Christ imagery into their writing, however riddling or inappropriate it may be, as a sop to a certain kind of reader or critic who feels a compulsion to ferret out such imagery or solve the riddle and then write a jargon-laden critique that will, it is hoped, advance a cause (a good grade, a degree, or tenure) as well as stimulate the sale of the book critiqued. Contemptible as I find this trend to be, even it inadvertently supports my thesis: The Gospel event does make its impact one way or another. Writers feel compelled to deal with it, for better or for worse. Perhaps I can join St. Paul in saying, "Notwithstanding, every way, whether in pretence or in truth, Christ is preached: and I therein do rejoice, yea, and will rejoice" (Philippians 1:18).

An overemphasis on reader subjectivity is a possible danger in our search for or recognition of Gospel elements in a work of literature. Aren't such elements likely to be more in the eye of the beholder than in the thing beheld, subjective rather than objective, eisegesis instead of exegesis, reading into instead of reading out of? Sometimes, no doubt, this is true. But granting this, it does not necessarily follow that my thesis is eliminated; it is only modified. If the Gospel event has not made an imprint on a specific literary work, it has had an impact on the Christian's perception of things. A Christian sees things—including belletristic literature—differently (and, I think, more perceptively as well). Thanks to the Holy Spirit, who through the Gospel has given faith in and understanding of the Gospel event, a Christian brings an added dimension also to the reading experience. Even on a purely human level this is true. One trained in Freudian theory, for example, sees meaning in *Hamlet* (to supply one instance) that the average reader misses—and may even stubbornly wish to continue to miss after he has encountered the Freudian interpretation! I, for one, believe that an interpretation of literature should be as objective as possible, that there should be something in the content, structure, symbolism, imagery, technique of a literary selection that the reader can point to in support of his interpretation. ("*Es steht geschrieben da.*") But, however objective our approach to literature is—and should be—the fact remains that any literary interpretation is affected by the experiences, background, education that we bring to that activity. What we get out of a book depends more than we care to admit upon what we bring to it. It does not follow from this that we should put a premium on subjectivity and reader whimsy. But it does follow that we should recognize the phenomenon, give it its due, and use whatever of value may accrue from it.

More serious than violating the substance or intention of a work of literature, I believe, is violating the spirit or tone of that work. Particularly is this true of books that are lighter fare: children's stories, tales of adventure, comedies. In a legitimate search for a moral or lesson (above all, a Gospel pattern or Gospel aspects), the reader must not make the mistake of chewing lemon meringue pie as if it were a porterhouse steak. Treating lighter genres too seriously is to sin against Alexander Pope's famous dictum to interpret a work of art "in the spirit the author writ" [sic]. We must be careful not to assign more freight to a literary genre than it is intended to carry. To see a lesson, moral, or Gospel element in a work of art must always be in keeping with the tone of the medium conveying that art. While adventure and humor may carry a serious message, we must not eliminate adventure and humor in the act of decanting that message. No one should reduce a work of art to a Sunday school lesson or a Gospel tract.

The Values of the Thesis

For those familiar with Christian doctrine, especially the doctrine of the Gospel, the presence of the Gospel in literature often gives Christian doctrine a new translation. Christian readers experience the joy of seeing familiar truths in unexpected settings and in new arrangements, the excitement of seeing much-loved doctrines in a fresh perspective. The result is considerable "reader identification"—always the mark of successful communication, whatever the genre.

But there is even greater value in such reader involvement than the being involved. To see Christian doctrine in a new perspective is sometimes to see it (really see it) for the first time—at the very least to see it better than before. Of course, there is always the possibility of altering the doctrine itself in the process of according it a new translation. Content can never be totally divorced from form. To change form can, admittedly, change the substance—and sometimes for the worse instead of for the better. But I fear that the dangers of not according Christian doctrine a new translation are even greater. The customary language for doctrine becomes so familiar we don't hear it, or, if we do, it goes in one ear and out the other. Familiarity may not only invite indifference, it may even breed contempt. But in belletristic literature Christian readers find the old wine of the Gospel in new wineskins and for that reason welcome it.

Not only does this increase our understanding of the Gospel—it's downright fun! It is reassuring to realize that the pivotal event in history we call the Gospel has hit our world with such impact that it has spilled beyond the bounds of Holy Scripture designed to contain and convey it. Isn't it thrilling to witness not only the Gospel's point of impact (in the Scriptures) but also to discover its ever-widening ripples (e.g., in literature). True, many of these ripples are faint and incomplete, nowhere nearly so recognizable and dependable as their source. But better some Gospel in unexpected places than none at all. So long as these ripples take us back to the point of impact of God's sufficient and accurate revelation in the Holy Scriptures, it argues their value and their purposiveness in God's scheme of things.

The presence of Gospel in literature can be equally effective for those unfamiliar with the Christian Gospel, even for those indifferent or hostile toward the Gospel. People who wouldn't be caught dead in a church may very well read a literary work that, perhaps unknown to them, contains Gospel. Their guard is lowered. Their defenses are down. In the familiar words of C. S. Lewis, the Gospel in literary format slips past "those watchful dragons" and "stained glass window associations" that have often inhibited the reception of the salvation story for those unacquainted with or inimical toward it.

Not only for those receiving the Gospel but also for those communicating it, the Gospel in literary format is helpful. Literature is rife with metaphor. Metaphor is a powerful vehicle for our Gospel witness. As the saying goes, "A picture is worth a thousand words." Metaphor is concrete rather than abstract, exciting rather than dull, understandable rather than perplexing, communicating rather than complicating. In my homiletics classes I have often risked the sweeping generalization that effectiveness in preaching is in direct proportion to the preacher's capacity for metaphor. Good literature (and especially poetry) can not only supply us with metaphors, but it can also serve as a catalyst to come up with our own metaphors to communicate the Christian Gospel.

Literature—at least good literature—suggests meaning as much as it states meaning directly (incidentally, a universally acknowledged literary virtue). It is implicit as well as explicit. It hints more than it spoonfeeds. In reply to a child in America who had written him for some writing tips, C. S. Lewis advised her not to use adjectives that merely tell the reader how the writer wants him or her to feel about the thing he is describing. "Instead of telling us a thing was 'terrible,'" Lewis continues, "describe it so that we'll be terrified. Don't say it was 'delightful,' make us say 'delightful' when we've read the description."[4] Exposure to the art of suggestion can refine the communication skills of public speakers. We can learn to supplement the explicit with the implicit in our Gospel communication. We can discover how ambiguity can enrich our clarity rather than obscure it. We can present levels of meaning without clouding, replacing, or negating the Gospel at its basic, simplest level. We can rise above cliché and pat formulas. Besides, style is more caught than taught. Overt, conscious plagiarism is a crime, and most of us are sufficiently ethical to avoid it. Yet all of us are "unconscious plagiarists," absorbing via some sort of osmosis the style of those we read. As one reads, so one writes. Like Luther, Donne, Herbert, Marvell, Shakespeare, Greene, and many others, we can take the ordinary and trivial and clothe it with Gospel significance. We can redeem the language, that very language that God chose as a medium—together with water, wine, and bread—for communicating the Christ-event. "Whether therefore [we] eat, or drink, or whatsoever [we] do [read? write? speak?]," we do it "all to the glory of God" (1 Corinthians 10:31).

Christ's incarnation and the Holy Scriptures constitute the ultimate precedent for the effectiveness of language—both that of the books we read and our own. To better communicate his plan of salvation, more specifically, his holiness and his love (his Law and Gospel), God sent his Son to our world as a human being. By entering our history, becoming flesh and blood, living, dying, and rising again on our planet, Christ gave us a more concrete, a more tangible, a more complete revelation of God's saving plan. If you will, Christ gave the doctrine of God's holiness and love "a new translation." To be sure Christ did more than reveal or translate the plan of salvation—he accomplished it! Still Christ's incarnation is revelation too, revelation at its best, communication in its most effective mode: the abstract made concrete. As the evangelist puts it, "The Word was made flesh and dwelt among us, (and we beheld his glory, the glory as of the only begotten of the Father,) full of grace and truth" (John 1:14).

In addition, God has inspired an account in human language of God's plan of salvation and its implementation through Jesus Christ. Ordinarily, we call it the Bible. First the Word becomes flesh, then the Word becomes words—the words of the Holy Scriptures. The same divine humility that prompted God to send his Son as "a baby at a peasant-woman's breast, and later an arrested field-preacher in the hands of the Roman police" is also the humility that prompted God to provide the Holy Scriptures.[5] In short, language is incarnational—not only the inerrant language of the Bible but also our own language. Errant as our language can be, it nevertheless is an effective, God-chosen medium to communicate God's love. Language has magic in it. It packs a wallop. Hence communicators of Christian doctrine harness the power of language to the power of God's Word, not with the false assumption that by their efforts they are helping God do his job but with the prayerful hope that through their efforts the Word of God "as becometh it, may not be bound, but have free course and be preached to the joy and edifying of Christ's holy people." God's method is not exclusion (God without human language) nor is it cooperation (God plus human language); rather, it is transformation (God through human language). With that truth in mind communicators of Christian doctrine tap the magic of language, exploit the medium in their continual efforts to tell "the greatest story ever told."

Finally, the presence of Gospel in belletristic literature can help to remove the false dichotomy between the secular and the spiritual that permeates so much of our everyday thinking and living. All things in our world coming from the hand of one Maker, the Triune God, can be expected to resemble God and, therefore, reflect a high degree of unity. True, Satan and sin shattered this unity, bringing about a divide between the spiritual and the secular—more specifically, driving a wedge between the arts and biblical revelation. But Christ's atoning life, death, and resurrection have changed all that. They have impacted creation as well as people. They have reversed the process initiated by Satan and sin and have begun to join together again what Satan and sin had put asunder. Jesus' parabolic method is a dazzling example of the successful marriage of the spiritual and the secular. It is a comfort to know that whenever I pick up a novel or scientific journal, attend a concert, or visit an art museum, I am not vacating the spiritual realm for the secular. It is just possible that even in these activities I may encounter the Good News. Whatever I encounter is, of course, no substitute for hearing God's Word in church or reading the Scriptures at home. At best, the Gospel I meet in the realm of nature and the arts is always supplementary—in addition to God's established means of grace, not in place of. But every time we are exposed to the Good News in unexpected places, we are multiplying our Gospel opportunities.

The Approach to the Thesis

Aware of both the potential dangers and benefits, we are now ready to explore the Gospel aspects of a variety of literary works, a total of eighteen in all. I am considering these selections under three headings.

Part One: Intentional Gospel Patterns in Literature. In this section I will deal with those selections in which the authors deliberately weave the saving acts of Christ and/or their significance into the fabric of their respective works. Literary critics agree that the Gospel is present in these works and that the recognition by the reader of such Gospel insertions is consistent with authorial intention. Although not every critic may comment on the Gospel's presence, every critic concedes its presence—or at least does not deny its presence. Some critics may like its inclusion, others may dislike its inclusion, but no one argues its absence.

Part Two: Possible Gospel Patterns in Literature. In this section I will deal with literary works to which some reputable literary critics have accorded "Christian interpretations" that involve some or many elements of the Gospel. Other equally reputable critics, however, question the presence of Gospel elements in the works under consideration. Although I do not intend to enter into the debate, readers should be aware that not every one agrees with the presence of the Gospel that I have noted in a specific work. In short, the presence of the Gospel in the literary selections considered in this section is much more tenuous than that of the works dealt with in the first part described above.

Part Three: Unintentional Gospel Patterns in Literature. In this section I will attempt to demonstrate how certain aspects of the Christian Gospel may invade—or at least be found in—literary works in which such invasion or discovery was clearly not at all the author's intention and in which works, to my knowledge, no other critic or reader has noticed such an invasion or shared such a discovery. Although I may attempt to make a case for the presence of Gospel in the selections considered in this section, that argument should be taken with a grain of salt. The Gospel found may well be in the eye of this beholder rather than in the literary work beheld.

Study guides related to the specific literary selection under consideration are appended to each chapter. Although the chapter itself in each instance will focus exclusively on the Gospel characteristics of the selection under consideration, the study guides will deal with literary aspects of that selection as well as its Gospel characteristics (under the assumption that this book may fascilitate discussions about the relationship between literature and the Gospel). It is my intent that the questions submitted in the study guides jog the reader's imagination and curiosity, not restrict the reader to the issues raised. It is my hope that these questions will help the reader to see the issues they raise, but not to see only those issues.

A brief bibliography is appended to each chapter of the book, directing the reader to secondary sources that will shed additional light on the literary and/or theological issues dealt with in that chapter.

Notes

1. For a more detailed analysis of the Gospel elements in *Till We Have Faces*, see my article "De-Gospelizing a Myth: C. S. Lewis's *Till We Have Faces*" in *Concordia Journal*, October 2003 (Vol. 27, No. 4), 323-329.

2. C. S. Lewis, T*he Lion, the Witch and the Wardrobe* (New York: Collier Books, 1950), pp. 8 and 12.

3. Despite the fact that the word sounds so forbidding and so eminently unreadable, "belletristic" is a handy short cut, a convenient way of embracing in one term all such literary genres as poetry, drama, short stories, and novels. In short, belletristic literature is nontechnical writing, writing that we would not ordinarily use as a textbook, reference work, or how-to-manual.

4. W. H. Lewis (ed.), *Letters of C. S. Lewis* (New York: Harcourt, Brace and World, 1966), p. 271.

5. C. S. Lewis, "Introduction" in J. B. Phillips, *Letters to Young Churches: A Translation of the New Testament Epistles* (New York: The Macmillan Co., 1951), p. viii.

PART ONE

Intentional Gospel Patterns in Literature

The presence of the Gospel in the selections considered in Part One is, to my knowledge, not denied by any reader or critic. There may, of course, be debate about the quantity, quality, and desirability of that Gospel presence.

CHAPTER ONE

The Silver Chair
by C. S. Lewis

Of the six works I have chosen to illustrate intentional Gospel patterns in literature, C. S. Lewis's *The Silver Chair* provides the most obvious demonstration. Actually, any member of The Chronicles of Narnia would suit our purpose. All readers of the Narnian tales see some resemblances between their content and the Christian Gospel—although not all agree on the quantity of those resemblances nor on their literary and/or theological quality.

Before we detail these resemblances, however, a caution is in order. The Chronicles of Narnia are not allegories. There is no one-to-one correspondence between the ingredients of the C. S. Lewis tales and biblical revelation. The minute we attempt to establish such a correspondence, we soon discover it will not work. At best the correspondence is only partial. This realization may impel us to the more modest claim that if the Narnian tales are not allegories, they are at least allegorical; that is, there are clearly some correspondences between elements of the chronicles and biblical revelation. But even this approach runs the risk of failing to see that the Narnian chronicles are children's adventure stories in their own right. They don't necessarily "stand for" or "represent" elements in Christianity.

A safer approach, one that allows the reader to appreciate the stories themselves and yet vibrate to their Gospel overtones, is to regard the Narnian chronicles as "suppositional" (an approach suggested by Lewis and popularized by Peter Schakel). That is, suppose that God created another world called Narnia. Suppose that this Narnia, like our Earth, in some sense "fell into sin" under the spell of a demonic creature (Jadis, alias the White Witch, alias the Lady of the Green Kirtle). Suppose that God in compassion resolves to save Narnia even as God saved our planet. Such a plan proceeding from the same divine Source will understandably bear some resemblance to God's plan for saving Earth. But God never repeats himself. Besides, Narnia is largely a world of fallen animals (ordinary, talking, and mythical animals). Even as God sent the Son as a person to save fallen people, so "the Emperor-over-the-Sea" (God) sends his Son, Aslan, as an animal (specifically, a lion) to save fallen animals. A lion is the shape the incarnation of the Second Person of the Trinity might have taken to save a largely animal world.[1]

This "suppositional" approach recognizes certain parallels between God's plan of salvation for Narnia and God's plan of salvation for Earth. At the same time this approach discourages air-tight equivalencies. Above all, the "suppositional" approach leaves each chronicle intact as a children's adventure story in its own right, rather than reducing it to a mere set of symbols for Christian events and teachings. Not to see any similarities at all between the Narnian tales and biblical revelation is to be imperceptive. But to see too many of them is to risk transforming narrative into religious tract.

Early hints in *The Silver Chair* that this chronicle might be something more than the account of the adventures of Eustace Scrubb and Jill Pole is that the former is described as "Son of Adam" and the latter as "Daughter of Eve"[2] and "Human Child" (22). That is, Eustace and Jill are not merely a boy and a girl. They are also representative of the human race.

Fleeing bullies at Experiment House, the school they attend, the two children resort to what Eustace calls Magic, calling upon Aslan for rescue. Yet in so doing Eustace avoids the temptation to draw circles and recite charms and spells for fear that "it would look as if we thought we could make [Aslan] do things" (7). "But really," he continues, "we can only ask him" (7). To their surprise, even as they call upon Aslan for help and run for an exit normally locked, Aslan answers. They find the exit open and escape. Later Jill learns from Aslan, "You would not have called to me unless I had been calling to you" (23). The entire episode suggests a lot about Christian prayer without ever using that theological term: a sort of magic, and yet too simple to be called that, for it's really "Ask, and it will be given you" (Luke 11:9); God's eagerness and alacrity in answering ("While they are yet speaking, I will hear," Isaiah 65:24); and the fact that it is God who prompted the request to begin with.

Eustace and Jill escape to "That Place." (Note the capital letters.) Eustace "pulled her [Jill] through the door, out of the school grounds, out of England, *out of our whole world* (my emphasis) into That Place" (12). Called "Aslan's country" in other Narnian chronicles, That Place is to Aslan and Narnians what God's home, heaven, is to Christ and Christians. It is shortly after the children's arrival in Aslan's country that we encounter the first major Gospel element in the novel. Approaching a cliff's edge below which yawns an incredibly deep chasm, Jill, more comfortable with heights than Eustace, "shows off" and bargains for more than even her customary courage can handle. Paralyzed by fear, Jill is unable to move away from the cliff's edge. In an effort to retrieve her, Eustace struggles with Jill and accidentally plunges over the edge. Quick as a flash, a lion (Aslan) appears and by blowing vigorously from his wide-opened mouth causes the fallen Eustace to float in the air like a feather to safety in the land of Narnia below.

It is easy to see in this dramatic episode some similarity to the biblical account of Adam and Eve's fall into sin. There are a male and a female; Jill, like Eve, is instrumental in her male companion's fall (not a metaphor in Eustace's case); and death seems to be the inevitable outcome for Eustace. So far, of course, we have only Law pattern. But Aslan's prompt rescue of Eustace introduces Gospel, a Gospel, however, that is different (at this point at least) from the proto-evangelium of Genesis 3—and it is that difference that inhibits treating the episode as an allegory. Aslan's manner of rescuing Eustace may call to mind the Holy Spirit (*ruach*, breath), or Jesus' breathing upon his disciples to empower them (John 20:22), or even (if we focus on Eustace) on the frequent Gospel metaphor in the Old Testament of being carried on the wings of an eagle. The biblical overtones are impossible to ignore. At the same time they elude precise and specific identification—a recurring paradox throughout Lewis's novels.

The "conversation" between Aslan and Jill that follows Eustace's fall and rescue introduces us to one of the greatest Gospel moments in *The Silver Chair*. Impelled by thirst, Jill seeks to get a drink from a nearby stream. However, the lion lies between her and the water. He invites her to drink. She asks him to go away, but he declines her request. She wants assurances that he won't do anything to her if she does drink. "I make no promise," the lion replies (21). "I daren't come and drink," Jill complains (21) even though she had acknowledged earlier that she is "*dying of thirst*" (20; Lewis's emphasis). If she doesn't drink, Aslan assures her, "you will die of thirst" (21). Volunteering to find water elsewhere, Jill is told, "There is no other stream" (21). Desperately, Jill drinks from the stream and finds the water to be more immediately and more permanently satisfying than any drink she had ever experienced. Although the lion doesn't eat her, as Jill had feared, he does force her to admit her complicity in Eustace's fall into the chasm by her "showing off" and tells her, "Do so no more" (22). Jill is surprised to find herself instinctively calling the lion, "Sir." "Then you are Somebody, Sir?" Jill asks. The lion replies, "I am" (23).

Look at the Gospel possibilities in this episode. So much of it is reminiscent of the encounter between Jesus and the woman at the well in the fourth chapter of John's gospel. The literal water becomes ultimately a metaphor for the water of salvation. Both the girl in the one case and the woman in the other case are persuaded to acknowlege their wrong-doing. The appellation "Sir" applied to Aslan is also applied to Christ ("Sir, I see that you are a prophet," John 4:19). Yet there are obvious differences too, not the least of which is that it is Jesus who, initially, asks the woman for a drink in John's account. And the "Do so no more" that Aslan urges upon Jill echoes a different biblical encounter between Jesus and a woman, the account of the adulterous woman in the eighth chapter of John's gospel, where Jesus tells the woman, "Neither do I condemn thee: *go, and sin no more*" (John 8:11; my emphasis). Aslan's "I am" reply (frequent in the Narnian chronicles) echoes the many "I am" statements of our Lord (suggesting the deity of both speakers). Aslan's observation, "There is no other stream," is faintly reminiscent of Jesus' claim, "I am the way, and the truth, and the life. No one comes to the Father except through me" (John 14:6). What we have in this remarkable episode in *The Silver Chair* is a host of tantalizing but imperfect echoes from a variety of biblical sources, suggesting that Lewis's Gospel inclusions are more like unforeseen leakage from his abundance of biblical knowlege rather than a conscious attempt at an allegory of the Gospel.

Commissioning Jill to join Eustace in a quest for Rilian, a lost prince and heir to the throne of Narnia, Aslan similarly "blows" Jill to Narnia, where Eustace had preceded her. But first he gives her Four Signs to guide them in their search. Despite there being four rather than ten, the reader immediately associates the signs with the decalogue, especially when Aslan urges Jill to memorize the signs, repeat them over and over, and depend absolutely upon their guidance. (See Deuteronomy 6:6-9.) Yet the repeated failure of Jill and Eustace to remember and follow the signs, with catastrophe in every instance averted only by Aslan's intervention, suggests the familiar truth that no one can keep the Law of God unless God assists. Human failure necessitates God's grace.

After a lengthy search riddled with many adventures, Jill, Eustace, and Puddleglum, their marshwiggle companion, are taken prisoner by the Earthmen of Underland and transported to their Queen. Upon their arrival at the Queen's palace, they learn that she is temporarily absent. In the meantime they are entertained by a young man who, unbeknownst to them (and even to himself), is the object of their search, Prince Rilian. He claims that the Queen has rescued him from an evil enchantment and has promised him a kingship in the Overworld. But, he confides to them, every night his evil enchantment returns for a period during which he is bound to a silver chair until the spell passes. Feeling the charm approaching, the young man voluntarily undergoes his confinement in the chair, warning the prisoners under no circumstances to listen to his pleas for help during that interval or to carry out any command he might issue. They agree. The spell begins. In the course of his supposed ravings, the young man divulges that now is really the hour of sanity and reality and that the time he is *not* bound to the chair is the period of evil enchantment. Jill, Eustace, and Puddleglum dutifully resist his pleas and commands—until he invokes their aid in the name of Aslan, one of the Four Signs Aslan had given Jill that they were to heed. Despite his fears of what might happen, Puddleglum persuades Jill and Eustace that they have no choice but to obey Aslan's sign. They free the young man, who then reveals himself as Prince Rilian. The Queen, he informs them, is the Lady of the Green Kirtle, the witch who had kidnapped and enchanted him.

Before they can escape, the Queen returns and subtly begins to put them all under an enchantment with her soothing sophistries accompanied by the music of her mandolin and the "sweet and drowsy smell" emanating from a green powder she sprinkled in the fireplace. Once again it is Puddleglum to the rescue. Bravely, he stamps out the fire, severely burning his webbed foot in the process, but ending the wicked enchantment. At that moment the beautiful Queen turns into a green serpent and coils herself around the Prince's legs. In the ensuing struggle they hack off the serpent's head. Not only is the group freed but so are all the creatures of Underland. Their silence is broken. They dance and talk and explode firecrackers.

Surely, the serpent form the Queen relapses into is reminiscent of the form Satan assumed when he corrupted Adam and Eve. And, surely, cutting off her head calls to mind for the Christian reader the words of Genesis 3:15: "He [the woman's seed] will strike her head."

But this is not the only echo of Genesis 3:15 in *The Silver Chair*. Another part of that Bible verse prophesies that Satan shall bruise the future Savior's heel. ("You will strike his heel.") Although Satan will "get the worst end of it," Christ, the victor, will not go unscathed. In the final chapter of *The Silver Chair*, just after witnessing the death of King Caspian, Prince Rilian's father, Aslan whisks Jill and Eustace back to Aslan's country. When they arrive, they see the body of King Caspian lying on the gravel bed of a clear stream (a common metaphor for death). Even Aslan weeps huge lion tears at the sight. Suddenly, he comands Eustace to pluck a thorn from a nearby thicket and jab it into the lion's right front foot. Reluctantly, Eustace obeys. When he plunges the foot-long thorn into Aslan's paw, a huge drop of blood issues from the wound, splashing into the stream immediately above the corpse of the king. Not only is King Caspian resurrected, but also his youth and vigor are restored. In the ecstatic reunion scene that follows, Eustace suddenly checks his mirth with a worried question, "Hasn't he—er—died?" Eustace's question causes the resurrected king to call Eustace an ass and it prompts Aslan to reply, "He has died. Most people have, you know. Even I have" (213).

In this scene are echoes of some familiar Christian teachings: physical death and subsequent bodily resurrection to life in heaven (alias Aslan's country) and the role of Christ's saving blood in effecting that miracle. But there is more in the scene—much more. The fact that Aslan's paw is wounded completes the echo of Genesis 3:15, the assurance that in this victorious struggle with Satan and sin Christ's heel would be bruised—it would be a painful and costly victory for him. The use of the thorn, for example, calls to mind not only the crown of thorns in our Savior's Passion but also the thorns (along with thistles and sweat, Genesis 3:18-19) symbolizing the consequences of the sin of Adam and Eve which necessitated the shedding of Christ's blood for salvation. The lion's tears remind the reader of Jesus weeping at Lazarus' tomb. The matter of fact, even humorous dismissal of Eustace's reservations about Caspian's prior death portray the joy we will experience at the time of our bodily resurrection. Tucked into the middle of this humorous exchange is an ever-so-casual allusion to the death of Aslan (Christ) and the incarnation that made that death possible. "He [Caspian] has died. Most people have, you know. Even I have." That same remark, incidentally, hints at the familiar syllogistic premise, "All men are mortal." Perhaps even the fact that Eustace plunges the thorn into Aslan's paw is not only a reminder of our involvement in our Lord's death (we were indeed there when they crucified our Lord), but also an encouragement to us to tell and apply "the saving Gospel" to the human condition. Whether these latter inferences can be legitimated or not, certainly the scene calls to mind an earlier incident in *The Silver Chair* where Puddleglum injures his foot in stamping out the deadly enchantment—an event not only functioning as dramatic foreshadowing of Aslan's wounded foot but also suggesting the scriptural parallel that we are to be little Christs by living vicariously.

This episode is the most Gospel-permeated in the entire novel, and it gives us a glimpse into Lewis's methodology. Look at all the Christian doctrines associated with a thorn-wounded lion's paw! So much from so little. Lewis's metaphors explode with possible meanings. Whenever Lewis throws a Gospel rock into the water, the reader not only recognizes the point of mpact but also experiences the thrill of seeing an ever-widening circle of doctrinal ripples. Where will it stop?

Immediately after Caspian's resurrection, Jill and Eustace are returned to England. Caspian, though now a permanent resident in Aslan's country, is allowed, at his request, temporarily to accompany them to see their world. He worries about the integrity of his request, but Aslan assures him, "You cannot want wrong things any more, now that you have died, my son" (254). The assurance echoes the Christian hope of God-given perfection in heaven. So Caspian and even Aslan accompany Jill and Eustace back to Experiment House, the place where the novel began. They destroy the school, ending its reign of bullyism and vacuous education. Despite the frequent (and possibly deserved) criticism leveled by critics and readers alike at this episode for trivializing the first moments of Caspian's new life in Aslan's country and for venting Lewis's beef with certain types of contemporary education, the scene does suggest the power of the Gospel for everyday behavior. It clarifies that the Gospel is a power for sanctification, not just for salvation; a power for this life as well as the next one.[3] After all, Caspian, Eustace, and Jill achieve what they do, not by their own power, but by the power of Aslan, who accompanies them.[4]

Finally, a word about Underland and the liberation of the Earthmen after the witch's death. What, if anything, does it signify? C. S. Lewis literary criticism is rife with suggestions about what it represents: 1) an image of the mythological world of the dead (Totenreich, Hades, Sheol);[5] 2) hell or, more specifically, the harrowing of hell; 3) purgatory; 4) a mere metaphor for the kingdom of darkness; or, most simply, 5) another fantasy world (like Narnia) that Lewis creates. In my opinion, the last suggestion is the simplest and most defensible. Although attractive arguments can be advanced for each of the first four positions, those arguments always, in my experience, break down in the face of challenging opposing arguments. We are reminded that this is a novel, after all, and not a theological treatise or a religious allegory. It is ultimately a fantasy tale designed to delight children—and the child in every adult. The question, "What does Underland stand for?" is, to use Falstaff's words, "A question not to be asked."

Notes

1. The lion is a superb choice. His majestic appearance, stern mien, terrifying roar, and powerful limbs are appropriate to the Second Person of the Godhead's divine nature. At the same time His sweet breath, soft fur, gentle feet, and kitten-like playfulness are appropriate to the Second Person of the Godhead's human nature. Besides, the lion metaphor has biblical warrant and Messianic implications. (See Jer. 50:44, Lam. 3:10, Hosea 11:10, and especially Rev. 5:5.)
2. C. S. Lewis, *The Silver Chair* (New York: Harper Collins Publishers, 1994), 40. All future page locations for citations from this book will be included in parentheses in the text of this chapter.
3. The title of the chapter containing this episode, "The Healing of Harms," seems to support this inference.
4. Reminiscent of Exodus 33:23 is the fact that Aslan, however, allows his enemies in this instance to see only his back (253).
5. Pagan religious beliefs and mythlogical phenomena in Lewis's works are at worst a distortion of biblical truth and at best a foreshadowing or reflection of that truth.

Study Guide for *The Silver Chair*

1. Notice Lewis's quarrel with modern education throughout the novel, especially in the opening and closing pages. In what respects is Lewis legitimately vulnerable to criticism for the inclusion of this subject? How can its inclusion be justified thematically? (See especially pages 187-189.) How can its inclusion be justified structurally? (Compare the first and third paragraphs of the opening chapter; then compare pages 1-2 with pages 254-257. What do both items in the foregoing comparison have in common?)

2. What hints does Lewis provide the protagonists in the novel that the invitation to the Autumn Feast on page 91 has a different meaning than the one understood by the protagonists? Read carefully "the moment of truth" on pages 134-135 and comment on Lewis's narrative skill in handling this episode. Point out an element of poetic justice in the episode.

3. How does humor enhance Lewis's narrative skill?

4. Notice Lewis's skill in making us more accepting of other creatures's value systems and, simultaneously, more suspicious of our own (e. g., the owls's fondness for night and the gnomes's fondness for subterranean life).

5. How are owl speech and giant speech consistent with their respective natures?

6. What refrain occurs frequently in Underworld? How does Lewis provide a pleasing variation?

7. How does Lewis achieve "unity in diversity" in The Chronicles of Narnia? (See especially pages 28, 46, 58, 61, 218, and 240.)

8. Itemize the ingredients in Puddleglum's characterization that make him one of Lewis's most memorable characters.

9. What people and place designations tip the reader off to the allegorical overtones of this novel?

10. How do the early pages of the novel enhance our understanding of prayer?

11. What are the allegorical possibilities of the "accident" that befalls Eustace early in the novel?

12. What characteristics and actions of Aslan associate him with Christ?

13. What biblical incident is echoed in the first encounter between Jill and Aslan?

14. How does Chapter 12 contribute to our understanding of evil? What is significant about the shape into which the Queen of Underworld changes? Compare this transformation with Prince Rilian's comment on page 161 about her race and agelessness.

15. What is the interpretative significance of the Dwarf's comment at the end of Chapter 15?

16. What might be the Christian equivalent to the signs? (See Deuteronomy 6:6-9.)

17. Note the mixture of Christianity and mythology in Lewis's portrait of Underland. What truth does Lewis mean to suggest through this combination? What is Underland? Why is this question difficult to answer? What caution should be inferred from this interpretative difficulty?

18. What action of Puddleglum parallels a later action by Aslan? What is the literary significance of this similarity? The theological significance?

19. What might be the Christian equivalent to Aslan's country (pages 10-26 and 250-254)?

20. What biblical incidents may be echoed on pages 254-255?

21. How does the last sentence of the novel serve Lewis's purpose? (See also page 232.)

22. Point out symmetry in the arrangement of the countries visited in this chronicle.

23. Explore Lewis's use of the four elements: fire, air, earth, and water.

For Further Reading

Adey, Lionel. *C. S. Lewis: Writer, Dreamer, and Mentor.* Grand Rapids: William B. Eerdmans, 1998.

Gibson, Evan K. *C. S. Lewis: Spinner of Tales.* Grand Rapids: Christian University Press, 1980.

Glover, Donald E. *C. S. Lewis: The Art of Enchantment.* Athens, Ohio: Ohio University Press, 1981.

Hooper, Walter. *Past Watchful Dragons: The Narnian Chronicles of C. S. Lewis.* New York: Collier Books, 1971.

Kilby, Clyde S. *Images of Salvation in the Fiction of C. S. Lewis.* Wheaton, Illinois: Harold Shaw Publishers, 1978.

Manlove, Colin. *C. S. Lewis: His Literary Achievement.* New York: St. Martin's Press, 1987.

———. *The Chronicles of Narnia: The Patterning of a Fantastic World.* New York: Twayne Publishers, 1993.

Myers, Doris T. *C. S. Lewis in Context.* Kent, Ohio: The Kent State University Press, 1994.

Sammons, Martha C. *A Guide through Narnia.* Wheaton, Illinois: Harold Shaw Publishers, 1979.

Schakel, Peter J. *Imagination and the Arts in C. S. Lewis: Journeying to Narnia and Other Worlds.* Columbia, Missouri: The University of Missouri Press, 2002.

———.(ed) *The Longing for a Form: Essays on the Fiction of C. S. Lewis.* Grand Rapids: Baker Book House, 1977.

———. *Reading with the Heart: The Way into Narnia.* Grand Rapids: William B. Eerdmans, 1979.

CHAPTER TWO

Brideshead Revisited
by Evelyn Waugh

In Romans 8:38-39 Paul says, "I am convinced, that neither death, nor life, nor angels, nor rulers, nor things present, nor things to come, nor powers, Nor height, nor depth, nor anything else in all creation, will be able to separate us from the love of God in Christ Jesus our Lord." The passage calls attention to the marriage of God's omnipotence to God's compassion. It assures us that God's almighty power is buttressing and implementing God's fabulous love. There is nothing namby-pamby about God's love. It has teeth in it. God is dead serious about saving us. God means business. God intends to see it through. Blessed are we!

A well-known poem that captures the assurance of Romans 8:38-39 is Francis Thompson's "The Hound of Heaven." In this ode Thompson uses the metaphor of a hound to describe God's relentless love—a strange metaphor when you consider the unflattering portrait of dogs, for the most part, in the Bible. The point of the poem is that God's love pursues us, hunts us, hounds us, harasses us to our salvation. God will not let us get away.

A different metaphor for God's persistent love emerges in *Brideshead Revisited*, an early twentieth century English novel by Evelyn Waugh. *Brideshead Revisited* is the story about the involvement of Charles Ryder, the protagonist, with the Flyte family residing at the family mansion called Brideshead. On a deeper level, however, the book turns out to be the story of the involvement of God, the real protagonist, with the Flyte family and the impact of that involvement on Charles Ryder. The novel focuses on God's dealings with the more ornery, resistant members of the

Flyte family—specifically three of them: Sebastain, an alcoholic; Julia, a divorcee and an adulteress; and their father, Lord Marchmain, a dropout from the Roman Catholic Church. The metaphor Waugh uses to describe God's dealings with these three is one borrowed from G. K. Chesterton's Father Brown detective stories: a twitch upon the thread.[1] To paraphrase the language of the novel, God catches the human being with an unseen hook and with an invisible line long enough to let the person wander to the ends of the earth, bringing him back with a twitch upon the thread.

Consider how God employs this hook and line approach on each of the three.

First of all, Sebastian. Sebastian and Charles Ryder become intimate friends at Oxford University. Loners most of the time, their only occasional social contacts are with a dissolute, disreputable crowd. Sebastian and Charles enjoy an increasing number of drinking orgies. Charles is an agnostic. Sebastian's contact with the Roman Catholic Church is largely ritualistic. He crosses himself, genuflects, dips his finger in holy water, but, unlike his friend, does believe the Gospel to be a historical fact. He candidly admits, however, that the Christian doctrines he believes to be true have had little impact on his everyday behavior, a behavior not at all distinguishable from that of his agnostic friend.

When Sebastian drives Charles to his Brideshead mansion, Charles is surprised to hear him refer to it not as his home, but as the place where his family lives. It becomes increasingly obvious to Charles that Sebastian is uncomfortable with his family and protects Charles from meeting them, viewing them as a threat to their newly-found friendship. Particularly, Sebastian is uneasy about his mother who, he admits, is a genuine saint, a persistent but devout practitioner of the faith. A teddy-bear that Sebastian always carries with him functions as a sort of security blanket for Sebastian and foreshadows the more dangerous refuge he will someday seek in the liquor he imbibes in such great quantity.

Things go from bad to worse for Sebastian. Arrested for drunk driving and flunking out of college, he becomes an alcoholic and eventually drifts out of the country into Africa, living there with a dishonorably discharged German soldier who sponges off him. Ultimately, Sebastian dies of alcoholism in a monastery hospital.

But now the surprise. Years later Charles learns that Sebastian was viewed by his monastery companions not at all with horror or disgust and not merely with amused detachment, but rather with genuine affection. They loved him and thought of him as "a good man" (304), "near and dear to God" (308), not only "a very holy . . . man" himself but capable of recognizing holiness in others (305). Sebastian died, most likely after another of his drinking sprees, showing by a flicker of his eyelid that he was conscious when they gave him the sacrament (309). His holiness, Cordelia informs Charles, was the outgrowth of his self-inflicted but God-guided suffering. Sebastian ran with the line most of his life, but God's repeated twitches upon the thread brought Sebastian safely back into God's net at last. Nothing, neither dissolute life nor disgraceful death—not even alcoholism—separated Sebastian from God's love for Sebastian in Jesus Christ.

Julia, Sebastian's sister, is an equally interesting case study of God's tenacious grace. Initially a hit in the London social swirl, Julia falls in love with and eventually marries Rex Mottram. Because he is a divorced man, the marriage is not sanctioned by Julia's church or family. The marriage turns out to be a disastrous mistake—ultimately even in Julia's eyes. Ostracized by both church and family, Julia becomes increasingly disillusioned with her husband and sues for divorce. On a ship sailing from New York to Southampton, Julia encounters Charles Ryder (who is about to divorce his wife), falls in love with him, and together they commit adultery. They decide to get married as soon as their respective divorce actions are complete.

But the marriage never comes off. After witnessing the deathbed conversion of her father (to be described below), Julia voluntarily withdraws from her illicit engagement to Charles, and Charles reluctantly accepts her decision. Julia admits that she has been bad—and will probably be bad again—but that the worse she is, the more she needs God. "I can't shut myself out from his mercy," she says almost frantically (340). Why this is happening she doesn't know—maybe it's a conspiracy of God to thwart the lovers (276), perhaps the power of a religious nursery jingle she recited in childhood (293), maybe because of the prayers of her family (340), possibly it's a private bargain between her and God (340)—but happening it is, and she can no longer escape it.

Once again God has twitched upon the thread in dealing with the Flyte family. Once again nothing—not even their own determination to pursue evil—separate them from God's love.

Most remarkable of those hauled in on God's line is Lord Marchmain, the head of the vagrant Flyte family. Living abroad with his mistress, Lord Marchmain rejects not only his wife but also his church. Even when he returns to Brideshead in order to die at home, he persistently—even embarrassingly—resists the efforts of the loyal Catholics in his family to persuade him to return to the church. He rudely dismisses a priest invited by the family to minister to his spiritual needs.

But the family persists. When Lord Marchmain is unconscious and near death, they "force" a priest upon their father. Charles Ryder vigorously opposes the action, describing it variously as "superstition," "hypocrisy," "trickery," "witchcraft," "tomfoolery," and "mumbo-jumbo." He threatens to discard whatever respect he has retained for the church if it comes now, when the sick man's mind is wandering and he is unable to resist, and then claim him as a deathbed penitent. But, to his own shock, even agnostic Charles, during the priest's administration of last rites to the dying man, begins to hope for some sign of consciousness from Lord Marchmain, some evidence of assent to the grace of God the priest is offering. The sign is given: Lord Marchmain voluntarily makes a recognizable sign of the cross and dies shortly thereafter. In the priest's own words as he leaves the house: "Well, now . . . that was a beautiful thing to see. I've known it to happen that way again and again. The devil resists to the last moment, and then the grace of God is too much for him" (339).

How does all of this affect Charles Ryder, the protagonist? No doubt, the Christian reader would prefer a sort of Damascus-road experience for Charles near the end of the novel, and have him—literally—live happily ever after. But Evelyn Waugh is too skilled a writer to tie up all the loose ends and contrive an ending that will strain reader credibility. He leaves the issue of what eventually happens to Charles Ryder uncertain. But Waugh makes it clear that God's dealings with the Flyte family do impact the protagonist, and he reminds us that both Cordelia and Lady Marchmain are praying for Charles (93, 138)—and they are accustomed to having their prayers answered! Ryder himself describes his reaction to God's dealings as similar to that of a hunter trapped by a blizzard in a lonely arctic cabin suddenly assaulted, just when he thinks the ordeal is over, by a subsequent avalanche sweeping away everything in its path including his present shelter (310-311, 326, 341). The analogy suggests that God's triumph over Charles Ryder is just a question of time, that God's invisible hook has caught him too and that, given a few twitches upon the thread, Ryder also will come—fighting and flopping—but blessed in his ignorance—into the safety of God's net.

Even the title of Waugh's novel may suggest the delightful inexorableness of God's love in Jesus Christ. Technically, that title refers to a mansion called Brideshead that the protagonist visits twice: the first time during World War I (the setting for the body of the novel), the second time ("revisited") years later during World War II (the setting for the prologue and epilogue framing the body of the novel). But the biblical bridegroom–bride metaphor for the Gospel informs the novel. God is the Bridegroom; the characters of the novel are the bride. "Brideshead," a synonym for "maidenhead,"[2] suggests that no matter how frequently and how despicably the bride misuses this particular feminine symbol of her marriage relationship with God, the Bridegroom, God, keeps coming back. God revisits the bride, the Church, never cavalierly overlooking her sin but never rejecting the sinner either, unshakable in love, relentless in pursuit of the bride's happiness, determined to cleanse her at any cost.[3]

Not all readers, understandably, will be happy at Evelyn Waugh's denominational bias. Some readers, undoubtedly, would prefer that the fish twitching on the Divine Fisherman's thread display more obvious goodness in their redeemed lives. However, the depiction, as far as it goes, is no more jarring than the vineyard owner of our Lord's parable paying full wages to the idle group last hired, Jesus calling a notorious tax collector into the intimate circle of his disciples, or the Savior promising immediate paradise to a thief executed with him. Whether entirely successful or not, Waugh intends to accent God's grace, not to endorse or encourage human evil. The moral of his novel is not "Go and sin some more," but rather, "Trust in the inexplicable mercy of God." His goal, I believe, has been to accent the ringing truth of Romans 8:38-39, that nothing—neither the phenomena Paul specifically mentions in those verses nor even human orneriness and human perversity—NOTHING can separate us from the love of God in Christ Jesus. Whether successful or not, I am convinced that his purpose is not to make us secure in our sins but rather to make us secure in God's love. Waugh does not intend to diminish the soul-threatening power of sin. Rather he means to emphasize that however great the power of sin is to destroy, the power of God's grace to save is greater. *Brideshead Revisited* accents the timeless power of God to express love for any person, at any time, under any conditions without soliciting clearance from any of us. Waugh, like St. Augustine, believes that God's mercy can be found during a person's fall from the bridge to the stream below.

Notes

1. Evelyn Waugh, *Brideshead Revisited* (Boston: Little, Brown and Company, 1945), 220. All future page locations for citations from this book will be included in parentheses in the text of this chapter.
2. That the words "brideshead" and "maidenhead" can be regarded as synonyms is clear from the extensive play on these two words in Thomas Hardy's *Jude the Obscure*.
3. This possibility is strengthened by the pun on "brideshead" Waugh himself suggests at the bottom of page 320. In response to Beryl's remark that she felt as though it were she who was leading in the bride in the ceremony of her marriage to Bridey, Lord Marchmain says, "It was said with great indelicacy. . . . Was she making a play on my son's name, or was she . . . referring to his undoubted virginity?"

Study Guide for *Brideshead Revisited*

1. What is unique about the structure of *Brideshead Revisited*? How does the title of the novel encapsulate its structure? What are the advantages of this arrangement of the book?

2. Describe the complex tone of the novel.

3. Comment on Waugh as a stylist and as an observer of human nature.

4. Demonstrate Waugh's uncanny skill at characterization.

5. What change of focus does Waugh announce on page 178? Is this change of focus, as one critic insists, a trick Waugh plays on the reader and a structural flaw in the novel?

6. Does Waugh have any other purpose in mind than to provide hilarious entertainment in his account of Rex's instruction for church membership?

7. Establish a connection between the title of Book II and the Gospel pattern in the novel.

8. Note the heavy use of dramatic irony on page 262.

9. How is the Gospel pattern in *Brideshead Revisited* amplified on page 288?

10. How might the passage at the bottom of page 302 and at the top of page 303 compel us to revise our thinking about the structure of the novel? Should *Brideshead Revisited* perhaps be divided into three parts?

11. Relate the last paragraph of Chapter Four (Book II) to the meaning of the novel.

12. Other than the fact that it poses the central question of the novel, what is the function of the discussion between Charles and Julia recorded on pages 324-330?

13. Is it a flaw in the novel that Lord Marchmain takes over the spotlight at the end?

14. Is the deathbed conversion of Lord Marchmain realistically presented? Has Evelyn Waugh written a novel, a Catholic tract, or a lampoon on Christianity?

15. Does Charles Ryder become a Christian?

16. Does the title of the novel have any thematic significance?

17. Point out significant symbols in the novel.

For Further Reading

Carens, James F. *The Satiric Art of Evelyn Waugh.* Seattle and London: University of Washington Press, 1946.

Cook, Jr., William J. *Masks, Modes, and Morals: The Art of Evelyn Waugh.* Cranbury, New Jersey: Associated University Presses, Inc., 1971.

Crabbe, Katharyn W. *Evelyn Waugh.* New York: Continuum Publishing Co., 1988.

Davis, Robert Murray. *Evelyn Waugh, Writer.* Norman Oklahoma: Pilgrim Press Books, Inc., 1981.

Garnett, Robert R. *From Grimes to Brideshead: The Early Novels of Evelyn Waugh.* London and Toronto: Associated University Presses, Inc., 1990.

Lane, Calvin W. *Evelyn Waugh.* Boston: Twayne Publishers, 1981.

Littlewood, Ian. *The Writings of Evelyn Waugh.* Oxford, England: Basil Blackwell Publisher Ltd., 1983.

Phillips, Gene D. *Evelyn Waugh's Officers, Gentlemen, and Rogues: The Fact Behind His Fiction.* Chicago: Nelson-Hall, 1975.

Wilson, John Howard. *Evelyn Waugh: A Literary Biography,* 1903-1924. London: Associated University Presses, Inc., 1996.

Wykes, David. *Evelyn Waugh: A Literary Life.* New York: St. Martin's Press, Inc., 1999.

CHAPTER THREE

The End of the Affair
by Graham Greene

Except for some stylistic variations, it's hard to believe that Graham Greene's *The End of the Affair* was not written by Evelyn Waugh. Not only were both authors adult converts to Roman Catholicism but also the same Gospel pattern that informs *Brideshead Revisited* permeates Greene's novel. That Gospel pattern is what is often called "The Hound of Heaven" motif (after the Francis Thompson poem by that name). How Romans 8:38-39 expresses God's relentless, persistent love for people in Jesus Christ has been pointed out in the immediately prior essay on *Brideshead Revisited*. An equally well-known biblical expression of this Gospel pattern—and one that may have inspired Francis Thompson's poem—can be found in Psalm 139:7-10: "Where can I go from your Spirit? Or where can I flee from your presence? If I ascend up to heaven, you are there; if I make my bed in sheol, you are there. If I take the wings of the morning and settle at the farthest limits of the sea, even there your hand shall lead me, and your right hand shall hold me fast." Could we not regard both the Waugh and Greene novels as dramatizations of the closing words of our Lord's Parable of the Great Supper: "Go out into the highways and hedges, and *compel* them to come in, that My house may be filled" (Luke 14:23; emphasis mine)?

Though presented in a decidedly non-sequential manner, the plot of *The End of the Affair* is a simple one. An author, Maurice Bendrix, interviews Sarah Miles, the attractive wife of a civil servant, in order to acquire authentic detail for the better development of the character of a government official in a future novel. Predictably, Bendrix falls in love with the interviewee and initiates an adulterous relationship with her.

In one of their assignations, their London trysting place is largely destroyed by a Nazi V-1 rocket. Looking for her lover in the debris, Sarah, unharmed, finds his body lying under a door, one arm protruding. Unable to lift the door, Sarah assumes that Bendrix is dead and in her panic breathes a prayer to God, "Let him be alive, and I will believe. . . . I'll give him up for ever, only let him be alive with a chance." 1 She then retreats to a more secure area of the demolished structure.

Some moments later Bendrix, knocked only unconscious by the blast, revives, extricates himself from the door on top of him, and finds Sarah. Startled, then pleased at the unexpected answer to her prayer, Sarah suddenly recalls—with pain—her careless vow to "give him up for ever" and reluctantly resolves to keep it. "Is one responsible for what one promises in hysteria?" she records in her diary (94). But she steels herself to do what she promised; she refuses to see Bendrix or return his phone calls.

Suspecting another lover, Bendrix, with the help of a detective named Parkis, spies on Sarah. Parkis not only reports that he has seen her visiting a certain Richard Smythe, but also hands over to Bendrix Sarah's diary that he had managed to procure. With morbid curiosity Bendrix plunges into her journal as a possible source for the identity of the rival who, he assumes, has replaced him in Sarah's affection.

That diary records conversations between Sarah and her lover, referred to vaguely only as "you" in the initial entries that Bendrix encounters, piquing Bendrix's curiosity even more. To his surprise—and the reader's—the lover is eventually identified as God! Many of the entries describe Sarah's reluctance to keep her vow but her inability to break it. She records efforts to renew her affair with Bendrix, but somehow God always foils those attempts. It develops that the Richard Smythe she has been seeing is merely an advocate for atheism whom Sarah visits in the hope of destroying the faith in God she has so unwillingly been gifted with. But Smythe's arguments only serve to convince Sarah of God's existence and love. God simply will not let Sarah go. "My disbelief made no difference to You," she writes in the diary entry for January 10, 1946 (113).

Once Bendrix (himself an atheist) discovers that he has only a divine opponent rather than a human one, he exults in the ease of the competition and renews his pursuit of Sarah. But she kindly and reluctantly rebuffs him, remaining loyal to God. Quite arbitrarily she catches a cold, develops pneumonia, and dies.

To spite the Lover who defeated him—and, paradoxically, whose existence he still refuses to accept—Bendrix talks Sarah's husband into cremating Sarah's body, Bendrix jeering at his Opponent, "Resurrect that body if you can!" (137). In the days that follow the funeral, the disclosures of Sarah's Christian faith snowball. A priest insists that she should have been given a Roman Catholic burial since Sarah had expressed an interest in joining his parish. An unwelcome encounter with Sarah's loquacious mother informs Bendrix that Sarah had been surreptitiously baptized as a child. Childhood books from Sarah's library contain scrawls betraying her preoccupation with God even in those tender years.

Apparently, her baptism "took" and "proved contagious" (to use Greene's imagery). Richard Smythe sheepishly confesses that he has abandoned his advocacy of atheism, the result of Sarah's influence on him and of her miraculous touch allegedly curing a disfiguration on his face. Parkis, the detective who spied on Sarah, expresses his admiration for the woman and acknowledges that the loan of one of her childhood books to Lance, his sick son, may have been a factor in his inexplicable recovery. Henry, Sarah's husband, not only charitably forgives Bendrix for cuckolding him but also begins to regret that he had not given his wife a Christian burial. At the report of all these "miracles," Bendrix struggles to insist that they are merely "coincidences." The novel ends with Bendrix complaining to God, "You've done enough. You've robbed me of enough . . . leave me alone for ever" (192).

The foremost feature of the Gospel emerging from the prior synopsis is the persistence, even insistence, of God's love. The Divine Lover will not quit—no matter what, He will not take no for an answer. Quite simply, God will not let Sarah go even when she struggles to escape. From a human perspective, God's love may seem troublesome; God appears to hound and harass. But from a divine perspective, God's love is saving and sanctifying, effecting our goodness and eternal happiness. Greene does not say all this, of course. In fact, he does not say it at all. After all, he's writing a novel, not a sermon. What preachers appropriately explain, artists appropriately suggest.

One wishes that Greene had emphasized the tenderness of God's love as much as he did its relentlessness. In Sarah's own words, "[God has] got mercy, only it's such an odd sort of mercy, it sometimes looks like punishment" (146). A mitigating factor, however, is that the perspective on God's love in this novel is largely that of an unbeliever, Maurice Bendrix, the protagonist, who finds God's love for Sarah inconvenient to his adulterous activities. In addition, Greene's portrait of God's saving activity errs in the direction of determinism rather than synergism (somewhat of a surprise from a Roman Catholic). But for all its heretical potential, Greene's picture of God's saving activity does underscore the biblical truth that our eternal salvation is God's doing, not ours.

This facet of the Gospel, God's monergism, is brought into sharper focus by the "reluctant convert" motif permeating *The End of the Affair*. Not only does Sarah herself, like St. Paul, "kick against the goads" but so does everyone else who gets tangled in the web of God's love for Sarah (and for them): Bendrix, Smythe, Henry, Parkis, and his son, Lance. The resistance of the last three mentioned is relatively mild, but that of Bendrix and Smythe is massive and aggressive. Yet by the end of the novel all of them find themselves, in varying degrees, swept up by God's overpowering love. Round and round God's love goes, and where it stops nobody knows.

Of these characters the ultimate fate of Bendrix is the most in doubt. Will Bendrix succumb to God's love or not? His closing words, "Leave me alone for ever," sound like a self-imposed hell. Yet a few passages in the novel suggest that Bendrix himself may be pulled into the orbit of God's love no matter how much he resists. The first is a dream Bendrix has of shooting at bottles in the booth of a midway at a fair. Even though all the bullets hit their targets, they bounce off without breaking them. In Bendrix's words, "I fired and fired, and not a bottle could I crack" (165). In another passage Bendrix concedes, "I felt like a swimmer who has overpassed his strength and knows the tide is stronger than himself" (189). Late in the novel Bendrix compares himself to the occasional character in his own writing experience that he had so much trouble successfully developing. If that character "had not been drawn," he had "certainly been dragged" (185). Then Bendrix makes the application to himself. "I can imagine a God feeling in just that way about some of us" in the divine drama that God authors (185). Ironically, Bendrix discovers that this very novel he has written (as the alleged mouthpiece of Graham Greene) was prompted by God. On the opening page he speculates whether he chose the images he uses "or did these images choose me? . . . if I had believed then in a God, I could also have believed in a hand, plucking at my elbow, a suggestion" (7). Even a careless prayer Bendrix mutters at one point, to be extricated from an undesired sexual encounter, he finds to his surprise to be answered. Like Sarah, he learns to be careful what you pray—it might just get answered. Clearly, all these instances portray the inability of Bendrix to ward off God's saving plan for Sarah. Possibly, they foreshadow also Bendrix's inability to ward off God's saving plan for himself. In my opinion, Bendrix's salvation is just a matter of time. Bendrix reminds me of the Gingerbread Man in the classic children's story who gleefully taunts each new threat he encounters with the refrain, "I ran away from [the baker, the farmer, the bull, etc.], and I can run away from you too, I can, I can."[2] But in the end he is snapped up by the fox, the author of the tale closing with the dubiously comforting assurance, "But, then, a Gingerbread Man is supposed to be eaten!" The Divine Fox, I believe, is too much for Bendrix, who "methinks, protests too much." After all, he is supposed be consumed by God's love.

    Wisely, Greene does not spell out this outcome. Bendrix's fate is left in doubt. Like any good artist, Greene neither ties up all the loose ends nor makes his story too good to be true. Bendrix is the protagonist with whom the author intends the reader to identify. He is we. And his future is a blank to be filled, even as ours is. That future can go either way, the way of perdition or the way of salvation. But if God decides, the way we go will be God's, the way of salvation. Come to think of it, neither does our Lord finish the account of the noble young man who "went away sorrowful: for he had great possessions" (Matthew 19:22), nor do we learn the final decision of the grumbling elder brother in the parable when his father invites him to join the celebration in honor of the just-returned prodigal son (Luke 15:31-32). The point in either instance seems to be that if any of us share the problem of the rich man or the elder brother, there still is time. The story need not be over.

What God intends the end of that story to be for us and for the characters in Graham Greene's novel is evident from the author's skillfully chosen title. *The End of the Affair* has multiple levels of meaning. It develops that the word "end" has at least three meanings: cessation, consequence, and goal. Thus *The End of the Affair* means 1) the cessation of the adulterous shenanigans between Sarah and Bendrix; 2) the consequences of the affair, its impact on their lives and the lives of others; and 3) God's end, God's saving and sanctifying objective, overruling and putting to good use the evil that the two have initiated. Even the word "affair" from the title, in the context of the rich ambiguity of the word "end," becomes more than a word with only sordid connotations. Sarah and Bendrix's unethical love affair is ultimately transformed into Sarah and God's divine love affair.

Two subsidiary religious themes in the novel, not Gospel in themselves yet relevant to the Gospel, have to do with prayer and miracles. Reference has already been made to God's answers to Sarah's desperate prayer for Bendrix's return to life and to Bendrix's thoughtless prayer (heretically through the intercession of "Saint Sarah") to be rescued from an unwanted woman. In both cases God came through with surprisingly swift answers. Noting that Sarah had died soon after praying in her journal, "Let me be happier. Let me die soon" (120), Bendrix wryly muses, "She seemed to have had a knack of getting her prayers answered even before they were spoken" (147). Although there is too much of the "be careful what you pray for you might just get it" in Greene's depiction of prayer, what he presents is an affirmation of the biblical "Ask, and it shall be given you." Besides, it is clear from the novel that Greene's intention is to accent the eagerness of God to answer prayer—not the power of supplicants to manipulate God with prayer. Artistically, Greene reinforces his accent on prayer with its comic counterpart in his portrait of Lance. Pretending to be sick as a ploy for facilitating Bendrix's entrance into Smythe's residence, Lance actually becomes sick in the house from wolfing down too much orange squash. "Be careful what you pray" is paralleled by "Be careful what you play"!

Greene's portrait of miracles is the other subsidiary religious theme in *The End of the Affair*. Inundated by the revelations of miracles in Sarah's lifetime and by miraculous happenings and conversions after her death, Bendrix stubbornly tries to dismiss them as coincidence. "I'll never lose my faith in coincidence," Bendrix insists to Henry (188). "I believe in magic even less that I believe in You," Bendrix scoffs at God. "Magic is your cross, your resurrection of the body, your holy Catholic church, your communion of saints" (164-165). "You can't mark a two-year-old child for life with a bit of water and a prayer," Bendrix continues. "If I began to believe that, I could believe in the body and the blood" (165). But as the miraculous continues to confront him, Bendrix despairs, "with a sense of weariness, how many coincidences are there going to be?" (189). Greene is too sophisticated to ram the supernatural and the miraculous down our empirical throats. But he does plant the seed of doubt in our positivist mind-set. In the words of Father Crompton, "I'm not against a bit of superstition. It gives people the idea that this world's not everything. . . . It could be the beginning of wisdom" (175).

The fact that the average reader probably anticipates only the first of the levels of meaning in the title of Greene's novel introduces us to the skill with which Greene conveys his Gospel theme. Expecting a book that may automatically flop open at the oft-consulted "juicy passages" concerning Sarah and Bendrix's affair (incidentally, there are no such passages), the reader ends up encountering God! The reader picks up a book ostensibly dealing with adultery and is assaulted by the Christian Gospel. Sarah herself in her journal muses over God's exploitation of her *eros* to bring her to *agape* (123). Even the more sophisticated reader who eschews cheap thrills and who welcomes materials dealing with both theology and art but ordinarily views them as best kept apart, will appreciate the artistry of Greene's mix of the two. There is nothing clumsy or cloying about Greene's religious theme; it does not intrude. The novel remains a novel. *The End of the Affair* is both good art and good theology.

We turn now to consideration of the suspension of disbelief devices (in addition to the title of the novel) by which Graham Greene accomplishes his artistic/theological goal. Suspension of disbelief techniques are designed to make the incredible more credible or the unpalatable more palatable.

As mentioned earlier, the protagonist and ostensible narrator of *The End of the Affair* is an unbeliever, Maurice Bendrix. Though vain and spiteful, Bendrix has a sufficient number of redeeming traits (intelligence, honesty, a sense of humor, etc.) to retain our respect. The reader—especially the non-Christian reader—will identify with him. He is an underdog for whom we pull, with the result that as he begins to learn from his errors, we learn also. Moreover, like the senior devil in C. S. Lewis's *Screwtape Letters,* Bendrix hisses at God and sticks out his tongue at the Good News. For the non-Christian reader these gestures of contempt provide a safety valve for his biases as Greene nudges him toward the truth of the Gospel. For the Christian reader, Bendrix's expressions of derision, blasphemous as they may seem, can provide a refreshingly new perspective on the Gospel. Seeing grace from a diabolic point of view may actually help some of us see grace—really see it—for the first time. We begin to comprehend the foolishness of God which is wiser than men [sic] and the weakness of God which is stronger than men [sic].

Richard Smythe, the apostle for atheism, is another suspension of disbelief tool in the novel with whom the more skeptical reader can identify. Given his rational arguments, he wins our respect. Given the strawberry-colored disfiguration on his cheek, he wins our sympathy. But the reader's skepticism begins to crumble with the failure of Smythe's arguments to dethrone God. The reader's possible hostility toward God begins to diminish when the God whose existence Smythe had attempted to deny miraculously cures the very facial flaw that had made Smythe's life so unhappy. The God Smythe had tried to reject renders good for evil!

The most effective suspension of disbelief tool in the novel is the inclusion of Father Crompton. Graham Greene's hidden agenda is to promote not only Christianity but also a certain brand of Christianity, Roman Catholicism. Rather than advocate Roman Catholicism frontally, Greene gives the anti-Catholic reader a safety valve through which to release negative feelings even as the author subtly nudges the reader in a pro-Catholic direction. Father Crompton is that safety valve. He has short, squat legs and a nose like a flying buttress. His answers to theological questions are pat and dogmatic. He dislikes socializing. "He had very limited small talk, and his answers fell like trees across the road"

(174). So unprepossessing a personality does Greene give Father Crompton that some Catholic readers weren't sure initially that Greene was helping their cause at all. The author may have honed this suspension of disbelief tool too well! For a time *The End of the Affair* had difficulty acquiring the Catholic *nihil obstat* and *imprimatur*. But Father Crompton turns out to be right in his assessment of Sarah's relationship with God and the Roman Catholic Church. Once again the unsuspecting reader may be drawn toward a more favorable view of Christianity/Roman Catholicism than prior to reading the novel.

The comical shenanigans of Parkis, the detective, and his sweets-addicted son, Lance, constitute Greene's most appealing suspension of disbelief technique. Parkis takes seriously his socially contemptible job of spying on adulterous people. He views it as a "vocation" requiring the utmost professionalism. "Every profession has its dignity," he says (76). He religiously trains his son to follow in his steps, yet is humorously protective, sparing him the more sordid aspects of the intimacies he interrupts. Plodding and painstakingly methodical, Parkis makes occasional blunders (which he calls "floaters"), the knowledge of which he tries to spare his son lest he lose confidence in his father. One such "floater," he learns too late, is the naming of his son. Parkis had called him Lance after Sir Launcelot, a knight of King Arthur's Round Table, because Parkis had assumed that Launcelot found the holy grail. He is crushed to learn from Bendrix that, instead, Launcelot was found in bed with Queen Guinevere. (Note, in passing, how this comic mixture of piety and adultery parallels the more serious theme of adultery and conversion that is the focus of the novel.) Yet, for all his bumbling, Parkis is a lovable person who comes to admire and prove loyal to the very Sarah whose suspected intimacies he was hired to disclose. He even attends her funeral, and when Bendrix spots him at the crematorium, he asks Parkis somewhat wryly, "Do you always follow your people as far as this?" (Note, again, how Parkis's relentless but loving pursuit of Sarah is a comic parallel to God's more significant relentless but loving pursuit of Sarah.)   The Parkis/Lance character portraits seem to be Greene's attempt to immerse the Gospel in humor, to sugarcoat the theological pill Greene hopes the reader will swallow to his spiritual health. Through laughter Greene hopes to facilitate the reader's entrance "into the joy of the Lord."

Permeating all these suspension of disbelief devices is Greene's ultimate suspension of disbelief device, the gradual yet incomplete disclosure of Greene's hidden theological agenda as well as the subtle hints from the very start of the existence of this agenda. An instance of gradual disclosure is Sarah's diary that Parkis steals for Bendrix. Both Bendrix and we begin the reading of that diary with the anticipation of discovering the identity of Bendrix's adulterous competitor and only find out near the end of that reading that Sarah's new lover is God! An instance of (artistically) incomplete disclosure is the unclarity of Bendrix's relationship with God at the very end of the novel. Subtle hints at the hidden theological agenda are present already on the opening pages, although the average reader may understandably miss them in enthusiasm for the interesting story in which Greene engages him. "If I had believed then in a God," Bendrix says on the first page as he ponders the mystery of whether he chose the words he is writing or whether they were given him (7). On the same page Bendrix speculates that Sarah's husband, too, must have grown to hate "that other, in whom in those days we were lucky enough not to believe." It is not until much later that even the perceptive reader learns that the "other" referred to is God, not some philanderer. Only a few pages later Bendrix corrects himself by admitting that the novel he is ostensibly writing is not about himself but about "Sarah, Henry, and of course, that third, whom I hated without yet knowing him" (35-36). "That third," although we may not suspect it at the time, turns out to be God. Even casual statements that are at best cliches and at worst instances of taking God's name in vain become ironically loaded with truth about God's presence and activity. Uncertain of what prompted Sarah to go out into the rain or where she went when she caught the cold that led to her death, Henry informs Bendrix, "She got up and went out a week ago, *God knows where or why*" (135; my emphasis). Henry employs a similar cliche when he tells Bendrix what Parkis had told him: "[Parkis] said she'd been kind to his little boy; *God knows when*" (169; my emphasis). Tired platitudes explode with theological profundity!

Notes

1. Graham Greene, *The End of the Affair* (London: Penguin Books, Ltd., 1975), 95. All future page locations for citations from this book will be included in parentheses in the text of this chapter.
2. This kind of language was actually used earlier by Sarah in a moment of rebellion against God: "Stop me if you can, stop me if you can" (116).

Study Guide for *The End of the Affair*

1. Note the many tantalizing hints with which the novel opens. What are the functions of these hints?

2. Demonstrate some of the ingredients that account for the charm of Greene's style.

3. How does the opening paragraph introduce both the structure and the theme of the novel? How does Greene prevent the Christian theme from coming on too strong?

4. Comment on Greene's technique of characterization.

5. What are the roles in the novel of Parkis and his son, Lance?

6. What is ironic about Lance's getting sick at Miss Smythe's house? What is the thematic significance of this incident? In this connection see the remarks about Parkis on pages 137 and 158.

7. What is the structural significance of the mistake Parkis makes in connection with Lance's name? The thematic significance?

8. What is surprising about both the format and especially the content of Book Three? Compare page 53 with page 123 and pages 89-90 with pages 123-124. Note how sharply context has altered the meaning of words that are repeated.

9. Point out in detail "the reluctant convert" motif in Sarah's conduct and "The Hound of Heaven" motif in God's actions.

10. Comment on the symbolic significance of the livid spots on Richard Smythe's cheek. Has his name any thematic significance?

11. Note Greene's frequent use of sexual imagery for the Gospel. In this connection, demonstrate levels of meaning in the title of the novel.

12. What is the thematic significance of the extended analogy on pages 185-186? The structural significance?

13. Does Bendrix become a Christian?

For Further Reading

Atkins, John. *Graham Greene*. London, Calder & Boyars Ltd. 1966.

Baldridge, Cates. *Graham Greene's Fictions: The Virtue of Extremity*. Columbia, Missouri: University of Missouri Press, 2000.

Boardman, Gwenn R. *Graham Greene: The Aesthetics of Exploration*. Gainesville, Florida: University of Florida Press, 1971.

Cargas, Henry (ed.). *Graham Greene*. St. Louis: B. Herder Book Co., n. d.

De Vitis, A. A. *Graham Greene*. New York: Twayne Publishers, 1964.

Gaston, Georg M. A. *The Pursuit of Salvation: A Critical Guide to the Novels of Graham Greene*. Troy, New York: Whitson Publishing Co., 1984.

Hynes, Samuel (ed.). *Graham Greene: A Collection of Critical Essays*. Englewood Cliffs, New Jersey: Prentice-Hall, Inc., 1973.

Kelly, Richard. *Graham Greene*. New York: Frederick Ungar Publishing Co., 1984.

Kunkel, Francis L. *The Labyrinthine Ways of Graham Greene*. New York: Sheed & Ward, 1959.

Kurismmootif, K. C. Joseph. *Heaven and Hell on Earth: An Appreciation of Five Novels of Graham Greene*. Chicago: Loyola University Press, 1982.

Miller, R. H. *Understanding Graham Greene*. Columbia, South Carolina: University of South Carolina Press, 1990.

Mudford, Peter. *Graham Greene*. Plymouth, England: Northcote House Publishers Ltd., 1996.

O'Prey, Paul. *A Reader's Guide to Graham Greene*. New York: Thames and Hudson, Inc., 1988.

Rai, Gangeshwar. *Graham Greene: An Existential Approach*. Atlantic Highlands, New Jersey: Humanities Press, Inc., 1983.

Stratford, Philip. *Faith and Fiction: Creative Process in Greene and Mauriac*. Notre Dame, Indiana: University of Notre Dame Press, 1964.

CHAPTER FOUR

Crime and Punishment
by Fyodor Dostoevsky

Crime and Punishment (in my opinion one of the greatest novels ever written) can be—indeed, should be—approached in many different ways: as a thrilling adventure story, as a psychological study of the criminal mind, as a philosophical work, and as a religious/theological novel. For the purpose of this thesis, we will approach it primarily as a religious/theological novel. But that dimension is only a part of the novel's greatness and richness. The whole (the novel) is greater than any of its features singled out for admiration—or even the sum of those features.

Many readers have interpreted the novel as a tribute to the power of love or to the value of suffering, Christian themes to be sure, but not exclusively Christian themes. Perhaps the best way to get at the specifically Christian/Gospel character of *Crime and Punishment* is to see in it the Gospel pattern of death and resurrection. Raskolnikov, the protagonist, proceeds from spiritual death to spiritual life through the intervention of Sonia, a Christ figure.

Raskolnikov's spiritual death is most obvious in his planned, even rehearsed, and eventually accomplished murder of an old pawnbroker and the gratuitous murder of her half sister when she blunders onto the scene of the crime. Murder is foul enough, but some of the factors prompting Raskolnikov's crime make his deed even more despicable. In the course of the novel Dostoevsky presents a variety of motives for Raskolnikov's crime: the desire for money to alleviate the poverty of his mother and sister;[1] an unconscious protest against the squalid environment he lives in (359); incipient insanity (358); the thrill or daring of it, a sort of morbid curiosity (360); Satan (360); and a Superman concept.[2] Although the humanitarian and environmental factors prompting Raskolnikov's crime may reduce the heinousness of his foul deed, the main motive—at least the one to which Dostoevsky devotes the most space—the Superman concept, increases the magnitude of his crime.

As a university student Raskolnikov had written an article advancing a Superman concept.[3] That article advocated the theory that society is divided into two classes, ordinary people and extraordinary people. The latter have the right to break the moral law on occasion to advance some great cause designed (in their opinion) to benefit humanity. Not only will these extraordinary people not stop at murder (if necessary) to further their cause, but they also will not even consider what they do to be a crime—although ordinary people will so view it according to their conventional moral standards. Raskolnikov regarded Napoleon, Lycurgus, and Mahomet to be examples of the extraordinary class. To implement his theory, to prove that he himself is a member of the extraordinary class, a sort of modern Napoleon, was a major factor in Raskolnikov's axe murder.

The heinousness of Raskolnikov's crime is skillfully foreshadowed through a dream he has. In the dream a man cruelly beats to death with a crowbar an old mare, unable to pull a wagon overloaded with drunken revelers, under the rubric that the mare is his property and that he can do with it as he pleases. Intensifying the depravity of the owner's mind-set and deed is the phenomenon of a woman laughing and cracking nuts for the duration of the ordeal (50-51). One bystander is so shocked at what he sees that he calls out to the owner, "Are you a Christian, you devil?" (51). Horrified at his "nightmare," but relieved to discover that it was only a dream, Raskolnikov promptly connects the dream to his contemplated crime: "Good God! . . . can it be, can it be, that I shall really take an axe, that I shall strike her on the head, split her skull open . . . that I shall tread in the sticky warm blood. . . . Good God, can it be?" (53). This dream episode is a microcosm of the murder that informs the main plot of *Crime and Punishment*.

As the dream foreshadows the egregious evil of Raskolnikov's crime, his confession to Sonia mirrors it. So horrible is the deed even in his own eyes that, like the murderer in the movie *Presumed Innocent,* Raskolnikov at first can confess it only in the third person. "He . . . did not mean to kill that Lizaveta . . ." he says, "he . . .killed her accidentally" (353). Unable to give the dastardly deed the words it deserves, Raskolnikov twice insists that Sonia guess at what he did rather than himself admitting it (353). For that matter, even when he was contemplating his crime, Raskolnikov was unable to give his evil deed the necessary evil words, referring to it, not as a murder or a crime, but rather as "that" (2), "this" (47), "It" (47), "the whole plan" (3), "this business" (3) "dream" (3), "project" (3), and "experiment" (53). So evil even in his own view is the deed Raskolnikov plots that he cannot call a spade a spade.

The evidence for Raskolnikov's spiritual corruption does not rest exclusively, however, on the murder of two old ladies and the circumstances related to that crime. There are more subtle indications. For example, early in the novel Raskolnikov tries to protect a drunken girl from a would be rapist stalking her and even pays a policeman to intervene; then suddenly he "repents" of his contemplated good deed and dismisses the officer with the cynical thought, "Let him take as much from the other fellow to allow him to have the girl. . . And why did I want to interfere? . . . Let them devour each other alive—what is it to me?" (45). In the opening pages of the novel Raskolnikov emerges as an irritable hypochondriac, isolated from others, ducking his landlady, and crossing the street to avoid his friend Razumihin. The very name "Raskolnikov" means "alienated," "detached." Raskolnikov is "like a tortoise in its shell" (25). His separation from both people and God is best symbolized by Raskolnikov's tossing into a river a coin given him "in Christ's name" moments before by a kind woman, an action accompanied by Dostoevesky's gratuitous explanation, "It seemed to him, he had cut himself off from everyone and from everything at that moment" (102). Obviously, something is rotten in the state of Raskolnikov's spirituality.

Raskolnikov's character and conduct are more than inhuman, they are diabolic. And for Dostoevsky "diabolic" is more literal than hyperbolic. Evil is not merely of human provenance; it is ultimately of Satanic origin. Demoniac possession is a reality in

Dostoevsky's portrait of evil.[4] "A strange idea [the crime] was pecking at [Raskolnikov's] brain like a chicken in the egg" (57). Having overheard someone say that the pawnbroker would be alone at precisely the time of his scheduled appointment with her, Raskolnikov "felt suddenly in his whole being that he had no more freedom of thought, no will, and that everything was suddenly and irrevocably decided" (56). As he approaches the pawnbroker's lodging, weaponless, he spies an axe under a porter's bench and seizes it with the remark, "When reason fails, the devil helps!" (65). There seems to be additional diabolic intervention (*diabolus ex machina*, to coin a term) when a wagon screens Raskoslnikov's entrance into the lodging, when there is an empty flat for him in which to hide after the crime as strangers approach him on the stairway, and when the porter is not home as Raskolnikov returns the axe. Sonia's later diagnosis removes any doubt of a Satanic role in Raskolnikov's evil when she cries out to Raskolnikov, "You turned away from God and God . . . has given you over to the devil!" ((360). One thinks of St. John's comment about Judas during the meal in the upper chamber right at the start of our Lord's Passion: "After he received the piece of bread, Satan entered into him. Jesus said to him, Do quickly what you are going to do." (John 13:27).

Separated from both God and man, Raskolnikov experiences occasional foretastes of that permanent separation called hell toward which he is headed.. "A gloomy sensation of agonizing, *everlasting* solitude and remoteness took conscious form in his soul . . . . the most agonizing of all the sensations he had known in his life" (92-93; my emphasis). "A special form of misery had begun to oppress him of late. . . . there was a feeling of *permanence*, of *eternity* about it; it brought a foretaste of *hopeless years* of this cold leaden misery, *a foretaste of an eternity* on a square yard of space'" (367; my emphasis). For Raskolnikov, "to feel like hell" is neither metaphor nor cliche.

To prevent the reader from despising Raskolnikov and dissociating from him, Dostoevsky gives his protagonist some redeeming qualities, a literary practice called dramatic hedging. Raskolnikov, even like Shylock and similar villains of literature, is not altogether bad. Anonymously, he leaves money for the poverty-stricken Marmeladov family when he first meets them. He is consistently generous, giving money to a street-singer, to a prostitute (no services rendered!), to fetch a doctor for the dying Marmeladov run over by a carriage, and to Marmeladov's destitute family after his death. He even asks Polenka, Marmeladov's daughter, to pray for him as he leaves the bereaved family.

But for Dostoevsky to attribute a few good qualities to Raskolnikov's character is more than the exercise of a literary convention. For him the duality in Raskolnikov, the mixture of good and evil in his make-up is a theological truth, the Christian doctrine of the old man and the new man in human personality. "It's as though he were alternating between two characters" (187). As Sonia puts it in a moment of dismay, "How could you give away your last farthing and yet rob and murder?" (355).

Which brings us to Dostoevsky's curious concept of "the double," a concept prominent in many of his novels.[5] He dramatizes the Christian doctrine of the duality of human nature by suggesting that among the acquaintances of such principal characters as Raskolnikov (of this novel), Ivan Karamazov (of *The Brothers Karamazov*) and Golyadkin (*of The Double*) there are people who constitute the embodiment, the personification, the logical outcome (unless corrected or inhibited) of their respective old man and new man. Razumihin, Raskolnikov's good friend, is Raskolnikov's "good double." (There by the grace of God can go Raskolnikov.) And Svidrigailov is Raskolnikov's "evil double." (There except for the grace of God goes Raskolnikov.) Thus Raskolnikov is strangely attracted to Razumihin, mystified why he is drawn to him, especially when feeling the urge to confess his crime. "Could I have expected to set it all straight and to find a way out by means of Razumihin alone?" (47). Frequently, Razumihin and Raskolnikov call each other "brother" (though they are not related), and even Raskolnikov's mother and sister regard Razumihin as "a relation" and "a son and a brother" (197, 272).

More to the point in our present focus on Raskolnikov's spiritual death and corruption is Dostoevsky's portrait of the protagonist's "evil double," Svidrigailov, one of the "creepiest" evil characters in all literature. It is an understatement when this evil man—a wife abuser, a pedophile, visited by ghosts, incapable of dreaming anything but nightmares, from whom children flee in terror—is told, "You should go to a doctor" (250). Svidrigailov himself is aware of the strange affinity between him and

Raskolnikov. "Didn't I say that there was something in common among us, eh?" he asks Raskolnikov (248). "I keep fancying there is something about you like me," he insists (254). "Wasn't I right in saying that we were *birds of a feather*?" (251; my emphasis). Raskolnikov, too, is uncomfortably aware of the horrifying affinity. He puzzles over the fact that the "man had some hidden power over him" (398). This "double-relationship" between protagonist and villain is further evidenced by numerous parallels between the two men: Both are cynics; both have nightmares; both feign sleep to avoid contact with unwanted visitors; both berate themselves for their occasional and inexplicable good deeds; both are afraid of water; both are in need of "fresh air"; and both have committed murder. "I don't know why I'm afraid of that man," Raskolnikov muses (255). Readers of Dostoevsky can clarify the mystery for Raskolnikov. "Because he's your double—your evil double—the portrait of the frightful thing you will become unless, by God's mercy, you mend your ways!"

Plagued by conscience, driven by suffering, harassed by Porfiry (the detective whose "psyching out" of the protagonist qualifies him for the Columbo of the nineteenth century), and horrified by his future, Raskolnikov seeks help of Sonia, a prostitute (but not by her choice). Rather she has been driven to her fate in order to combat the poverty of her family, that of the alcoholic Marmeladov. Raskolnikov became acquainted with her when Marmeladov was run over and killed by a carriage. Raskolnikov is perceptive enough to note the difference in their respective evil: His is by choice; hers is by circumstance. His suffering is self-imposed; hers is other-imposed.

It is clear that Dostoevsky intends Sonia as a Christ-figure of sorts. Like Christ she is innocent (relatively), yet she "becomes sin" (2 Corinthians 5:21) for the sake of her family. "Where is the daughter," Marmeladov cries in his famous drunken speech, "who gave herself for her cross, consumptive step-mother and for the little children of another? Where is the daughter who had pity upon the filthy drunkard, her earthly father, undismayed by his beastliness?" (20). "Sonia Marmeladov, the *eternal* victim so long as the world lasts:" (39; my emphasis) At the end of the novel Raskolnikov recognizes that she "was *with him forever* and would follow him to the ends of the earth" (453; my emphasis). (See Matthew 28:20.) At one point he even bows down to her, dropping to the ground and kissing her foot with the explanation, "I did not bow down to you, I bowed down to all the suffering of humanity" (279).

It is to this Christ-figure, Sonia, to whom Raskolnikov repairs for help. Actually, his first major visit to Sonia is ostensibly to help her, to make her realize that if she continues in her present life of prostitution, she'll end up dead. But he learns that despite her misery and bleak future, she trusts unswervingly in God. "He does everything," she quietly whispers to Raskolnikov (281). As they converse, he spies a Russian New Testament in her room. He is startled to learn that Lizaveta, the pawnbroker's half sister whom he had also murdered, had given it to Sonia and that the two had been good friends. Impulsively, he asks her to read him the account of Lazarus's resurrection, the biblical miracle that Porfiry had earlier mentioned to him in the course of interrogating Raskolnikov about the crime. Sonia obliges Raskolnikov—but reluctantly. She is no careless hawker of precious Christian truths. She is not one to cast pearls before swine or holy things to dogs. Raskolnikov "understood only too well how painful it was for her to betray and unveil all that was her *own*. He understood that these feelings really were her *secret treasure*" (283; Dostoevky's emphasis). After the reading, Raskolnikov, on the verge of confession, only hints at his crime by promising that if he comes back, he'll tell her who killed Lizaveta.

He keeps his promise, returns to Sonia's lodging, and confesses—clumsily, reluctantly, and without remorse. She urges him to confess to the authorities and embrace his punishment, promising to share his imprisonment in Siberia. She instructs him also to go to the crossroads and kiss the ground as a symbol of his crime against all people and of his having defiled the earth (361, 452). As he leaves her lodging, Raskolnikov asks for a cross. Sonia offers one, again a gift from Lizaveta. Almost he takes it, then shrinks back from it and decides to wait until he is ready for it. Nor does Sonia force the cross on him.

That confession to the public authorities does not come easily for Raskolnikov. Even when he goes to the police station to make a clean breast of it, he learns that Svidrigailov, the only person (besides Sonia) who knew of Raskolnikov's guilt and who had threatened to blackmail him, had killed himself. Technically, Raskolnikov is now safe from the rigors of the law. Stunned, he leaves the police station—only to be driven back by the pleading eyes of Sonia as she waits outside. Much to the officer's surprise, Raskolnikov returns and confesses to the murder—precisely at the time when, humanly speaking, he had no need to confess.

There are numerous remarkable features, deserving of comment, in Raskolnikov's visits to Sonia. First, there is the irony of a murderer and a harlot reading the Scriptures together. One is reminded of our Lord's comment about tax collectors and prostitutes going into the kingdom of God before scribes and Pharisees (Matthew 21:31). Then there is a sort of poetic *in*justice in the fact that it is Lizaveta's Bible and Lizaveta's cross that are instrumental in initiating Raskolnikov's transformation. He gave her death—physical. In return, she gives him life—spiritual. Unlike the widow Paul speaks of in 1 Timothy 5:6, who "is dead even while she lives," Lizaveta, in a sense, "lives while she's dead"! Then there is the emergence of a foil relationship between Raskolnikov and Sonia, a sharp contrast between the two made vivid against the background of a number of similarities between them. Both had committed crime: murder by one, prostitution by the other. Both, in a sense, had killed a life: Raskolnikov in the past and Sonia in the future (her own) if she persists in prostitution. "You have laid hands on yourself," Raskolnikov tells her. "You have destroyed a life . . . your own" (286). But there the similarities end. Raskolnikov's crime is selfish; Sonia's crime is sacrificial. Raskolnikov denies God (279), but Sonia trusts God unreservedly. There is the lesson to be learned from Sonia's missionary technique: to avoid in our Christian witness not merely constipation of the spirit but also the opposite malady of diarrhea of the mouth. There is Dostoevsky's skillful use of a device to unify his plot: using the very miracle account of Lazarus's resurrection that Porfiry had casually introduced earlier (227) as a catalyst for a major shift in the direction of the plot.

But that miracle account is more than a device to tighten the structure of Dostoevsky's lengthy novel. The account of Lazarus's resurrection, as we have seen, initiates the change in Raskolnikov's character from bad to good. Actually, any scriptural account containing the Gospel of salvation and character transformation here on earth through Jesus' life, death, and resurrection could have done that for Raskolnikov. But here is where the genius of Dostoevsky is especially evident. He chooses a Gospel account which not merely effects the change in Raskolnikov but also, simultaneously, symbolizes the nature of that change: from death to life. Even as Lazarus was physically resurrected, so Raskolnikov is spiritually resurrected. To put it simply, the account of Christ's resurrecting Lazarus from the grave not only begins the change in Raskolnikov. It also dramatizes that change. It suggests the death and resurrection Gospel pattern that informs this novel. After Raskolnikov had confessed his crime to Sonia, we are told, "A feeling long unfamiliar to him flooded his heart and softened it at once. He did not struggle against it" (354). Just before his confession at the police station, Raskolnikov gives a coin to a beggar woman who responds, "God bless you" (402). Note how this incident parallels, yet contrasts, an earlier incident when Raskolnikov, mistaken for a beggar, receives a coin from a woman, given "in Christ's name," and then throws the money into the river. Even as the earlier action symbolizes his rejection of God and other people, so the later action signifies his growing acceptance of God and others. The transformation is evidently underway. But, unlike Lazarus's resurrection, the transformation is not instantaneous. Spiritual resurrection, realistically, comes harder and takes more time.

That's why Dostoevsky attached the Epilogue to his novel. Some (notably Ernest Simmons) have criticized this addition as anticlimactic, as a dull footnote to an otherwise exciting presentation. Some argue that the novel should have ended with Raskolnikov's electrifying confession at the police station. That opinion is not without merit. But, really, Dostoevsky needed the Epilogue for the completion of his theme, Raskolnikov's spiritual regeneration. Even in Siberia Raskolnikov resists the change that has begun. Late in the Epilogue we are told that he recognized "his criminality, only . . . the fact that he had been unsuccessful and had confessed it" (467). But Sonia patiently and unobtrusively persists, loyally bestowing on him her love and understanding. Then one day it happens. Raskolnikov embraces her and weeps, and Sonia recognizes that the moment for which she had longed had come. In Dostoevsky's words, their "pale faces were bright with the dawn of a new future, of a full resurrection into a new life" (471). The novel ends with the words, "But that is the beginning of a new story—the story of the gradual renewal of a man, the story of his gradual regeneration, of his passing from one world into another, of his initiation into a new unknown life" (472).

Even the structure of the novel—not just the content—reflects this death and resurrection pattern. Raskolnikov's visit to Sonia in which she reads to him the biblical account of Lazarus's resurrection occurs near the midpoint of the novel, thus dividing the novel into two easily recognizable parts. In the first part Raskolnikov visits Alyona, the pawnbroker; in the second part Raskolnikov visits Sonia, the prostitute. Murder is the high spot in the first part; confession is the high spot in the second part. There is a rehearsal for each of these actions in each part, "a dry run," so to speak, preceding the contemplated activity. Above all, death in the first part is paralleled by life in the second part. Form reinforces content—another aspect of Dostoevsky's genius.

Early in this chapter I specified two other ways to get at the role of the Gospel in *Crime and Punishment,* the way of love and the way of suffering. Because these two routes need not be exclusively Christian routes, I chose not to pursue them. But inadvertently, in my depiction of Sonia's relationship with Raskolnikov I have, in fact, dealt with the power of love as a Gospel pattern after all. Her reading of the biblical account of Lazarus's resurrection and her comments on that account were the Gospel in words. Her patience, loyalty, and unobtrusive love for Raskolnikov were the Gospel in actions. The verbal was reinforced by the visual. The two cannot really be separated in Christian witness. It is a truism that words—even Gospel words—without accompanying deeds are relatively ineffective.

I do feel, though, that the other route to the Gospel, the way of suffering, deserves more than the passing reference I have given it in view of the prominence of the theme of suffering in the novel. The Bible says, "We must through much tribulation enter into the kingdom of God" (Acts 14:22). *Crime and Punishment* is a dramatic demonstration of that truth. Whether suffering is self-imposed (as in the case of Raskolnikov) or other-imposed (as was true of Sonia, her parents, and her siblings), God can use those sufferings to steer the victims into the kingdom of God. Two notable examples of this (besides Raskolnikov and Sonia, whose sufferings I have dealt with briefly) are Marmeladov and his wife, Katerina Ivanovna. Marmeladov's famous drunken speech in the tavern early in the novel (20) has even been referred to as "The Gospel according to Marmeladov." In it he pictures God's mercy on Judgment Day to suffering sinners such as Sonia and himself. Katerina Ivanovna is a consumptive, most of her life exposed to abuse and abject poverty. Coughing blood, ridiculed by guests at the funeral dinner she gave for her husband, eventually maddened by society's rejection of her, Katerina dies in her misery. In another stroke of genius, Dostoevsky has Raskolnikov discover on her pillow a "certificate of merit" (once given her for her skillful dancing before the governor), symbolizing her status also in the sight of God. Literarily pleasing, this symbol, however, is theologically disturbing. Does Dostoevsky portray suffering as redemptive because it drives us to Christ, who redeems? If so, his presentation accords with the Scriptures. Or does Dostoevsky portray suffering as redemptive, *per se*? Katerina's words shortly before her death seem to suggest the latter : "I have no sin. God must forgive me without that. He knows how I have suffered" (373). If so, Dostoevsky's view dilutes the truth of salvation by God's grace alone, apart from human merit. Equally troublesome is the ingredient of masochism in Dostoevsky's concept of suffering. Marmeladov, especially, embraces suffering for its supposed benefits. "Know, sir, that such blows are not a pain to me, but even an enjoyment" (21). Later he calls his sufferings "a consolation" (23). Yet the central episode of the novel, Sonia's reading the biblical account of Christ's resurrection of Lazarus, and Raskolnikov's subsequent transformation clearly put suffering back into a more orthodox perspective.

Notes

1. Fyodor Dostoevsky, *Crime and Punishment*, Constance Garnett, tr. (New York: Bantam Books, 1981), 357. All future page locations for citations from this book will be included in parentheses in the text of this chapter.
2. The multiplicity of motives impelling Raskolnikov to murder is considered by some critics to be a flaw in the novel. They feel that neither Raskolnikov nor Dostoevsky could make up his mind about the motivation. This may well be the case, but I disagree that the variety of motives is a weakness in the novel. Realistically, a criminal doesn't always know his own mind. Further, Dostoevsky's depiction of numerous motives is a tribute to the mystery of evil, another whole that is often greater than the sum of its parts.
3. See especially pages 225-231. Although usually associated with Nietzsche, the Superman concept has been credited by Nietzsche himself to Dostoevsky, who, in turn, derived some of the theory from Hegel.

4. This is especially clear from the very title of one of his novels, *The Possessed* (sometimes also translated *The Devils*).
5. Notably (besides *Crime and Punishment*) *The Brothers Karamazov* and *The Double*.

Study Guide for *Crime and Punishment*

1. Note the element of the grotesque in Dostoevsky's descriptions of people and places. Evaluate the realism of these descriptions.

2. What does the name "Raskolnikov" mean? What is the possible spiritual significance of the meaning of his name? Connect the meaning of Raskolnikov's name with the actions described at the middle of pages 101 and 102.

3. How does Dostoevsky convert the stylistic vice of vagueness into a virtue in the opening pages? Does this technique suggest anything about the nature of evil?

4. What similarity does Dostoevsky find between the actions of Dounia and Sonia? Whose actions are "worse"? Why? Of what is Sonia representative or symbolic? Contrast the motives for Sonia's "crime" with the motives for Raskolnikov's crime. Note the vicarious element in the actions of Sonia and Dounia.

5. How do the girl-of-the-street incident and Raskolnikov's dream about the horse add to our understanding of evil? What other accent in Dostoevsky's writings is evident in the latter episode?

6. What role do the following incidents play in Raskolnikov's contemplated crime: the dream about the horse, the letter from Pulcheria, the encounter with Marmeladov, and the encounter with the girl-of-the-street?

7. Why might it be said of Dostoevsky's evil characters that they are "possessed"?

8. Find instances of diabolic coincidence ("providence in reverse").

9. Describe Raskolnikov's Superman concept.

10. Describe and evaluate Dostoevsky's concept of suffering. Note particularly "The Gospel according to Marmeladov" on page 20.

11. Mark passages which, in your opinion, interpret life or accord with human experience. Note especially in the opening pages the characterization of Marmeladov's wife and of Raskolnikov's mother.

12. Demonstrate particularly from Raskolnikov's conduct during and after his crime and from the relations between him and Porfiry that *Crime and Punishment* deserves to be called a psychological novel.

13. Enumerate Raskolnikov's good deeds. What is Dostoevsky's literary purpose in bringing these to our attention? What is his theological purpose in so doing?

14. What are Razumihin's roles in the novel?

15. What is Dostoevsky's attitude toward the Progressives and Progressive viewpoints? What is Luzhin's function in the novel?

16. How does Dostoevsky's use of irony enhance the readability of the novel?

17. Demonstrate specifically the cat and mouse game that Porfiry plays with Raskolnikov. With what other analogy does Dostoevsky describe their relationship?

18. What is the significance of Raskolnikov's dream recorded on pages 240-241? Point out in this instance how dream and reality merge. Make a connection between this dream and the incident that immediately follows it.

19. Pay careful attention to the characterization of Svidrigailov, particularly how he concretizes Dostoevsky's understanding of evil.

20. Demonstrate in detail that Svidrigailov is Raskolnikov's "double."

21. What is the structural significance of Raskolnikov's visit to Sonia (in Part Four: Chapter Four)?

22. How is the murdered Lizaveta "reactivated" in the plot of the novel?

23. Note the role that the biblical account of Lazarus's resurrection plays in the novel. Why did Dostoevsky choose this particular narrative? Would the account of a different biblical miracle have been equally appropriate?

24. What is Sonia's dramatic relationship in respect to Raskolnikov? Evaluate her missionary technique.

25. What functions does the mysterious accuser (pages 236-237) serve in the novel?

26. Find instances of non-verbal communication.

27. Why does Luzhin attempt to pin a theft on Sonia? What is ironical about the way in which his attempt is thwarted? How does this episode serve the main plot?

28. What is the significance of Sonia's advice to Raskolnikov to kiss the earth prior to confession of his crime to the police? (See pages 361 and 452-453.)

29. What is the significance of the certificate of merit on Katerina Ivanovna's deathbed?

30. Note Raskolnikov's attempt to explain to Sonia the motives for his crime. What accounts for his inability to pinpoint the exact cause of his misdeed? Is this failure a weakness or a strength in the novel?

31. What is the "journey" that Svidrigailov takes? How do his frequent allusions to it enhance the merit of the novel? What stylistic device used earlier in the novel reappears in the allusions to this journey?

32. Establish a connection between Svidrigailov's dreams and his character. What is the symbolic function of the dream described on pages 438-439? How do his dreams reinforce Dostoevsky's concept of reality?

33. What is the connection between the news of Svidrigailov's death and Raskolnikov's attempt at confession?

34. How are the Luzhin/Dounia and the Svidrigailov/Dounia episodes woven together?

35. Find unity devices late in the novel.

36. Note the true-to-life difficulties Raskolnikov experiences in attempting to confess his crime.

37. Comment on the meaning and significance of Raskolnikov's dream in the hospital.

38. Evaluate Dostoevsky's handling of Raskolnikov's conversion. Does this conversion help or hurt the novel?

39. Note the association of Sonia and Christ on page 453.

40. Itemize the references to the Gospel pattern of death and resurrection in the closing pages of the novel.

41. What is the significance for Christian readers of D. H. Lawrence's criticism of *Crime and Punishment* as bad art, of being too allegorical?

42. What other interpretations of the novel (not specifically "Christian") are possible?

For Further Reading

Amoia, Alba. *Feodor Dostoevsky*. New York: The Continuum Publishing Co., 1993.

Bregor, Louis. *Dostoevsky: The Author as Psychoanalyst*. New York: New York University Press, 1989.

Cox, Roger L. *Between Earth and Heaven: Shakespeare, Dostoevsky, and the Meaning of Christian Tragedy*. New York, Chicago, San Francisco, 1969.

Edgren, C. Hobart. *Of Marble and Mud: Studies in Spiritual Values in Fiction*. New York, 1959.

Fuelop-Miller, Rene. *Fyodor Dostoevsky: Insight, Faith, and Prophecy* (tr. Richard and Clara Winston). New York: Charles Scribners Sons, 1950.

Gide, Andre. *Dostoevsky* (tr. Arnold Bennett). New York: Alfred A. Knopf, 1926.

Gunn, Judith. *Dostoyevsky: Dreamer & Prophet*. Oxford, England: Lion Publishing, 1990.

The Huttarian Brethren (ed). *The Gospel in Dostoyevsky*. Ulster Park, New York: Plough Publishing House, 1988.

Jackson, Robert Louis (ed.). *Twentieth Century Interpretations of Crime and Punishment: A Collection of Critical Essays*. Englewood Cliffs, New Jersey, 1974.

Jones, John. *Dostoevsky*. Oxford, England: Clarendon Press, 1983.

Magarshack, David. *Dostoevsky*. New York: Harcourt, Brace & World, Inc., 1961.

Mathewson, Rufus. *The Positive Hero in Russian Literature*. New York, 1958.

Mochulsky, Konstantin. *Dostoevsky: His Life and Work* (tr. Michael A. Minihan). Princeton, New Jersey: Princeton University Press, 1967.

Simmons, Ernest J. *Dostoevski: The Making of a Novelist*. New York: Oxford University Press, 1940.

CHAPTER FIVE

The Wayward Bus
by John Steinbeck

In *The Wayward Bus* and in *The Old Man and the Sea*, the last two novels to be considered in this first part, "Intentional Gospel Patterns," we see a different kind of intentional use of the Christian Gospel. To be sure, the insertion of the Gospel in these novels is every bit as deliberate as in the previous works considered in this section. The presence of the Gospel in both *The Wayward Bus* and *The Old Man and the Sea* is too obvious and too abundant to be written off as accidental or incidental, and to my knowledge no critic denies Steinbeck and Hemingway's use of the Gospel in their respective novels. Yet neither of these authors appears to have any vested interest in the Gospel they utilize. They display no evangelistic fervor for it or any particular commitment to its truth claims. Although not overtly contemptuous of the Christian Gospel, they don't take seriously its power to give eternal life or, for that matter, its power to transform human personality in this life. At best, the Christian Gospel is *a* guide, only one among many guides or cultural forces that impact on human life. Steinbeck and Hemingway use the Christian Gospel exclusively for literary purposes; neither seems to have any interest in demonstrating or promoting that Gospel, however indirectly and artistically, for its own sake.

Specifically, Steinbeck in *The Wayward Bus* displays a somewhat lighthearted stance toward Christianity, a stance intoned early in the novel in his description of Alice's coffee urn as "a great godlike silver effigy which may, in some future archaeological period, be displayed as an object of worship of the race of

Amudkins, who preceded the Atomites, who, for some unknown reason, disappeared from the face of the earth."[1] Steinbeck is amused by Christians—as he is amused by most everyone in his *dramatis personae*—and he loves them as he loves most everyone. Steinbeck is tolerant. He lives and lets live. He is a sort of genial host who hopes that everyone is having a good time. He looks at people with all their flaws and eccentricities from the sideline rather than from a pinnacle. Even more than a merely charitable observer, he is a participant in the human condition, sharing the foibles of those who amuse him. He is flesh of their flesh, bone of their bone, and skin of their skin. Like the rock-and-roll singer Chuck Berry in his famous "Ding-a-ling" song, Steinbeck would accept those who sing out of tune or do their own thing, even those who refuse to participate in the communal singing. (And I would wager that Steinbeck would even join the singer in good-naturedly dedicating an entire verse "to those who will not sing.") Witness, for example, Steinbeck's treatment of Pimples, the acne-peppered, gauche lover filled with the juices of concupiscence. Even though Steinbeck portrays him as ridiculous—and deserving of our ridicule—he simultaneously persuades us to pull for Pimples in realizing his goal of having the protagonist call him by his real name, Kit, rather than by his demeaning nickname.

Steinbeck neither attacks nor promotes the Christian Gospel in *The Wayward Bus*. That Gospel is simply a cultural phenomenon, having a degree of ritualistic and emotional impact on people but certainly possessing no salvific power and no particular claim to truth. To Steinbeck Christianity is a sort of mythology to be adapted for literary use like the Greek or Arthurian mythologies.[2] Jesus Christ clearly does things to characters considered in previous chapters: Eustace, the Flyte family, Sarah Miles, and Raskolnikov. Not so with Juan Chicoy, the protagonist of *The Wayward Bus*. In Steinbeck's presentation Jesus Christ is merely a sort of "hero" to whom Juan Chicoy, in his own limited sphere and limited way, deserves to be compared. In short, Steinbeck uses the Gospel to magnify Juan Chicoy rather than Jesus Christ. This intentional use of the Gospel—but for non-Gospel purposes—will become increasingly evident as we consider the wealth of Christian Gospel materials present in *The Wayward Bus*.

First, consider the genre. The novel is an allegory or, at the very least, allegorical—a genre more amenable than other types to a moral (if not a Gospel) truth. Steinbeck clues us in to this possibility by prefacing the book with a citation from the classic medieval allegory *Everyman,* especially with the line "By fygure a morall playe" [sic]. Like other well-known allegories (*The Canterbury Tales, The Divine Comedy, The Pilgrim's Progress*), *The Wayward Bus* involves a journey, a trip from here to there—specifically, a trip from Rebel Corners (a name easy to associate with hell) to San Juan de la Cruz (a name easy to associate with heaven). For this journey a bus is used. Like the ship in Katherine Anne Porter's *Ship of Fools* (another allegory), that bus contains a cross-section of humanity, representative people, types as well as individual personalities. Juan Chicoy, the bus driver, even treats the group as a microcosm of society, a miniature democracy, when he addresses them on the issue whether it's safe or not to cross a flooded bridge: "Now, I'm willing to take a vote and do anything the majority of the passengers want to do. I'll make a run for it and take a chance, or I'll take you back and you can make other plans. It's up to you" (168). Barely visible on the front bumper of the bus is the faded inscription *"el Gran Poder de Jesus"* ("the great power of Jesus"). Those words may be ironic, suggesting the contrast between appearance and reality, and the fact that the inscription is faded may suggest Steinbeck's lack of seriousness about the power of the Gospel in the workaday world. The name painted over the inscription, "Sweetheart," plus the fact that the cargo the bus carries, besides passengers, consists of pies may even suggest the sentimental and saccharine nature of Christianity in Steinbeck's view. Nonetheless, the inscription is still present—for whatever reason.

There are other items suggesting a Christian context for the novel. Three times the passengers encounter religious signs emphasizing the word "Repent!": once along the road (180) and twice on the banks of cliffs (196, 226). Again, it is difficult to see little more in these signs than an authorial attempt at verisimilitude as the bus travels through a slice of California, and it is equally difficult to read into these signs anymore than an amused view of Christianity on the part of the author. In one instance, a profanity that slips from the lips of Norma, "Oh, Jesus Christ, let it happen!" (157) can, in its context, constitute also a half-hearted prayer.[3] Given the allegorical nature of the novel, Van Brunt, forever spouting predictions of gloom and dispensing judgments right and left, can be viewed as a sort of Old Testament prophet.

Less easy to write off as coincidence or satire is the religious symbol inside the bus and the bus driver's relationship to that symbol. Sharing the company of a baby shoe, a tiny boxing glove, and a kewpie doll, all hanging from the windshield of the bus, and a revolver and a bottle of whisky in the glove compartment, there is prominent on the dashboard a small statue of the Virgin of Guadalupe (15-16), "looking benignly back at the passengers" (118). Of this statue Steinbeck says, "This was Juan Chicoy's connection with eternity. It had little to do with religion as connected with the church and dogma, and much to do with religion as memory and feeling" (15). "Juan Chicoy, while not a believer in an orthodox sense . . . would nevertheless have been uneasy driving the bus without the Guadalupana to watch over him. His religion was practical" (15). "Juan was not a deeply religious man. He believed in the Virgin's power as little children believe in the power of their uncles. She was a doll and a goddess and a good-luck piece and a relative" (183). When the bus approaches a deep, water-filled hole in the road, Juan seeks guidance of the Virgin's statue: "Shall I take a chance?" (193). Moments later, after toying with the idea of deserting his troublesome passengers, Juan, glancing at the statue on the dashboard, vows, "I'll get them through if you want me to" (195), a vow he reaffirms a page later, "I'll keep my word . . .I'll get through if I can" (196). In exchange for having (eventually) kept his end of the bargain, Juan requests the Virgin to arrange to have Alice, his wife, sober when he returns home (259).

The most significant vehicle for the Gospel in *The Wayward Bus* is the protagonist himself, Juan Chicoy. Note his initials, J. C., suggesting an association with Jesus Christ and bringing to mind other famous J. C.'s in literature, such as Jim Casey in *The Grapes of Wrath*, Joe Christmas in *Light in August,* and Jean Charlot in *The Tenth Man*. Like Jesus, Juan bears scars (stigmata, if you will): a scar on his cheek and an amputated finger (10). Early in the novel, while repairing his bus, Juan scrapes his knuckle when a wrench slips, and blood flows from the wound. As he sucks the wound, Juan says, "You can't finish a job without blood" (19). (Is this a cavalier dismissal of the seriousness of his injury? Or does it echo the Savior's cry from the cross, "It is finished"?) Also, like Jesus, Juan undergoes "a temptation in the wilderness." Should he desert his passengers when the bus gets stuck and run off to

Mexico? Or should he see them through to their destination? For a time (most unlike the Son of God) Juan succumbs to the temptation to abandon his mission and seek personal pleasure. He deliberately gets the bus stuck in the mud, admitting to the Virgin on the dashboard, "All right, all right . . . so I cheated a little" (199). Under the pretext of seeking help, Juan leaves the bus to consider the alternatives of freedom or duty and to enjoy an unsought sexual encounter with one of the passengers. Prominent among his reflections during his absence from the bus is his nostalgic memory of his boyhood participation in a midnight mass in "a great, dim cathedral" (204). Ultimately, Juan repents of his abandoning the bus. "Juan didn't feel good about it now. Not the way he thought he would. It didn't seem as good or as pleasant or as free" (201). "Something went haywire," he later admits when he resolves to return to the bus (222). "It went sour. The Virgin of Guadaloupe let me down. I thought I fooled her. She doesn't like fooling. She cut the heart out of it" (242). And so he returns to extricate the bus and drive his passengers to St. John of the Cross.

What are we to make of all this? Certainly, Steinbeck does present the Christian Gospel as a guide to Juan Chicoy, as one of many factors playing a role in the protagonist's development and crises-survival. Although Steinbeck casts doubt upon Christianity's historicity, dogma, and truth claims, he does seem to respect its ritual and its emotional impact. This diluted version of Christianity plays some role (albeit in a negative, "killjoy" fashion) in preventing Juan Chicoy from selfishly abandoning his passengers. Yet that same version of Christianity fails to keep Juan from an illicit sexual encounter. Here, of course, we must remember the Steinbeck ethic: Fornication is, in his value system, at worst a venial slip and maybe even a "virtue" of sorts, the mark of a masculine personality and a strong leader; whereas an anti-social sin like deserting a group of people in their need remains a "mortal" sin in the Steinbeck code. What we have in *The Wayward Bus,* at best, is an anemic version of the Christian Gospel playing a limited role in human affairs. Even as the sign along the road urging repentance was just one among many signs, all advertising secular goods (180-181), so Christianity is just one of many cultural forces operative in the novel. There are simply too many wayward passengers (including the driver) on this "wayward bus" to warrant a different conclusion.

But Steinbeck does not so represent Christianity in order to cut it down to size. Rather, he uses elements of Christianity to elevate the character of his protagonist, Juan Chicoy. Juan is a practical man: realistic, objective, "natural," "a noble savage," incapable of self-deception. He exudes masculinity. He is a leader: competent, confident, courageous. There is nothing mean about him. He is "good" by most secular standards, but hardly pious. He is the kind of man Steinbeck admires. To suggest and symbolize that admiration, Steinbeck give him the initials J. C., putting him thereby into the company of another great man (but no more than that in Steinbeck's view), Jesus Christ. Like Jesus, Juan is a "savior" of sorts, but only in a secular, this worldly sense, not in the eternal, other worldly sense believed by most proponents of Christianity. The machinery of the Christian Gospel is obviously present in *The Wayward Bus*, but it is present only for a literary purpose, namely, to give stature to Steinbeck's protagonist.

Notes

1. John Steinbeck, *The Wayward Bus* (New York: Penguin Books, 1995), 6. All future page locations for citations from this book will be included in parentheses in the text of the chapter.
2. In fact, Steinbeck makes frequent use of Arthurian mythology in a number of his novels.
3. As we will see later in my analysis of the novel *Of Mice and Men*, Steinbeck attempts to use profanity as a vehicle for the Gospel.

Study Guide for *The Wayward Bus*

1. What bearing might the description of Alice's coffee urn on page 6 have on the quality of the Gospel elements in *The Wayward Bus*?

2. Describe Steinbeck's attitude toward the characters and the topics he introduces in the novel.

3. Demonstrate Steinbeck's ability in characterization. For example, do you find yourself identifying with or "pulling for" the characters you laugh at? Do you find yourself liking characters whose conduct technically doesn't deserve admiration? Do any of the characters grow? Should Steinbeck be faulted for directly describing the characters rather than indirectly letting them describe themselves through their words and actions? Can you infer from Steinbeck's characterizations the Steinbeck code of morality?

4. Comment on Steinbeck's ability to interpret life.

5. Which character in the novel functions as a catalyst to the action and interaction that occur on the bus?

6. Note instances of skillful transition in subject matter. Compare, for example, the top of page 147 with the bottom of page 148, the middle of page 158 with the middle of page 162.

7. What similarity do you note between the name of the bus and part of its cargo? What might Steinbeck be suggesting through this correlation?

8. What features of the novel tempt the reader to treat it as an allegory? What is the significance of this genre for a Gospel pattern?

9. Note how secular interpretations of the novel invariably contain spiritual elements.

10. Detail the evidence for a Gospel pattern in the novel. Does this pattern enhance the Christian Gospel? Why does Steinbeck employ Gospel imagery?

For Further Reading

French, Warren. *John Steinbeck* (2nd edition, rev.). Boston: Twayne Publishers, 1975.

_____. *John Steinbeck's Fiction Revisited*. New York: Twayne Publishers, 1994.

Levant, Howard. *The Novels of John Steinbeck: A Critical Study*. Columbia, Missouri: University of Missouri Press, 1974.

Lisca, Peter. *John Steinbeck: Nature and Myth*. New York: Thomas Y. Crowell, 1978.

Marks, Lester Jay. *Thematic Design in the Novels of John Steinbeck*. The Hague: Mouton, 1969.

McCarthy, Paul. *John Steinbeck*. New York: Frederick Ungar Publishing Co., 1980.

Tedlock, Jr., E. W. and C. V. Wicker (eds.). *Steinbeck and His Critics: A Record of Twenty-Five Years*. Albuquerque: University of New Mexico Press, 1957.

Timmerman, John H. *John Steinbeck's Fiction: The Aesthetics of the Road Taken*. Norman, Oklahoma: University of Oklahoma Press, 1986.

CHAPTER SIX

The Old Man and the Sea
by Ernest Hemingway

Much that was said in Chapter Five about Steinbeck's use of the Christian Gospel in *The Wayward Bus* applies to Hemingway's use of the Gospel in *The Old Man and the Sea*. Both authors deliberately insert Gospel elements into their respective novels, but not for Gospel purposes. Gospel imagery in both works is too obvious and too frequent to be dismissed as accidental or incidental. But in neither writer is there an undercurrent of serious commitment to the truth claims of that Gospel or to its saving and sanctifying power in human experience. If there is any difference at all between Steinbeck and Hemingway in this respect, it is that the latter's use of the Gospel is not so overtly comic or light-hearted; it is more poignant. But, like Steinbeck, Hemingway uses Gospel elements to elevate the character of his protagonist, Santiago, and to ennoble his struggle with the huge marlin that he caught and attempted to protect from attacking sharks. As was true of Steinbeck, Hemingway's Gospel insertions are strictly for literary purposes; there is no demonstrable secondary goal of advancing the Christian message.

The inclusion of Gospel elements in *The Old Man and the Sea* is so abundant that the Christian reader must ward off the temptation to overstate the case. A prominent theme in the novel is the interdependence of man and nature, a sort of bond or brotherhood between the two based on likeness and love, on similarity and affection. Santiago's ruminations about turtles suggest this brotherhood and the bases for it. "*He was sorry for them all.* . . . Most people are heartless about turtles because a turtle's heart will beat for hours after he has been cut up and butchered. But the old man thought, *I have such a heart too, and my feet and hands are like theirs.*"[1] The old man's eyes, too, are "the same color as the sea" (10). Repeatedly, Santiago expresses his love for nature and nature's creatures. "He always thought of the sea as *la mar* which is what people call her in Spanish when they love her" (29). He calls the stars "his distant friends" and is happy that he does not have to kill the stars or the moon or the sun as he does his "friend" and his "true brother," the fish (75). Even when he kills a fish, he does so out of kindness, to spare it a lingering and painful death (39). Flying fish are Santiago's "principal friends on the ocean," and he is "sorry for the birds" (29). Porpoises are his "brothers like the flying fish" (48). When a bird perches on his boat, Santiago converses with it, concluding, "Take a good rest, small bird. . . . Then go in and take your chance like any man or bird or fish" (55). When the bird leaves, Santiago misses his company (56). In stalking the huge marlin, Santiago 'lets that mind be in him which is also in a fish,' thinking as the marlin thinks (and suspecting the marlin of thinking as the man thinks). Although he believes the marlin to lack man's intelligence, he considers the creature to be more noble than man and more capable otherwise (63). In fact, the old man invents a sort of counterpart to the Trinity when he muses, "There are three things that are brothers: the fish and my two hands" (64). For two entire pages Santiago entertains the reader with a delightful soliloquy about whether or not it is a sin to kill the fish (105-106). Are people worthy of eating him? Santiago wonders. Maybe it would be better if the fish were to kill him! (92). One of the most poignant passages in the novel is Santiago's reaction to a shark chomping off about forty pounds from the captured marlin lashed to his boat: "When the fish had been hit it was as though he himself were hit" (103). (Are we talking some sort of Gospel vicariousness here?) Santiago addresses the remainder of the marlin carcass as a companion in hunting (115). The best symbol of man's brotherhood with nature is the picture of the fisherman and his catch "sailing together lashed side by side" and Santiago's uncertainty about who is bringing whom to shore (99). And the best symbol of man's interdependence with nature is the line by which the fisherman and his catch are joined when the fish is hooked: "Now we are joined together and have been since noon. And no one to help either one of us" (50).

It is tempting to view this communion between man and nature so attractively depicted in Hemingway's novel as a reflection of something faintly Christian: perhaps, the delightful bond that prevailed between Adam and the animals in the Garden of Eden before Satan and sin spoiled that relationship; even better, the beginning of that restoration of nature Christ also effected by his redemption of humankind on the cross (See Romans 8:19-23). But it is just as easy to see in Hemingway's portrait of man and nature a sort of romanticized, poetic version of Darwinian evolution, especially those passages in the novel that detail the likenesses between man and animal. Such a conclusion is all the more warranted by Santiago's frequent assertions that he must triumph over the creatures he loves and resembles. Remember that Santiago told the bird perched on his boat to go in and take his "chance like any man or bird or fish." Despite all the affection Santiago expresses for the marlin he caught, the old man means to triumph over him and kill him. "Fish . . . I love you and respect you very much. But I will kill you dead before this day ends" (54). "The fish is my friend. . . . But I must kill him" (75). Santiago even invokes the help of the Virgin Mary for this killing: "Blessed Virgin, pray for the death of this fish. Wonderful though he is" (65). Although verbalizing no love for the marauding sharks as he does for other creatures of the sea, the old man does express his intention of attempting to be their master. "I am too old to club sharks to death," he concedes. "But I will try it as long as I have the oars and the short club and the tiller" (112). Later he resolves,"I'll fight them until I die" (115). One might see in Santiago's paradoxical treatment of other creatures a parallel to the Scripture's "The Lord disciplines those whom he loves" (Hebrews 12:6); that is, "the fish whom Santiago loves, he kills." But one might just as easily see in Santiago's stance toward other creatures an echo of Darwin's "survival of the fittest." If Santiago can't join them, he'll beat them! After all, Santiago concedes a cruel streak in nature. "Why did they make birds so delicate and fine as those sea swallows when the ocean can be so cruel? . . . [S]he can be so cruel and it comes so suddenly and such birds that fly, dipping and hunting, with their small sad voices are made too delicately for the sea" (29).

Neither the Christian nor the Darwinian conclusion in my opinion is warranted. Both in this instance are eisegesis, not exegesis, and I do not mean to advance either view as serious interpretations of Hemingway's intent. My only purpose in mentioning these conflicting conclusions is to show that the evidence Hemingway provides can cut both ways, given a reader predisposition toward one view or the other. The title of the novel itself, for all its apparent simplicity, captures the ambiguity of Santiago's stance toward nature. In "the old man and the sea," the "and" is the troublesome word. If I say, "David and Jonathan," we think of friendship between the two men. If I say, "David and Goliath," we think of an adversarial relationship between them. So it is with "the old man and the sea." Are the two companions (the old man with the sea)? Or are they adversaries (the old man versus the sea)? Or is Hemingway simply announcing the principal *dramatis personae* of his novel with no intention of implying any specific kind of relationship between them?

Clearly, we must turn elsewhere for the Gospel elements in Hemingway's novel. They are not hard to find. They abound in two areas: 1) in the Christian context for the novel and, above all, 2) in the numerous parallels between Santiago and the Lord Jesus.

First, the Christian context. The fish is a well-known Christian symbol. There is frequent use of the number "seven," a sacred number in Christian tradition. Santiago's name means "Saint James," the same name borne by one of our Lord's twelve disciples and a biblical writer. Though hardly a saint in the traditional hyperbolic sense of the word, Santiago is a man of courage and compassion. He even prays after a fashion (65), although the sincerity of that prayer may be suspect in the light of a later prayer spoken as he begins to pull his big catch in: "Now that I have him coming so beautifully, God help me endure. I'll say a hundred Our Fathers and a hundred Hail Marys. *But I cannot say them now*" (87, my emphasis).Twice Santiago admits that he "went out too far" (116, 120), a statement that could be viewed as a sort of "fall" (due to pride) and as also containing the seeds of some kind of "repentance."

More impressive are the numerous similarities between Christ and Santiago. Both are fishermen. Both are teachers. Both have disciples: Jesus has the twelve and Santiago has the loyal

Mandolin, who late in the novel peers into the old man's hut (122) as John and Peter peered into Jesus' tomb, who resolves to forsake his family and follow Santiago (125), but who, like the twelve, still has much to learn (126). On the very first page of the novel, there is specific reference to a forty-day period during which Santiago had not caught a fish,[2] bringing to mind Christ's forty-day temptation from Satan prior to the start of his mission. Like Jesus, Santiago has "no place to lay his head"; for a pillow he has to use his own trousers stuffed with newspaper (24). Musing whether he might better have not been a fisherman, Santiago adds in his defense, "But that was the thing I was born for" (50). Does this statement echo our Lord's confession before Pilate, "For this I was born, and for this I came into the world, to testify to truth"? (John 18:37). Echoing the Lord's Passion suffering, the ordeal between Santiago and the big fish begins at noon and lasts three days (46, 50, 86). Like Christ, Santiago is scorned and jeered at, but he does not reciprocate (11). The old man carries the mast on his shoulder at the start of the novel (15); he had once been "in the cross-trees of the mast-head" and "at that height [he] saw much." (71) At the end of the novel he shoulders the mast again, begins to climb up the hill with it, falls once, and has to sit down five times before he reaches his destination (121). He sleeps in the hut "with his arms out straight and the palms of hands up," at the sight of which his disciple, Mandolin, weeps (122). Like Christ, Santiago is given a relieving drink (124). Prior to this variety of crucifixion, there are frequent references to the scars on Santiago's hand and the lash marks on his back. When asked at the end of the novel, "How much did you suffer?" Santiago replies, "Plenty"(126), even as our Lord suffered beyond measure. Yet despite the intensity and nobility of Santiago's epic struggle, the novel ends with a waiter and a woman casually failing to appreciate the significance of the skeleton remnants of the marlin they see lashed to the old man's boat. Santiago's accomplishment, like that of Christ, appears to be more failure than success. This fisherman also was "without honor in his own country." But in both cases, the men are "destroyed but not defeated" (103).

The most explicit Christ image in the novel occurs on page 107. "'Ay,' he said aloud. There is no translation for this word and perhaps it is just a noise as a man might make, involuntarily, feeling the nail go through his hands and into the wood." At this point, one rends his garments and exclaims, "What further need have we of witnesses?" The Christ images are there; in fact, they abound. And while some critics do not deal with them, no one denies their presence.

Although the tone of Hemingway's allusions to Christ and the Gospel is less lighthearted, more reverent, than that of Steinbeck, those references are not especially intended to call attention to Christ and the Gospel. They are, rather, designed to win our admiration for Santiago. Despite the old man's lowly origin, humble occupation, and social insignificance, Hemingway suggests that Santiago is a hero who deserves to be placed into the circle of history's greatest figures, Jesus Christ included. His epic struggle with the fish he caught and with the sharks who devoured that fish merits comparison to the heroic struggle of Christ with his enemies.

That Santiago rather than Christ is the focus of Hemingway's comparison between the two is clear from the fact that Christ imagery is not the only way in which Hemingway seeks to magnify Santiago. Actually, the Christ imagery is just one of many strategies Hemingway employs. Nor am I especially referring to the customary literary techniques by which Hemingway solicits our admiration for Santiago: the depiction of Santiago's integrity, honesty, and courage; the poignancy and humanity of Santiago's soliloquies and reflections; the respect and reverence the disciple, Mandolin, accords his master, thereby eliciting similar respect and reverence from the reader. I refer, more emphatically, to the other champions, besides Christ, with which Hemingway juxtaposes Santiago, the lions, for example. Repeatedly, Santiago dreams of them; one of those dreams, in fact, is the subject of the last line of the novel. As a man dreams, so is he. The lion is the king of beasts. Ergo, Santiago is "king" among men. Joe DiMaggio, a baseball great, is another example. "I must be worthy of the great DiMaggio who does all things perfectly even with the pain of the bone spur in his heel," Santiago muses (68). Later he reflects, "I think the great DiMaggio would be proud of me today. I had no bone spurs. But the hands and the back hurt truly" (97). After killing a huge shark Santiago soliloquizes, "I wonder how the great DiMaggio would have liked the way I hit him in the brain?" (103-104). These comparisons become all the more valid (to Santiago at least) when he recalls that DiMaggio's father was a fisherman (68, 105). Once, long ago, Santiago had even been called "The Champion" when he bested a strong, athletic black man, Cienfuegos, "who was the strongest man on the docks," (69) in a hand-wrestling match of twenty-four hours duration. Cienfuegos was a champion, DiMaggio was a champion, Christ was a champion. The point? Santiago is a champion too.

Hemingway's use of the Gospel does not especially glorify that Gospel. But it does show the impact of Gospel on literature regardless of the intent of those writers who employ it. Gospel shows up in unexpected places. It is a tool in unexpected hands. "Christ is proclaimed in every way, whether out of false motives or true; and in that I rejoice" (Philippians 1:18).

Notes

1. Ernest Hemingway, *The Old Man and the Sea* (New York: Charles Scribner's Sons, 1952), 37 (my emphasis). All future page locations for citations from this book will be included in parentheses in the text of the chapter.

2. Actually, the total duration of Santiago's trial was eighty-four days, but Hemingway does single out forty of that total for specific mention.

Study Guide for *The Old Man and the Sea*

1. Note the complexity, subtlety, and skill of the point of view in this narrative.

2. Demonstrate especially from the boy's remarks to the old man at the beginning of the novel Hemingway's skill in suggesting a truth rather than overtly stating it. What is the structural function of the boy in respect to the old man?

3. Enumerate prominent refrains in the novel. What do they do for the structure of the novel? For the realism of the novel? For the characterization of Santiago?

4. Find descriptions that demonstrate Hemingway's careful observation of detail and his ability to enter into the thinking of an old fisherman.

5. How does the conversation between the woman tourist and the waiter at the end of the story serve the novel?

6. What are the principal traits of Santiago's character?

7. What ingredients of "the Hemingway code" surface in this novel? For instance, what is the relationship between man and nature? What is paradoxi-

cal about the relationship? What are the bases for this paradoxical relationship? How does the central incident of the novel symbolize this relationship? (See the last full paragraph on page 50 and the middle paragraph on page 99.)

8. Point out levels of meaning in the apparently simple title of the novel. Does the title merely describe the *dramatis personae*? Or a companionship? Or a conflict?

9. Enumerate the parallels between Santiago and Christ.

10. Does Hemingway use Gospel imagery for Gospel purposes? Or does he use the religion of Christ in order to advance a religion of man? If the latter is the case, what is the religion of man that Hemingway proposes?

For Further Reading

Atkins, John. *The Art of Ernest Hemingway: His Work and Personality.* London: Spring Books, 1952.

Baker, Carlos (ed.). *Ernest Hemingway: Critiques of Four Major Novels.* New York: Charles Scribner's Sons, 1962.

_____. *Hemingway: The Writer As Artist.* Princeton, New Jersey: Princeton University Press, 1963.

Baker, Sheridan. *Ernest Hemingway: An Introduction and Interpretation.* New York: Holt, Rinehart and Winston, Inc., 1967.

Brenner, Gerry. *Concealments in Hemingway's Works.* Columbus, Ohio: Ohio State University Press, 1983.

_____. *The Old Man and the Sea: Story of a Common Man.* New York: Twayne Publishers, Inc. 1991.

Dillon-Malone, Aubrey. *Hemingway: The Grace and the Pressure.* London: Robson Books, 1999.

Donaldson, Scott. *By Force of Will: The Life and Art of Ernest Hemingway.* New York: Viking Press, 1977.

_____ (ed.). *The Cambridge Companion to Hemingway.* New York: Cambridge University Press, 1996.

Gajdusek, Robert E. *Hemingway in His Own Country.* Notre Dame: University of Notre Dame Press, 2002.

Hays, Peter L. *Ernest Hemingway.* New York: The Continuum Publishing Co., 1990.

Kiley, Jed. *Hemingway: A Title Fight in Ten Rounds.* London: Methuen & Co., Ltd., 1965.

Moddelmog, Debra A. *Reading Desire: In Pursuit of Ernest Hemingway.* Ithaca, New York: Cornell University Press, 1999.

Nagel, James (ed.). *Ernest Hemingway: The Writer in Context.* Madison, Wisconsin: University of Wisconsin Press, 1984.

Rovit, Earl. *Ernest Hemingway.* New York: Twayne Publishers, Inc., 1963.

PART TWO

Possible Gospel Patterns in Literature

The presence of the Gospel in the selections considered in Part Two is much more tenuous than in the works analyzed in Part One. In the books studied in the first part of this book, the inclusion of Gospel was assumed. The only debate was over the degree of its presence, its purpose, and its quality. But in the works considered in this second part, the very presence of the Gospel is at issue. Of course, there is usually a degree of Gospel present; otherwise, there would be no basis for argument. But that Gospel presence is too minimal, conventional, accidental, or incidental to add up to any coherent and meaningful pattern that every reader can recognize. What Gospel is seen and the significance of what is seen are to a high degree in the eye of the beholder rather than in the specific selection beheld. If not difficult to establish the presence of the Gospel, it is at least hard to demonstrate any theological or literary rationale for its presence. Those finding Gospel themes may feel compelled to make a case for its presence and meaning—a procedure often inviting refutation by other equally capable readers. I am not suggesting that all positions are equally valid. But I am saying that there is enough ambiguity in the selection under discussion to justify the possibility of opposing positions. In short, there is room for argument.

CHAPTER SEVEN

Sir Gawain and the Green Knight

Sir Gawain and the Green Knight, a poem of probable fourteenth century provenance and of uncertain authorship,[1] is a good canidate for debate about whether or not it contains Gospel. It is loaded with Christian allusions. But it is easy to conclude that these allusions are simply a reflection of the culture in which the poem was written. The unknown author may not even have been conscious of their inclusion; he may have simply been reflecting the times and the environment in which he was working. One could argue that the presence of these allusions is no more significant than the mention of a church building in the description of a town in some contemporary novel. In other words, the Christian allusions in the Gawain poem may be incidental, merely geographical or chronological in function. Or they may be conventional or stereotyped insertions simply suggesting a Christian context but no particular Christian or even literary purpose.

Besides, these Christian allusions are not alone in *Sir Gawain and the Green Knight.* There are nearly as many pagan allusions, also possibly reflecting the milieu of the poem. "Some critics have been at pains to interpret. . . Sir Gawain in terms of pagan ritual in spite of the often declared Christian purpose of the writers."[2] For that matter, the chivalric code and the courtly love tradition permeate the poem, too, both of which were often as much at odds with the Christianity of the times as they were inextricably mingled with it. Given this blend of Christian, pagan, chivalric, and courtly love elements, how can one single out the Christian elements for special interpretative consideration and blithely ignore the rest of the mix? Why make a Gospel mountain out of a Gospel molehill?

There is another factor giving one pause in approaching the question of possible Gospel in *Sir Gawain and the Green Knight*: There are so many other features in this remarkable poem worth talking about. No consideration of the poem dare ignore or minimize these features. To begin with, the versification of the poem is significant.[3] Equally worth consideration is the symmetrical structure of the poem.[4] Meriting discussion also are the elements of chivalry and courtly love already alluded to. Finally, the strain of charming, delicate humor in the poem should not be overlooked. Gawain, for instance, must not only resist the seductions of the Host's wife, but he must do so without offending her or violating the conventions of the code of courtly love. (See, for example, 69, 70, 83, and 87.) In brief, he cannot simply say to her, "Get out of here, you slut!" Nor can he even bolt his bedroom door.

A Gospel interpretation of *Sir Gawain and the Green Knight* is a possibility, but no more than that. At best, it is only one of a number of interpretations accorded the poem. Many readers, with considerable justification, regard the poem as merely a superbly narrated and structured adventure story. Brian Stone, translator of the Gawain poem, makes reference to the attempt to interpret it exclusively in terms of pagan ritual, although neither he nor I agree with that position. Nearly all interpretations of the poem involve spiritual and/or Christian elements, but most of these readings of the poem are not necessarily Gospel interpretations involving the usual Christian understanding of the meaning of the Lord's person and work.

The first such interpretation of *Sir Gawain and the Green Knight* regards the poem as a tribute to the power of evil. Sir Gawain, though portrayed as effeminate and treacherous in Malory's better known treatment of the Arthurian circle, is still a noble hero in this earlier portrayal by the author of the Gawain poem. Yet look what happens to this fine specimen of King Arthur's Round Table knighthood. Although Gawain survives the assaults on his chastity, he does accept from his would-be seducer a green girdle that allegedly will protect him when the Green Knight later attempts to behead him (Gawain having beheaded the Green Knight—without harming him—in their first encounter). Nor does Gawain level with the lady's husband, Gawain's host, Sir Bertilak, about the green girdle she has given him when the two men exchange their respective winnings as they had done twice before. Neither does Gawain make mention of the green girdle when he goes to confession to seek absolution prior to his appointment with the Green Knight. Moreover, Gawain flinches when the Green Knight makes a pass at him with his axe in the beheading attempt. "But here your faith failed you, you flagged somewhat, sir," the Green Knight says to Gawain at the time (109). Although the Green Knight credits Gawain for avoiding unchastity and materialism, he does accuse him of a lapse in courage: "for love of your life, which is less blameworthy" (109). Gawain agrees. In the same stanza he acknowledges, "How ill I behaved" (110). When the Green Knight (really Sir Bertilak in disguise) returns to Gawain the green girdle to keep permanently (Sir Bertilak's wife had tempted Gawain at her husband's behest), Gawain consents to wear it only as a badge of his moment of disgrace, "in token that he was taken in a tarnishing sin" (113). Later, among his peers at the Round Table, Gawain blushes at any reference to the girdle he wears and admits that sin cannot ultimately be concealed (114).

The point seems to be, according to this view, that if evil can shake a paragon of virtue like Gawain, how much more should ordinary people like us be on our guard against its baneful influence. To paraphrase Luke 23:31, "If these things happen to a green tree (like the noble Gawain), what will happen in the dry tree (like sinful us)?" Ergo, give evil its due and be on guard.

A more common interpretation is quite the opposite: The poem is a tribute to the goodness of Gawain in particular and to human potential in general. Gawain did the best he could. The point of the poem is to demonstrate what a fine chap Gawain was, whether pitted against the supernatural (the beheading game) or the natural (the chastity test). We see in this knight our potential for goodness. Though we may not match him in respect to bravery and purity, we are encouraged to emulate him. Who of us could have so successfully resisted the charming hostess, especially in decolletage? In addition, Gawain survived the transitional temptation between the seduction attempt and the return beheading game, the temptation to fail his appointment with the promise that no one would ever know of his failure (100). Nor does he flinch at the Green Knight's second pass with the axe. And when to his surprise Gawain survives the third stroke of the axe with merely a slight wound, he challenges the Green Knight to battle. The Green Knight himself calls his opponent "the most perfect paladin ever to pace the earth" (109). The strongest evidence for the view that the poem is a tribute to the goodness of Gawain (and, by extension, a tribute to our potential for goodness) is the fact that King Arthur's knights wear a girdle thereafter as a badge of honor, as "an everlasting honor to him who had it" (115).

Brian Stone, the translator of the Penguin Classics edition of *Sir Gawain and the Green Knight* agrees. "[Gawain's] failing is so slight, and he behaves so nearly like a paragon throughout, that the poem becomes a celebration of Christian knightly virtue" (14-15).

In my opinion, the two interpretations above put asunder what the unknown author of the Gawain poem has joined together. The two interpretations can easily be combined into one cohesive whole, the central symbol of the girdle joining the two views. Gawain wears the girdle as a token of his corruption by evil. His peers wear the girdle as a tribute to his courage and chastity. The point suggested? However much we properly decry evil, we share in it; we therefore admire those who battle it successfully. We are to be harsh on our self but charitable toward others. We recognize the worst that evil can do, but we praise those who survive its onslaughts and hope for the best in our own struggle with evil. This view seems congruent with the motto of the Green Garter appended to the poem, "*Hony Soyt Qui Mal Pence*" (Let him be ashamed who thinks evil).

The above interpretations clearly contain Christian elements. But those elements are not uniquely Christian. Other religions and ethical systems, too, decry evil and encourage good. And however "Christian" these interpretations may seem, there is nothing in them remotely resembling the Christian Gospel of salvation by God's grace through Jesus Christ. Rather, the above interpretations are strictly moralistic, with a strong suggestion of salvation through character rather than through Christ.

Two minority interpretations of *Sir Gawain and the Green Knight* do, however, approximate Gospel patterns. At least one critic has linked the poem with Matthew 16:25, claiming that Gawain nearly lost his life by trying to save it (in accepting the green girdle for protection) but that he eventually found his life by being willing to lose it (in his ultimately submitting to the three strokes of the Green Knight's axe). With more legitimacy another critic sees in the prominence of the color green in the poem the triumph of spring over winter, of life over death, a triumph buttressed by Gawain's survival of the beheading attempt. The Gospel pattern suggested is the death and resurrection pattern, so common in literature and so unique to the Holy Scriptures. Attractive as these views are in explaining the whole, there seems to be little explicit evidence in the poem to support them. The views, I fear, flirt with the danger of eisegesis.

A Gospel interpretation with considerable merit, I believe, is that the Gawain poem is a depiction of our pilgrimage through life in which we, in the language of Ephesians 6:12, "struggle . . . not against enemies of blood and flesh" (e. g., the chastity temptation [the natural]) but, above all, "against the spiritual forces of evil in the heavenly places" (e. g., the beheading game [the supernatural]).[5] To prevail in this struggle we need God's grace given in Christ Jesus.

Early in the poem it is said of Gawain that he is in danger of being "beheaded by an *unearthly being* out of *arrogance*" (47, my emphasis). There we have it: Both "flesh and blood" ("arrogance") and "principalities and powers" ("unearthly being") are identified as Gawain's enemies. Mention has already been made of the Green Knight possibly being Satan in disguise. Should the Green Knight be a supernatural being, the poet reminds us that supernatural help is available: "Our Lord can certainly see / That his own are in safe hands" (101). The green chapel, too, the site near which Gawain keeps his appointment with the Green Knight, is viewed by Gawain as a house of Satan. "At such might Satan be seen / Saying matins at midnight" (102). Moments later Gawain calls the chapel "the most evil holy place I ever entered" (103).

For this battle against his own evil nature and Satan as well, Gawain cannot rely on his own resources. He needs God's grace in Jesus. The poem abounds in reminders that this help is not only needed but is also available. Both Arthur and Guinevere commend Gawain to Christ as he leaves for his adventure (44). Was this reminder casual piety (like our modern goodbye)? Or was it a serious benediction freighted with Gospel theology? As he nears Sir Bertilak's castle, Gawain thanks Jesus and Saint Julian, "who had given him grace" in finding this lodging in the wilderness (50). Pleased at his host's initial hospitality, Gawain thanks him and adds, "May Christ make good your grace!" (52). Again, how much theology should we see in this conventional reply? When confronted the second time with the lady's temptation to fornication, Gawain says, "So save me God!" (79). Is this a sincere appeal for God's protection? Or is it a mild oath expressing Gawain's alarm? A similar cry from Gawain's lips, "God shield me!" occurs during the third temptation, at which point the poet editorializes, "And peril would have impended / Had Mary not minded her knight" (87). Between the temptation from the lady and his appointment with the Green Knight, Gawain seeks out a priest to confess his sins and to be enlightened "on how he might have salvation in the hereafter" (91). As Gawain exits Sir Bertilak's castle for his appointment with danger, a porter prays God "to grant that Gawain would be saved" (98). Saved from what? From death at the hands of the Green Knight? Or from eternal damnation? The word "saved" is ambiguous. In any event, Gawain sounds most serious when, shortly before his meeting with his antagonist, he vows, "Being given to God's good care, / My trust in Him shall be shown" (101). Even the Green Knight assures Gawain that his sins have been absolved (110), and the poet reminds us as Gawain sets out on his return to Arthur's castle that "his life [has been] saved by grace" (113). Most importantly, the poem concludes with the prayer, "Now Christ with his crown of thorn / Bring us his bliss evermore" (115).

What are we to make of all this evidence? Its quantity is sufficient for a Gospel interpretation. But what about its quality? Are these statements serious theology? Or are they simply pious cliches? Whatever the answer, it easily can be based on a circular argument. Does the Gospel interpretation arise out of the inherent quality of the Gospel evidence? Or does a predisposition for the Gospel (or against it, for that matter) season the objective evidence with the subjective quality it desires?

Certainly, if this Gospel interpretation of the poem is embraced, it enriches the symbolism of the poem. Given this interpretation, the girdle becomes a symbol of work-righteousness, of trust in our own strength, in our pilgrimage through life; and the pentangle becomes a symbol of the panoply of God with which we equip ourselves and in which we trust. Further, the poem becomes a fuller, more realistic portrait of our Christian pilgrimage in that it recognizes both the role of the natural and the supernatural in that journey. Best of all, the poem's accent on the supernatural enemies, "principalities, powers and the rulers of darkness," justifies the inclusion of the pagan element so obvious in the poem. That pagan element is no longer just a cultural appendage. It is, rather, an integral part of those satanic powers that war against our salvation.

Yet, candidly, there are weaknesses in this Gospel interpretation, not the least of which is that it seems out of tune with the red-blooded adventure and the subtle but winsome humor that inform the poem. And, as hinted above, the view may be taking too seriously conventional, stereotyped statements of piety. A Gospel interpretation may, in Shakespearean metaphor, be making a cannon bullet out of a bird-bolt. Also, Protestant readers may object that the view of God's grace the poem presents is infused grace rather than accredited grace, grace not solely God's but God's grace mingled with human merit. This objection is perhaps the easiest to cope with. One can hardly expect a Protestant view of grace in a pre-Reformation work of poetry! And even a Protestant, it seems, would prefer some Gospel in a poem to none at all.

Notes

1. The best argument for its authorship, in my opinion, is that it was penned by the author of *Pearl, Cleanness,* and *Patience. Sir Gawain and the Green Knight* exists in the same manuscript as these poems, there are similarities in style, and, like *Pearl, Gawain* consists of 101 stanzas. (There is even a reference to a "pearl" in the 95th stanza of *Gawain.*) Only trouble is, we don't know who wrote *Pearl* and the other works in this manuscript.
2. Brian Stone, tr., "Introduction" to *Sir Gawain and the Green Knight* (New York: Penguin Books, 1974), 13. All other future page locations for citations from this book will be included in parentheses in the text of the chapter.
3. The poem is an instance of alliterative verse, characterized by patterned alliteration rather than patterned rhyme. The only rhyme occurs in what is called the bob and wheel at the end of each stanza (five lines, the first containing one iambic foot, the next four each containing three iambic feet, and all five lines rhyming ababa.)
4. The structure can be viewed in terms of twos: two mentions of Troy, one at the start and one at the end; two Christmas festivals; two possible beheading incidents; two tests for the hero, one natural (chastity) and the other supernatural (courage); two sides to the Sir Bertilak's character, gruesome and jolly; two contrasting women at Bertilak's castle, one ugly, one beautiful; above all, two central symbols in the poem, the shield and the girdle, informing parallels in the plot.

It is just as easy to view the structure of the poem in terms of threes: three tests for Gawain (if one includes the transitional temptation he experiences to get credit for not fulfilling his vow to meet the Green Knight for a return beheading event); three assaults on Gawain's chastity (one kiss concluding the first, two kisses the second, and three kisses the third); three hunts (a deer, a bear, and a fox); three exchanges of winnings between Gawain and Sir Bertilak; three green's (knight, girdle, chapel); three prominent geographical settings (Arthur's palace, Bertilak's castle, and the green chapel).

More subtle are the correspondences between Gawain's mood and his environment and especially the correspondences between the huntings of the deer, bear, and fox and the simultaneous pursuit on Gawain's chastity by the Host's wife.

5. Some critics consider the Green Knight to be Satan in disguise. See 182 of the Penguin edition.

Study Guide for *Sir Gawain and the Green Knight*

1. Familiarize yourself with the authorship question of *Sir Gawain and the Green Knight*.

2. Identify the motifs of the poem and note how carefully the author has woven them together.

3. Why is it important to keep in mind that Gawain is a romance hero rather than an epic hero or a novel hero?

4. Familiarize yourself with the unique metrical structure of the poem.

5. Itemize in detail the elements of the code of chivalry and of the code of courtly love which permeate the poem.

6. Note the occasional allusions to Fortune or Fate. What is the medieval understanding of the relationship of Fate to God?

7. Find both pagan and Christian elements in the poem. What bearing does the presence of either of these elements have on the possibility of a Gospel pattern in this poem?

8. Study carefully the poet's exposition of the Pentangle. In what respects does the Pentangle encapsulate the strange mix of elements that constitute the poem?

9. Itemize the techniques Gawain employs to ward off the Hostess's temptations. What complicates his efforts to resist her? What is ironic about the temptation scene?

10. Enumerate the signs of weakness which Gawain shows. What actually motivates Gawain to accept the green girdle?

11. What techniques does the Green Knight employ to terrorize Gawain?

12. Does Gawain feel that he has passed his test? Do those who know him feel that he has? Relate these differing evaluations of Gawain to the interpretation of the poem. How does the girdle unite these conflicting evaluations?

13. Note the transitional temptation Gawain experiences on the way to the green chapel, and comment on its thematic and structural significance.

14. Establish a connection between Matthew 16:25 and the meaning of the poem. Evaluate the validity of this connection.

15. Establish a connection between Ephesians 6:11-12 and the meaning of the poem. Evaluate the validity of this connection. (For instance, what significance do the Pentangle and the girdle acquire, given this interpretation? How does this interpretation resolve the problem of the pagan element in the poem? Does the poem really celebrate God's grace—or rather man's potential for goodness?)

16. Attempt to organize the structure of the poem in terms of twos and threes. Note also how correspondences between Gawain's mood and his environment, between the three hunts and the three bedroom scenes, and between the Green Knight and the Host enhance the structure of the poem.

17. Note the surprising amount of humor in this story of adventure, danger, and testing.

For Further Reading

Andrew, Malcolm and Ronald Waldron (eds.). *The Poems of the Pearl Manuscript: Pearl, Cleanness, Patience. Sir Gawain and the Green Knight.* Exeter, Devon: University of Exeter Press, 1987, 1996.

Blanch, Robert J., Miriam Youngerman Miller, and Julian N. Wasserman (eds.). *Text and Matter: New Critical Perspectives of the Pearl-Poet.* Troy, New York: The Whitston Publishing Co., 1991.

Blanch, Robert J. (ed.). *Sir Gawain and Pearl: Critical Essays.* Bloomington, Indiana: Indiana University Press, 1966.

Borroff, Marie. *Sir Gawain and the Green Knight: A Stylistic and Metrical Study.* New Haven, Connecticut: Yale University Press, 1962.

Brewer, Derik and Jonathan Gibson (eds.). *A Companion to the Gawain Poet.* Cambridge, England: D. S. Brewer, 1997.

Condren, Edward I. *The Numerical Universe of the Gawain Pearl Poet: Beyond Phi.* Gainesville, Florida: University Press of Florida, 2002.

Fox, Denton (ed.). *Twentieth Century Interpretations of Sir Gawain and the Green Knight: A Collection of Critical Essays.* Englewood Cliffs, New Jersey: Princeton University Press, 1968.

Howard, Donald R. and Christian Zacher (eds.). *Critical Studies of Sir Gawain and the Green Knight.* Notre Dame, Indiana: University of Notre Dame Press, 1968.

Johnson, Lynn Staley. *The Voice of the Gawain-Poet.* Madison, Wisconsin: University of Wisconsin Press, 1984.

Marti, Kevin. *Body, Heart, and Text in the Pearl-Poet.* Lewiston, New York: The Mellen Press, 1991.

Moorman, Charles. *The Pearl-Poet.* New York: Twayne Publishers, 1968.

Prior, Sandra Pierson. *The Fayre Formez of the Pearl Poet.* East Lansing, Michigan: Michigan State University Press, 1996.

Putter, Ad. *An Introduction to the Gawain-Poet.* London and New York: Longman, 1996.

Stanbury, Sarah. *Seeing the Gawain-Poet: Description and the Act of Perception.* Philadelphia: University of Pennsylvania Press, 1991.

CHAPTER EIGHT

Of Mice and Men
by John Steinbeck

Most critics regard Steinbeck's *Of Mice and Men* as one of his best efforts. Nearly everyone notes its numerous structural merits. Like *Madame Bovary, Brideshead Revisited,* and the Parable of the Laborers in the Vineyard, *Of Mice and Men* is a clear example of the frame or bookend device, that is, the novel ending as it began. The pool where George and Lennie appear at the beginning of the novel is the very same locale where George, as an act of necessary kindness (in his view), shoots Lennie at the end of the novel. This frame or bookend device extends even to minutiae: a heron, a watersnake, the play of light and shadow on adjacent mountains, sycamores, Lennie's reference to ketchup, his thoughts of Aunt Clara, and his love of rabbits are all mentioned at the end as they were at the beginning. George Milton and Lennie Small, the protagonists, are obviously foils: The one is small; the other—despite his ironic name—is large; the one has street-smarts, the other is incapable of making his way through the workaday world. Dramatic foreshadowing is another excellent feature of the book's tightly structured unity. Lennie's affectionate but rough petting of mice and puppies leading to their death foreshadows his "petting" of Curley's wife's hair leading to her death, the "crime" that undoes George and Lennie's dreams of owning property by compelling George to kill Lennie lest he fall into the hands of a lynching party. Even the manner of Lennie's death, a pistol shot in the back of the head, is foreshadowed by the execution of Candy's mangy old dog in the middle of the novel, also with a pistol shot to the back of the head. Here again, the dramatic foreshadowing permeates the minutiae. Lennie has dog-like traits: retrieving a dead mouse, hands described as "paws,"[1] a voice that growls (72), urged on by cries of "Get 'im" (63), threatened with a "collar" (72). The heron at the pool devouring the water snake present is a microcosm of Lennie's ultimate fate.

There is less unanimity on other aspects of the novel. Is it a tragedy? Or a tragi-comedy? If it is a tragedy, is it a character tragedy? Or a fate tragedy? Or a combination of the two? Above all, what does the novel mean? What is it trying to tell us about life? Most agree that the novel is more than an adventure story or a character sketch.

Many readers connect the "moral" of the story with its title, a fragment of the familiar excerpt from Robert Burns's poem, "To a Mouse" : "The best laid schemes o' mice and men / Gang aft aglay." The desire for companionship, best symbolized by George and Lennie's traveling together and Lennie's continuous urge to pet, and the wish to own a piece of property and enjoy its fruits directly, best symbolized by the protagonists' plan to own land and raise rabbits—these are the "best laid schemes" of George and Lennie. Others want in, Crooks the black and Candy the amputee. Even Curley's wife, a flirt and a troublemaker, at least yearns for companionship. "An' what am I doin'?" she asks. "Standin' here talkin' to a bunch of bindle stiffs . . . an' likin' it becuase they ain't nobody else" (78). But, alas, the plans of George, Lennie, Crooks, and Candy go awry ("gang aglay"), Curley's wife being the catalyst for the failure. Her threat to blackmail Crooks with a false rape charge causes Crooks to withdraw from the plan. Above all, her gratuitous association with Lennie causes him to "accidentally" kill her when he "pets" her hair and "can't" let go. The end of the dream is a bullet in the back of Lennie's head. In the pessimistic words of Crooks to Candy, "You'll talk about it a hell of a lot, but you won't get no land. You'll be a swamper here till they take you out in a box" (75). Or Crooks to Lennie: "Nobody never gets to heaven, and nobody gets no land" (74). It is a piece of pessimism confirmed by George himself: "I think I knowed from the very first, I think I knowed we'd never do her" (94).

Rather than focusing on the poignant disappointment of the unrealized dreams in *Of Mice and Men* (and attributing it to character flaw or fate), Warren French, for one, accentuates the maturity of coming to terms with the disappointment ensuing from schemes that "gang aft aglay." Dreams of rabbits and a small parcel of land may be childish. Crooks and George's assessments are not signs of pessimism or cynicism; they are, rather, the beginning of wisdom. These men are growing up, adjusting to the world that is rather than pursuing a false dream. It is an interpretation reinforced by the Arthurian pattern found in so many of Steinbeck's novels. The ideals of chivalry, the aspirations of romantic love, the search for the Holy Grail are gradually replaced by unrealized goals, the dissolution of companionship, adultery, and death. The knights of the Round Table grow up—and so do George, Crooks, Candy, and others. It is an interpretation perhaps too contemporary for some in its faddish exaltation of unhappiness over happiness, but it is an interpretation, nonetheless, validated by objective evidence in the novel.

Given the prevalence of Gospel in *The Wayward Bus* (cf. Chapter Five) and the appearance of Gospel in other Steinbeck works such as *The Grapes of Wrath* and *East of Eden,* one should be prepared for the possible emergence of Gospel in *Of Mice and Men* as well. Only trouble is, there are many Steinbeck novels without Gospel elements altogether. And if they are present in *Of Mice and Men,* their presence is arguable and, above all, add up to no particularly coherent or meaningful pattern. But let's look at the evidence.

The use of the first letters of the biblical names of Cain and Abel, "C" and "A," so painstakingly carried out in the names of the characters in *East of Eden,* surfaces in part also in *Of Mice and Men.* Many names begin with a "C" (too many to be happenstance): Crooks, Candy, Carlson, Curley, Curley's wife, and Clara, suggesting perhaps that they, like Cain, fail to be their brother's keeper. Trouble is, Crooks and Clara are too sympathetically portrayed to deserve that classification. Nor are there any characters whose names begin with an "A," although the fact that George's name doesn't begin with a "C" may be enough in Steinbeck's plan to separate him from the rest and associate him with Abel, especially since George was very definitely "his brother's keeper" in respect to Lennie, even when he kills him. Assuming that George is "the Abel" in contrast to all the other "Cain's," we have at best only a biblical pattern, not a Gospel one. Failure to be our brother's keeper is a violation of God's Law, being our brother's keeper is a keeping of God's Law, but both are Law, not Gospel. The most a Cain and Abel pattern proves is that Steinbeck had the Bible and Christianity on his mind when he wrote the novel.

Turning to the last names of the protagonists is a bit more promising. George Milton: the "Milton" part might bring to mind John Milton's works, especially *Paradise Lost* and *Paradise Regained,* both of which could correlate to George and Lennie's property aspirations and dashed hopes. Lennie Small: The "Small" part could, with a little imagination, be associated with "one of these little ones" (Luke 17:2) or "the least of these who are members of my family" (Matthew 25:40), for which Jesus showed such compassion.

Then there is Slim: "the prince of the ranch" (33), a natural leader, who exudes masculinity. Actually, Slim is more than a man's man, he is a God-figure. His "face was ageless" (33), he has "God-like eyes" (40), he moves "with a majesty only achieved by royalty" (33). "There was a gravity in his manner . . . that all talk stopped when he spoke" (33). "His authority was so great that his word was taken on any subject" (33). Candy looked at him to appeal the decree that his old dog should be executed; he hoped "to find some reversal," and "Slim gave him none" (47). Slim is capable of awesome deeds, such as "killing a fly on the wheeler's butt with a bull whip without touching the mule" (33). Even George's voice takes on "the tone of confession" (40) when talking to Slim. Twice Slim excuses or "forgives" acts, Lennie's crushing of Curley's hand (64) and George's execution of Lennie (107).

The best evidence, in my opinion, is the time frame of the novel: not only three days but the very same three days as those that were the setting for our Lord's crucifixion, burial, and resurrection, Friday through Sunday (49). If the association is valid, then what is being called to our mind is definitely a series of Gospel events.

Given the assumption that there is something faintly biblical or religious about the novel, the lengthy and repeated paeans to the rabbits Lennie and George hope to own someday resemble something liturgical. Facetiously, I call the tribute to rabbits on pages 13-15, "The Order of Rabbits" or "The Litany of Rabbits."

The passage contains dialogue, repetitions, even italicized sections. "George's voice became deeper," and he says his parts "rhythmically as though he had said them many times before" (13). Lennie has his parts "by heart" (14). And even though Lennie "know[s] all of it," he regards George as the more qualified to speak the lines: "It ain't the same if I tell it" (14). Lennie repeats parts of this "liturgy" right before he is killed at the end of the novel. It is interesting that Crooks associates Lennie's dream of rabbits with heaven (74), although the association for Crooks at the time is a cynical one.

The most arresting—albeit blasphemous—evidence is the association of Lennie with Christ, especially in the frequent profanities in the novel. "Jesus Christ, you're a crazy bastard," George says to Lennie (4). Come to think of it, Jesus' relatives thought that he was "beside himself" (Mark 3:21). "Jesus Christ, Lennie," George says later. Is "Lennie" vocative? Or is his name an appositive? (This close juxtaposition of the names "Jesus" and "Lennie" occurs frequently in the novel.) When Curley sees the corpse of Lennie lying on the sand at the end of the novel, he exclaims, "Got him, by God." No doubt, Curley intended profanity. But could his words be a description of Lennie's present locale—"by God"? In the presence of all this profanity, the pious reader may wonder, "What possible good can come out of this particular Nazareth!" Yet the association of Lennie with Christ, forced as it may seem initially, acquires some respectability when one considers that both Jesus and Lennie are powerful but tender. And, of course, both are executed.

I would like to believe that there is some Gospel fire in all this biblical smoke, but I can't pinpoint it. The evidence in the novel is too abundant to ignore—but too fragmented to constitute an identifiable pattern. Most of the evidence seems to prove only that the Bible was a part of Steinbeck's reading experience and that his familiarity with it leaks out in his writing, even as his acquaintance with the Arthurian epic does. At best, the biblical/Gospel imagery in *Of Mice and Men* universalizes the particular episode Steinbeck portrays so poignantly. Maybe the images, especially when applied to Lennie, are meant to elevate his character by putting him into good company, no less than that of Jesus of Nazareth. These would be valid literary uses of biblical/Gospel images. At worst, the inclusion of these references may reflect a literary fad, the presence of Christ images so often found in works by Faulkner, Hemingway, O'Connor, Vonnegut, and other recent and contemporary authors. But the strictly Gospel images in Steinbeck's *Of Mice and Men,* if actually present, are too random, incidental, and profane to constitute, in my opinion, the inclusion of Gospel for purposes, even secondarily, of respecting or advancing the Gospel.

Notes

1. John Steinbeck, *Of Mice and Men* and *Cannery Row* (New York: Penguin Books, 1986), 63 and 92. All future page locations for citations from this book will be included in parentheses in the text of the chapter.

Study Guide for *Of Mice and Men*

1. Point out specific virtues of Steinbeck's writing style.

2. Compare the setting of the end of the story with that at the beginning of the story, and comment on its structural significance.

3. Describe the opposite characteristics of George and Lennie. What is the literary name for this deliberate contrast in characterization?

4. Demonstrate in detail how superbly Steinbeck foreshadows the end of the story throughout the novel.

5. Identify prominent symbols in the novel.

6. Enumerate the principal characteristics of the *dramatis personae.* Are the characters true-to-life?

7. What interpretation of the novel is suggested by its title? What variation to this interpretation is suggested by the frequency of the "trap" image in the novel?

8. What evidence is there that Steinbeck may have intended this novel as a paean to maturing, growing up? How would the Arthurian pattern that some find in this novel reinforce this particular interpretation?

9. What is significant about the fact that so many names of characters begin with the letter "C"? How does George's name fit into this pattern?

10. Comment on the Gospel possibilities of the names George Milton and Lennie Small.

11. Is Slim a God-figure?

12. What is the time frame of the novel?

13. What liturgical elements can be found in the repeated passages about rabbits?

14. Note the frequent association of Lennie with Christ. Are many of these associations profanity or profundity?

15. On the basis of your answers to Questions 9-14, evaluate the possibility of a Gospel pattern in this novel.

For Further Reading

French, Warren. *John Steinbeck* (2nd edition, rev.). Boston: Twayne Publishers, 1975.

———. *John Steinbeck's Fiction Revisited*. New York: Twayne Publishers, 1994.

Levant, Howard. *The Novels of John Steinbeck: A Critical Study*. Columbia, Missouri: University of Missouri Press, 1974.

Lisca, Peter. *John Steinbeck: Nature and Myth*. New York: Thomas Y. Crowell, 1978.

Marks, Lester Jay. *Thematic Design in the Novels of John Steinbeck*. The Hague: Mouton, 1969.

McCarthy, Paul. *John Steinbeck*. New York: Frederick Ungar Publishing Co., 1980.

Tedlock, Jr., E. W. and C. V. Wicker (eds.). *Steinbeck and His Critics: A Record of Twenty-Five Years*. Albuquerque: University of New Mexico Press, 1957.

Timmerman, John H. *John Steinbeck's Fiction: The Aesthetics of the Road Taken*. Norman, Oklahoma: University of Oklahoma Press, 1986.

CHAPTER NINE

A Handful of Dust
by Evelyn Waugh

Though not as popular or well-known as *Brideshead Revisited*, Evelyn Waugh's *A Handful of Dust* is viewed more favorably by literary critics. Many consider it the best work in the Waugh canon. All the good features for which a sophisticated reader looks in a work of art are abundantly present: three dimensional characterization, incisive wit, subtle humor, penetrating insights on human nature, understatement, suggestion, dramatic foreshadowing, poetic justice, dramatic irony, symbolism, form reinforcing content—you name it.

In the context of these overpowering attractions, the possibility of Gospel content in the novel may not even come to the reader's mind. And certainly no novel—at least on the surface—would seem to be less eligible for that possibility. Introducing the subject of Gospel inclusion may seem as abrupt and arbitrary as Mr. Todd's unexpected question of Tony in the middle of a thoroughly secular conversation, "Do you believe in God?"[1] And even if the subject is introduced, the average reader, upon completion of the novel, may share Tony Last's sentiment (in a different context): "The last thing one wants to talk about at a time like this is religion" (158).

To begin with, there is the title: *A Handful of Dust* is a phrase excerpted from T. S. Eliot's *Waste Land* (note that title too). The full line reads, "I will show you fear in a handful of dust." That title calls to mind the biblical pronouncement, "You are dust, and to dust you shall return" (Genesis 3:19). The title suggests that *A Handful of Dust* is to the Waugh canon what Ecclesiastes is to the biblical canon with its initial theme of doom, "Vanity of vanities! All is vanity" (Ecclesiastes 1:2).

The tone of the novel reinforces the tone of the title. From Mrs. Beavers' initial designs on the pocketbooks of those house owners for whom she contracts to do interior decorating to the novel's closing depiction of the transformation of the glory of Hetton House into a silver fox farm managed by mediocre heirs, the tone of *A Handful of Dust* is cynical and pessimistic, a tunnel with no light at the end, a dark cloud devoid of silver lining. A marriage disintegrates, a child dies in a fall from a horse, and the protagonist's search for a fabled lost city ends in his being condemned to eke out the remainder of his earthly existence reading Dickens novels aloud to a crazed plantation owner in the South American jungle.[2] Scenes of foolish and fickle savages in the jungle alternate with scenes of grasping, designing people in an allegedly more civilized England, the point of the juxtaposition being that savagery is rampant everywhere.

Accenting the dark content of the novel are the frequent animal images Waugh employs—carnivorous images rather than the cuddly kind. Mrs. Beaver and her son, John Beaver, "prey" on people and "gnaw" on their houses and incomes in order to build their own "dam." Jock Grant-Menzies pursues women and raises pigs. The boy John Andrew describes Lady Cockpurse as a monkey who eats nuts and gibbers and chatters and lashes around with her tail as she endeavors to catch and devour big, juicy fleas (56). A shameless blonde bears the name Mrs. Rattery; she attempts to console Tony during his bereavement with a game called Snap in which one of them plays the role of a hen clucking, "Coop-coop-coop," and the other the role of a dog barking, "Bow-wow." A "ravenous tiger," "furtive jackel," and "ponderous elephant" replace the idyllic ox and ass in Mr. Tendril's oft-repeated Christmas sermon as he loses the thread of his comparisons (79). Skinned rabbits from "the stinkeries" are fed to the silver foxes that have taken over Hetton House at the close of the novel. Together, these images portray a dog-eat-dog kind of society.

Form matches content. The structure of the novel reinforces its dire events and the foreboding tone in which those events are narrated. "English Gothic," the title of Chapter Two, is echoed by the titles of Chapters Four and Seven, "English Gothic - II" and

"English Gothic - III" respectively. "English Gothic" depicts the glories of Hetton House romantically in terms of time-honored traditions and rooms named after the knights of King Arthur's Round Table. But in "English Gothic - II" we are told, "A whole Gothic world had come to grief. . .there was now no armour, glittering in the forest glades, no embroidered feet on the greensward; the cream and dappled unicorns had fled. . ." (209). When we arrive at "English Gothic - III," the Gothic mansion has been replaced by *Bleak House*, the dreary name of the dreary Dickens novel Tony Last is compelled to read aloud to his crazed host. The chapter titles and their content depict the devolution of the glory that was once Hetton House.

Add to all this one crushing fact, namely, that Tony arrives at the fabled city for which he is searching only in delirium. When he awakens to reality again, that reality consists of living in the forced society of the maniacal Mr. Todd "until death do them part." How can there be Gospel in so pessimistic and cynical a world view as that provided in Waugh's *A Handful of Dust?*

Oddly enough, it is that very city that rouses the suspicion of Gospel inclusion in Waugh's presentation.[3] When first introduced in the novel, that city is simply one of the goals of the geographical and archaeological expedition Dr. Messinger has persuaded Tony Last to join. But Waugh soon suggests that he may have more in mind that just a curious discovery. On the ship bound for South America, a fellow passenger asks Tony where he is going and what he is looking for. "To tell you the truth, I am looking for a city," Tony replies. In surprise the stranger responds, "Sounded just like you said you were looking for a city." "Yes," Tony answers. "That *was* what you said?" returns the stranger. Again Tony replies, "Yes" (211). The persistent curiosity of the stranger arouses a similar curiosity in the reader. It calls attention to the possibility that there may be more than meets the eye in this city that has been so casually mentioned.

Such is the case. Just a few pages later the city, previously written with a lower case "c," begins to be capitalized. Dr. Messinger says that he heard about it from the Pie-wie Indians, adding, "None of them had ever visited the City, of course, but they *knew about it*" (220; Waugh's emphasis). Then Dr. Messinger points out that every tribe has a different name for the City. "The Pie-wies call it the 'Shining' or 'Glittering,' the Arekuna the

'Many Watered,' the Patamonas the 'Bright Feathered'" (220-221). At this point I have scribbled in the margin of my copy of the book, "Would Americans call it 'Heaven' or 'Paradise'?" (showing the tentative conclusion to which Waugh's "bait" had led me at this juncture!). Tony ponders the city in his heart at night. "He had a clear picture of it in his mind. It was Gothic in character, all vanes and pinnacles, gargoyles, battlements . . . *a transfigured Hetton*" (222, my emphasis). Tony populates the city with groves and streams and daisies, "a tapestry landscape filled with heraldic and fabulous animals" (222). This recalls the words of Hebrews 11:10, "He looked forward to the city that has foundations, whose architect and builder is God." Could Tony be among the "they" spoken of in Hebrews 11:14-16? "People who speak in this way make it clear that they are seeking a homeland. If they had been thinking of the land that they left behind [Tony's England?], they would have had opportunity to return. But as it is they desire a better country, that is, a heavenly one." Might Tony be among those who have concluded that "here we have no lasting city, but we are looking for the city that is to come"? (Hebrews 13:14).[4] When Tony arrives at the city (in delirium),[5] it is everything he dreamed: gilded cupolas and spires of alabaster, blossoms floating in the breeze, trumpets sounding from the glittering walls (283).

That Waugh may have intended an association of this city with the city of God seems possible in the light of the fact that in Tony's delirium Ambrose announces, "The City is served" (283). Ambrose was the bishop who around 1600 years ago baptized St. Augustine, the author of *The City of God*.

Note, too, the name of the person who persuaded Tony to join him in the search for a city: Dr. Messinger. It is a name that tempts the reader to think of the messengers of God—prophets, apostles, preachers—who proclaim the good news of the city of God. It is this Dr. Messinger, moreover, whose initial oath, "Oh, for God's sake," at Tony's continuous scratching of insect bites is mysteriously repeated a few lines later, "Oh, for God's sake" (236). Is Waugh suggesting through this otherwise pointless repetition that their mission, too, is "for God's sake"? Perhaps "'Twere to consider too curiously, to consider so" (Hamlet, V, i, 198). But it wouldn't be the first time that profanity in literature has had Gospel significance.[6]

Other names are suggestive. For example, the name of the protagonist, Tony Last. Could the name suggest that Tony is among those "*last* who will be first" ? (Mathew 19:20 and 20:16, my emphasis). Or might the name remind us of the scriptural truth that "the one who *endures* [lasts] will be saved"? (Mark 13:13, my emphasis). Another example is the name of Tony's jungle host/captor, Mr. Todd. Omit the last letter and you have the German word "*tod*," meaning death. Is "Tod (d)" the channel Tony must go through in order to arrive at "the transfigured Hetton," the City (of God)?[7] Even the name of Tony's Gothic home, Hetton, is not totally unlike "Heaven" in its pronunciation.

The structure of the novel is an argument that cuts both ways. We have already seen how the three chapter titles containing the phrase "English Gothic" portray Tony's world as deteriorating from romanticism to utter pessimism. But the similarity in their titles, as well as the similarity in two other chapter titles (Chapter One, "*Du Cote De Chez Beaver*," and Chapter Six, "*Du Cote De Chez Todd*") suggests a certain symmetry, perhaps even harmony, in Tony's world. If there is disaster, there is at least design in that disaster. If there is chaos, there is at least a degree of organization of that chaos. Might there be a divine plan behind the devolution from Gothic I to Gothic II to Gothic III? Might I, II, and III fail so that Tony can thereby be prepared for Gothic IV, "a transfigured Hetton"—Heaven itself?

Late in the book Mr. Todd tricks Tony into a drug-induced sleep. During that period Mr. Todd removes Tony's watch and gives it to three Englishmen looking for the missing man. Todd intends the gift to be a souvenir by which the Englishmen can prove Tony's death back home and claim a reward. The missing watch symbolizes Tony's death from time. Time has stopped for him. But the death from time need not be the end; it could be the necessary preparatory step for existence in eternity. In fact, eternal life may be the only thing Tony has left for him. Similarly, in the last chapter the tower clock at Hetton perversely strikes fourteen, symbolizing that indeed "the time is out of joint." But this need not imply that there is not a world beyond time where all is harmony.

Perhaps the realization that all is "a handful of dust" is not the last word but simply the necessary prerequisite for attaining the City of God. The fact that the human creature is dust and "unto dust returns" does not eliminate the possibility that that handful of dust—after Tod(d)—will be raised again.[8] The ambiguity just stated seems to be encouraged by the tantalizing admission of Mr. Todd, "They say that it is possible to bring dead people to life after they have begun to stink, but I have not seen it done" (289). The statement, a masterpiece of equivocation, seems to encapsulate the interpretative ambiguity of the entire novel.

Two other factors faintly support the possibility of Gospel in *A Handful of Dust*. The first is Waugh's conversion to Roman Catholicism just a few years before publication of this novel. It does not follow from this biographical truth that *A Handful of Dust* is a vehicle for the expression of Waugh's newly found faith. But, at the very least, it does raise the possibility that it could be.[9]

The other factor is the witness of *Brideshead Revisited*. This book, as we have seen in Chapter 2, contains a clear and intentional Gospel pattern. The novel plainly evidences Evelyn Waugh's familiarity with Christianity and, more specifically, with Roman Catholicism. Interpreting one book in the light of another in the same canon is a hermeneutical principle recognized as valid in both biblical and literary criticism.[10] The fact that there is clear Gospel in one book does not suggest that it need be present in another book by the same author. But it does increase the likelihood of such an occurrence.

The question of whether or not there is Gospel in *A Handful of Dust* is a vexing one, and the reader may despair of resolving the issue. The pros and cons seem to weigh equally quantitatively and qualitatively, and a number of the arguments cut both ways. Certainly the novel can be read and appreciated without resolution or even consideration of the matter. Indeed, the novel should be read in any case, so great a work of art it is. Wrestling with the issue of its Gospel potential is one (but only one) of the charms of this outstanding book. Perhaps, Shakespeare can come to our rescue. The title of one of his plays, *As You Like It*, and the subtitle of another play (*Twelfth Night*), *What You Will*, seem to invite the reader to interpret these plays with a high degree of subjectivity. As long as the reader's interpretation is not solely or primarily based on personal capriciousness or whimsy but rather on objective evidence—even conflicting evidence—there does seem to be room for interpreting *A Handful of Dust* as you like it and as you will.

Notes

1. Evelyn Waugh, *A Handful of Dust* (Boston: Little, Brown and Company; 1962), 291. All future page locations for citations from this book will be included in parentheses in the text of this chapter.
2. Read the especially ominous descriptions of this activity on pages 290, 294, 297, and 301-302. As one reader quipped, "These passages sound like hell because they *are* hell" (at least symbolically).
3. Some of the views that follow have been encouraged by the authors listed in the bibliography at the end of this chapter.
4. See also Hebrews 12:22 and Psalm 127:1.
5. The fact that Tony sees this city only in delirium is, of course, a telling argument against the Gospel truth suggested.
6. See Chapter Eight.
7. Here is another weak aspect of the possible Gospel interpretation of the novel. In Tony's case, he arrives at his City (in delirium) before Tod(d) rather than after Tod(d).
8. If this is the view that Waugh intended, he clearly hasn't told us so. To hypothesize a Gothic IV is, I must admit, an argument based on Waugh's silence.
9. In acknowledging this possibility, we must guard against what C. S. Lewis has called "the personal heresy," the assumption that a work of art reflects the author's biography or beliefs. It may do so, but it need not do so, Lewis argues. To read a work of art for the primary purpose of determining the character of the author's life and views is as foolish as ordering a meal at a restaurant in order to learn about the chef's life and opinions. The meal is to be enjoyed for its own culinary artistry!
10. No less a person than T. S. Eliot has reminded us that every Shakespeare play, for example, must be interpreted in the context of the entire Shakespeare canon.

Study Guide for *A Handful of Dust*

1. Demonstrate Waugh's skill in characterization. Note how in some instances the name of a person is subtly suggestive of that person's character. Note Waugh's use of dramatic hedging in his portrait of Tony Last.

2. Find passages in which Waugh skillfully abstracts or generalizes the three dimensional aspects possessed by many of the novel's characters.

3. Document the following ingredients in Waugh's style: suggestion, dramatic irony, simple irony, refrain, understatement, humor, metaphor, poetic justice.

4. How does dramatic foreshadowing enhance the structure of the novel? For example, consider carefully the renaming of John Andrew's horse, the animal imagery of Mr. Tendril's Christmas sermon, and the name Jenny mistakenly ascribes to Tony.

5. What factors account for the hilarious humor of Tony and Jock's drinking bout and of Tony's attempt at staged adultery as grounds for divorce?

6. Demonstrate poetic justice in Tony's hypocritical hospitality toward Beaver at the start of the novel and in Brenda's lie about studying economics.

What is the relationship between these instances of poetic justice and the title of the novel?

7. What is the structural function of the numerous parallels in the novel? In this connection, note the similarities between the titles of Chapter 1 and Chapter 6; also Chapter 2, Chapter 4, and Chapter 7. Do these parallel titles have a thematic function as well?

8. Read carefully the account of Tony's delirium on pages 279-283 and comment on its stylistic merit, its structural purpose, and its thematic function.

9. Note how *A Handful of Dust* is preoccupied with "What will people think?" and how frequently it points out the error of human assessments.

10. What interpretation of the novel is suggested by its title?

11. How does the chapter entitled "In Search of a City" suggest a possible Gospel pattern? In this connection, see Psalm 127:1; Hebrews 11:10, 14-15; Hebrews 12:22; Hebrews 13:14. How do the names Todd and Tony Last support this pattern? How do the title of the novel, its last chapter, and its last paragraph argue against the presence of a Gospel pattern? What passage on page 289 encapsulates the ambiguity of the book's relationship to a Gospel pattern?

12. Find notable symbols in the book, especially those in its closing pages.

For Further Reading

Carens, James F. *The Satiric Art of Evelyn Waugh*. Seattle and London: University of Washington Press, 1946.

Cook, Jr., William J. *Masks, Modes, and Morals: The Art of Evelyn Waugh*. Cranbury, New Jersey: Associated University Presses, Inc., 1971.

Crabbe, Katharyn W. *Evelyn Waugh*. New York: Continuum Publishing Co., 1988.

Davis, Robert Murray. *Evelyn Waugh, Writer*. Norman Oklahoma: Pilgrim Press Books, Inc., 1981.

Garnett, Robert R. *From Grimes to Brideshead: The Early Novels of Evelyn Waugh*. London and Toronto: Associated University Presses, Inc., 1990.

Lane, Calvin W. *Evelyn Waugh*. Boston: Twayne Publishers, 1981.

Littlewood, Ian. *The Writings of Evelyn Waugh*. Oxford, England: Basil Blackwell Publisher Ltd., 1983.

Phillips, Gene D. *Evelyn Waugh's Officers, Gentlemen, and Rogues: The Fact Behind His Fiction*. Chicago: Nelson-Hall, 1975.

Wykes, David. *Evelyn Waugh: A Literary Life*. New York: St. Martin's Press, Inc., 1999.

CHAPTER TEN

Measure for Measure
by William Shakespeare

Not every play by Shakespeare lends itself to the thesis of this book. Only in some of his plays, in my reading experience, have literary critics found a Gospel pattern or Gospel echoes: *All's Well That Ends Well, Cymbeline, Hamlet, Henry the IV, Part One, King Lear, Measure for Measure, Othello, Pericles, Prince of Tyre, The Tempest, Twelfth Night,* and *The Winter's Tale.*

Measure for Measure, like every other Shakespeare play, has been accorded a host of interpretations—including a Gospel interpretation. Many of the more common interpretations of the play include Christian/biblical/religious/ethical elements, but seldom does one encounter a Gospel interpretation, that is, one in which some saving event of Christ's earthly career and/or its significance plays a major role in the plot. Gospel interpretations are definitely in the minority.

To put a Gospel interpretation of *Measure for Measure* in proper perspective, we need to briefly examine a number of the majority interpretations of the play.

First, there is the interpretation reflecting the title of the play. That title, *Measure for Measure,* is echoed late in the play when the returning Duke Vincentio decrees that Angelo, the deputy ruler during the Duke's absence, who (it is thought at the time) had put Claudio to death with undue severity and haste for unchastity, should himself be summarily executed for having committed a similar crime. Says the Duke,

> "An Angelo for Claudio, death for death"
> Haste still pays haste, and leisure answers leisure;
> Like doth quit like, and measure still for measure.[1]

In its immediate context the passage sounds as if it is advocating "an eye for an eye and a tooth for a tooth," more specifically echoing Jesus' words from the Sermon on the mount, "The measure you give will be the measure you get" (Mattthew 7:2)—a decidedly biblical echo but, most assuredly, not a Gospel one. But in the larger context of the entire play (a play in which nobody—not even Angelo and Claudio—gets seriously hurt), Shakespeare demonstrates that mercy should be measured out as well as justice, even suggesting that a measure of mercy should always accompany the justice that is measured. The moral conveyed by the title, then, is a variant of the Golden Rule: In the measure you want people to treat you, so measure out to them.

Then there are the perennial interpretations frequently accorded numerous Shakespeare plays. Some scholars suggest that all of Shakespeare might be summed up in the saying that "appearance isn't reality." That theme, so often found in Shakespeare's works, surfaces also among the interpretations of *Measure for Measure*. One of the reasons Duke Vincentio gives for putting the governance of Vienna into Angelo's hands during his absence is to determine whether "this well-seeming Angelo" is as good as he is reputed to be. As the Duke puts it,

> That we were all, as some would seem to be,
> From our faults, as faults from seeming, free (III, ii, 39-40).

Later the Duke repeats the concern:

> O, what may man within him hide,
> Though angel on the outward side! (III, ii, 271-272).

This interpretation has the virtue of conforming to the hermeneutical principle of "interpreting Shakespeare with Shakespeare."

Another perennial interpretation is the Aristotelian Golden Mean, that is, to avoid excesses or extremes and to strive for balance. *Measure for Measure* is concerned with finding the appropriate middle point between justice and leniency, betwen prudishness and immorality. The characterization of the *dramatis personae* seems to support this understanding of the play. If Duke

Vincentio is too lax, Angelo is too severe. If Pompey and Lucio are too cavalier about immorality, Isabella is too severe in her chastity. If Claudio is too fearful of death, Barnardine is too indifferent toward it. Only the Provost, the unnamed jailer, initially seems to represent the happy medium. One critic has suggested that the name of one of the *dramatis personae*, Mistress Overdone, is intended by Shakespeare to encapsulate all the excesses of the play. Everything from Elbow's stupidity to Pompey's stalling tactics is "overdone." Indeed, the theme of avoiding extremes and striving for balance is frequent in Shakespeare, and to see this concern as central also in *Measure for Measure* is validated by the interpretative principle of interpreting one play in the light of all the plays Shakespeare wrote.

Among the less frequent and less comprehensive interpretations of *Measure for Measure* is that the play is a study in evil. Evil is widespread, touching everyone from Angelo at the top of the social scale to Barnardine at the bottom. Vienna is rife with evil. According to Duke Vincentio it is a place where he has "seen corruption boil and bubble / Till it o'errun the stew" (V, i, 358-359), where "faults [are] so countenanced that the strong statutes / Stand . . . as much in mock as mark" (V, i, 360-362). The so-called reputable are no better than the so-called disreputable. Usury is no better than bawdry; charging interest begets illegal coins much the same as fornication begets illicit children (III, ii, 1-10). When houses of prostitution are razed in the suburbs (at Shakespeare's time "the bad part of town"), those in the city are spared because " a wise burgher put in for them" (I, ii, 96). Lucio, for all his levity in respect to evil, makes the shrewd comment that everyone scrapes out from the ten commandments the restriction that forbids his pet sin (I, ii, 7-15). Nor can mere legislation eliminate evil. In the words of Pompey, "Though you change your place, you need not change your trade" (I, ii, 103-104), a sentiment echoed by Lucio, "It is impossible to extirp it quite . . . till eating and drinking be put down" (III, ii, 103-104). Lest this study of evil be too negative in character to rise to the level of the play's moral, *Measure for Measure* does suggest a positive feature in evil, namely, that good can come from it:

> They say best men are molded out of faults,
> And, for the most, become much more the better
> For being a little bad (V, i, 503-505).

A variation of the contention that *Measure for Measure* is a study in evil is that the play is a study in temptation. Focusing on Angelo, some conclude that the moral of the play is the cliche, "There but for the grace of God go I." Angelo (and the reader) learn the truth of 1 Corinthians 10:12, "So if you think you are standing, watch out that you do not fall."

Another contention is that the play is an analysis of the character of law, specifically, that law cannot be viewed as a completely neutral, impersonal, objective entity. One can never take refuge in the defense, "It is the law, not I, condemn your brother" (II, ii, 105).[2]

More defensible (because more of the play is concerned with the issue) is the view that *Measure for Measure* is a study in death, especially the proper reaction to it. We have already noted that if Claudio is too fearful of death, Barnardine is too indifferent toward it. And, one might add, Pompey is too flippant about it. No doubt, the most memorized and most quoted passage from the play—on a par with Hamlet's soliloquies—is Duke Vincentio's lengthy lecture on death to the condemned Claudio at the beginning of Act III. Because of its central position in the play, its length, and its poetic merit, it is, a strong contender for what the play is about.

I turn now to a possible Gospel interpretation of *Measure for Measure*, an approach advanced especially in Bryant's *Hippolyta's View* and hinted at in Goddard's *The Meaning of Shakespeare* and Parrott's *Shakespearean Comedy*. Bryant maintains that the play celebrates the *felix culpa* ("the fortunate fall") doctrine of Christian theology and that the plot with its bed trick echoes the vicarious atonement of Christ.

The lines cited earlier suggesting that good can come from evil could support the *felix culpa* doctrine. And there does seem to be general agreement among interpreters that grace or mercy prevails over justice in this play—a view that may or may not be connected with the Christian Gospel. But there is additional—and more specific—evidence. Angelo (as his name suggests) is an angel who, like his counterpart Satan, succumbs to temptation and becomes a fallen angel. Angelo is referred to as an "archvillain" (V, i, 65) and "the devil" (V, i, 32). He himself comments, "Let's write 'good angel' on the devil's horn. / 'Tis not the devil's crest" (II, iv, 16-17). By way of contrast, Duke Vincentio could be the God-figure in the play. At one point Angelo says of him, "Your Grace, like power divine, / Hath looked upon my passes" (V, i, 416-417).³ Shakespeare expanded the Duke's role from his sources. Vincentio is a master of ceremonies, a *primum mobile*, if you will, who sets the universe of the play into motion with his plans and travels, a catalyst for all the action that transpires. Like God he is concerned about evil, specifically the evil in Vienna, and about the reformation of society. Like God he concerns himself with people, their needs, and their character development, such as the testing of Angelo and the comforting and molding of Claudio, Isabella, Mariana, Barnardine, and even to a degree the irascible Lucio. At one point the Duke verbalizes his role as a variety of Providence:

> But I will keep her [Isabella] ignorant of her good
> To make her heavenly comforts of despair
> When it is least expected (IV, iii, 117-119).

In combatting the hypocritical Angelo's disguise of holiness by persuading Mariana (Angelo's rejected betrothed) to disguise herself as Isabella in an amorous tryst Angelo has arranged with Isabella, the Duke is aping a divine method celebrated in *Piers Plowman* and *Paradise Lost*, that of fighting disguise with disguise. Since Satan disguised himself as a serpent, Gods Son, in battling Satan, disguised himself as a man. Since Satan introduced sin into the world through the tree of the knowledge of good and evil, Jesus conquered sin through the tree of the cross. In the words of the Passion collect, "He [Satan] who by a tree once overcame likewise by a tree might be overcome." It is this Gospel methodology the Duke imitates in his plan, describing it thus:

> So disguise shall, by the disguised,
> Pay with falsehood false exacting
> And perform an old contracting (III, ii, 280-282).

Given the Duke's role as a sort of Providence in the play, the notorious *deus ex machina* in *Measure for Measure* becomes less intrusive. When Angelo prematurely orders the beheading of Claudio, the Duke and Provost are at a loss as to how they can save Claudio's life. It so happens that just that morning a prisoner named Ragozine had died, a person who—it just so happens—

physically resembles Claudio, thus enabling the Duke and the Provost to send Ragozine's head to Angelo in place of Claudio's. Along with the pirate ship that retrieved Hamlet enroute from Denmark to England, this incident in *Measure for Measure* is perhaps the most glaring *deus ex machina* in all Shakespeare. If, however, Duke Vincentio is a sort of *deus ex machina* in person, the substitution of Ragozine's head for Claudio's might be precisely the sort of thing we should expect. God's interfering in the normal and expected sequence of things could be what the play is all about. In the words of the Duke: "O, 'tis an accident that heaven provides!" (IV, iii, 82).

The heart of the Gospel interpretation of *Measure for Measure* is, of course, the famous bed trick, a device used once before by Shakespeare in *All's Well That Ends Well.* To save her brother from the executioner's block, Isabella has been asked by Angelo to yield her body to his lust, an arrangement that the "enskied and sainted" Isabella predictably declines. The Duke, however, persuades her to pretend to agree to an assignation with Angelo and then assures her that he will send Mariana, once legally betrothed to Angelo and still in love with him, in Isabella's place, a substitution possible in the darkness of the area chosen for the amorous tryst. Since in Elizabethan thinking engagement was tantamount to marriage, Mariana would commit no sin and Angelo would sin only in intent rather than in deed. Best of all, Isabella's chastity and Claudio's head would be spared. Blasphemous as it might at first appear, this substitution of Mariana for Isabella has been viewed as a microcosm of the cross-event, where Christ, who is actually without sin, was "made sin for us" and bore the consequences of sin in our behalf, thereby sparing us from eternal death and damnation. The bed trick is seen as a miniature of Christ's atonement. That, Bryant argues, is the Gospel pattern in *Measure for Measure.* In the Duke's own words to Isabella, "By this is your brother saved, your honor untainted, the poor Mariana advantaged, and the corrupt deputy scaled" (III, i, 279-282).

Does this Gospel interpretation have any merit? Certainly, it is a possibility. But that can be said of so many interpretations of Shakespeare's plays. Shakespeare is a generalist. So vast is his knowledge (including knowlege of the Scriptures), so profound are his insights, so universal are his interests, and so great is his genius that, unwittingly, he has something for everybody in his plays. The reader can find what he wants in Shakespeare's works, not just because he wants it, but because Shakespeare has probably put it there. Shakespeare is all things to all people. Whoever reads him feels included. Shakespeare is too much a generalist to saddle him with so specific a Gospel interpretation as we have just examined. But given some of the absurdities, for example, in the Freudian approach to Shakespeare's plays, the so-called Christian interpretations are no more forced or contrived. In fact, they strike me as reasonable by comparison. Were we able to ask Shakespeare himself to resolve the issue, he would probably shrug his shoulders and say, "As you like it, what you will, but come to the play!"

Notes

1. William Shakespeare, *Measure for Measure*, The New Folger Library Shakespeare, eds., Barbara A. Mowat and Paul Werstine (New York: Washington Square Press, 1997), V, i, 465-467. All future locations for citations from this play will be included in parentheses in the text of the chapter.
2. See Angelo's eloquent (but faulty) defense of the law's impartiality in Act II, Scene i.
3. Here is an instance where Shakespeare, who never missed an opportunity to pun, may be credited with an unintended pun because of linguistic changes since Shakespeare's time. The word "passes" is a clipped version of "trespasses." And certainly Angelo's trespasses could be seen also as "passes" by a contemporary reader!

Study Guide for *Measure for Measure*

1. Why is this play called "a dark comedy," "a problem play"? What is the relationship between these genres and a Gospel interpretation of *Measure for Measure*?

2. What reasons does Duke Vincentio give for turning over the government to Angelo? Are these reasons consistent? How does his transfer of power to Angelo serve the drama? In view of his dramatic function, need the Duke's motives be consistent?

3. How does the function of the name "Angelo" change as the play progresses? Comment on the skill Shakespeare employs in naming other *dramatis personae*.

4. Why is it essential to the appreciation of this play to understand the Elizabethan theology of engagement?

5. What motives for sentencing him does Claudio attribute to Angelo?

6. Note the contrast between Angelo and Lucio in their respective attitudes toward Claudio's "crime." What is Lucio's dramatic function in respect to Angelo? Who else stands in this same relationship to Angelo?

7. How do Elbow and Pompey enhance the comedy of *Measure for Measure*?

8. Notice how Shakespeare has individualized the unnamed Provost. What are his possible functions in the play?

9. Note how Isabella's opening remark immediately characterizes her. What other trait does Claudio ascribe to her in I, ii, 182-184? Demonstrate from the initial encounter between Isabella and Angelo that Claudio is correct.

10. In what sense is Isabella's polite remark to Angelo, "Heaven keep your Honor safe," ironic?

11. What important truth does Angelo learn about himself in his initial meeting with Isabella?

12. Enumerate the arguments Angelo employs to seduce Isabella.

13. Note the many profound passages about death in this play.

14. Is Isabella too severely righteous to be genuinely good?

15. Is there any merit to one critic's contention that Barnardine is the real hero of the play?

16. What is the technical name for the "accident" that allows the Provost to substitute Ragozine's head for Claudio's in IV, iii, 74-82? Is the use of this device dramatically defensible? What bearing, if any, might its inclusion have on the Gospel interpretation?

17. Is Duke Vincentio kind or cruel? Is his conduct always ethical? Is his characterization consistent? Is it proper to apply the usual canons of characterization to him? What is his probable role in the play?

18. Enumerate those characteristics of the ending of *Measure for Measure* that are typical of Shakespearean comedy.

19. Read V, i, 465-468, and its immediate context carefully. What is the apparent meaning of the title of the play? In terms of the larger context of the entire play, is there possible ambiguity in the meaning of the title?

20. Distinguish between episode and subplot. What might constitute the subplot in this play? How is it both structurally and thematically connected with the main plot?

21. What interpretation of this play is suggested by the title? What perennial themes appear in this play? How might the name of Mistress Overdone encapsulate one of these perennial themes? Find evidence for special themes in *Measure for Measure*. (For instance, what does the play say about evil, temptation, the nature of the law, death.?)

22. Enumerate the possible Gospel echoes in *Measure for Measure*. Do they constitute a significant and convincing pattern?

For Further Reading

Bache, William B. *Measure for Measure As Dialectical Art.* Lafayette, Indiana, 1969.

Battenhouse, Roy W. *Shakespearean Tragedy: Its Art and Its Christian Premises.* London and Bloomington, Indiana, 1969.

Bryant, J. A. *Hippolyta's View: Some Christian Aspects of Shakespeare's Plays.* Lexington, Kentucky, 1961.

Burgess, William. *The Bible in Shakespeare.* New York, 1903.

Campbell. Oscar James. *Shakespeare's Satire.* Oxford: Oxford University Press, 1943.

Chambers, Sir Edmund K. *Shakespeare: A Survey.* London: Hill and Wang Drama Book, 1925.

Cox, Roger L. *Between Earth and Heaven: Shakespeare, Dostoevsky, and the Meaning of Christian Tragedy.* New York, Chicago, San Francisco, 1969.

Craig, Hardin. *An Interpretation of Shakespeare.* Columbia, Missouri: University of Missouri Press, 1948.

Dean, Leonard (ed.). *Shakespeare: Modern Essays in Criticism.* Oxford: Oxford University Press, 1963.

Geckle, George L.. (ed.). *Twentieth Century Interpretations of Measure for Measure: A Collection of Critical Essays.* Englewood Cliffs, New Jersey, 1970.

Goddard, Harold. *The Meaning of Shakespeare.* Chicago: University of Chicago Press, 1973.

Hunter, Robert Grams. *Shakespeare and the Comedy of Forgiveness.* New York and London, 1965.

Lascelles, Mary. *Shakespeare's Measure for Measure.* London: De Graff, 1953.

Lawrence, William Witherle. *Shakespeare's Problem Comedies.* New York: Macmillan, 1960.

Leavis, F. R. *The Common Pursuit.* New York, 1964.

Ornstein, Robert (ed.). *Discussions of Shakespeare's Problem Comedies.* Boston: Heath, 1961.

Parrott, Thomas. *Shakespearean Comedy.* New York, 1962.

Soellner, Rolf and Samuel Bertsche (eds.). *Measure for Measure: Text, Source, and Criticism.* Boston: Houghton Mifflin Co., 1966.

Tillyard, E. M. W. *Shakespeare's Problem Plays.* London: Chatto & Windus, 1950.

Toole, William B. *Shakespeare's Problem Plays: Studies in Form and Meaning.* London, The Hague, Paris, 1966.

CHAPTER ELEVEN

The Fall
by Albert Camus

In *The Fall* by Albert Camus, the protagonist, Jean-Baptiste Clamence, encounters a stranger in the *Mexico City,* a bar in Amsterdam, and carries on a number of sustained but interrupted conversations with him extending over a period of days. All we get to read are Clamence's contributions to those conversations. What his companion contributes we can only infer from the protagonist's replies. In short, Jean-Baptiste Clamence does all the talking. To read the book is like listening to a telephone conversation when you can hear only one party talking. Were this novel a poem we could call it a dramatic monologue. Camus's *The Fall* is a prose counterpart to that poetic genre, of which Robert Browning's "My Last Duchess" is perhaps the best-known example.

The genre Camus has chosen is admirably suited to the protagonist. Clamence is self-centered and egotistic; hence a prose variation of the dramatic monologue is an ideal vehicle for these characteristics. Form matches character. It is not only what Clamence talks about but also the fact that he does all the talking that reveals his character.

Look at his character in more detail—to begin with, his self-centeredness and egotism. That Clamence is self-centered is clear from his own admission: "I was always bursting with vanity. I, I, I is the refrain of my whole life."[1] "For more than thirty years I had been in love exclusively with myself" (100). That he is egotistic is evident from his fondness for high places. "I have never felt comfortable except in lofty places" (23). For that reason, he goes on to say, he prefers the bus to the subway and the top deck of a ship to the lower levels. In his past performances as a lawyer, he yearned to occupy not the floor of the courtroom, but the rafters, "like those gods that are brought down by machinery [*deus ex machina*] . . . to transfigure the action. . . . After all, living aloft is still the only way of being seen and hailed by the largest number" (25). He desires to forgive the pope, not especially from compassion, but because "that's the only way to set oneself above him" (127). Sicily is his favorite place "especially from the top of Etna" (43). Were he to be arrested and sentenced to death, he would prefer decapitation. "Above the gathered crowd, you would hold up my still warm head . . . and I could again dominate" (146).

The portrait gets worse. Clamence is "a billy goat for lust" (95). "My kingdom was the bed," he boasts (86). The only women he claims to exempt from his lust are the wives of his friends—except that when the opportunity arises in that circle, he adheres to his principle by no longer including their respective husbands among his friends (58-59)! That admission by the protagonist betrays another of his characteristics, extreme cynicism. "I have no . . . friends; I have nothing but accomplices" (73). "Something must happen—and that explains most human commitments" (37). "Fortunately there is gin, the sole glimmer of light in this darkness" (12). He claims to be more intelligent than everyone else, then deflates himself with the addition that most every imbecile shares the same conviction (29). He concedes that he possesses the virtue of patriotic loyalty to France, but the origin of this virtue was sheer accident; he discovered its presence one day when a passing German soldier stole the affections of a stray dog Clamence had just started to befriend. Clamence's newly adopted role of being "a judge–penitent" sounds promising. The reader assumes that Clamence is going to repent of some of his past judgments. Not true! Rather, Clamence is embracing penitence in the cynical hope that doing so will give him a clearer right to judge others. Clamence stands the biblical injunction on its head by eliminating the first "not" from Jesus' dictum, "Do not judge, that you may not be judged" (Matthew 7:1). Add to all this an impulsive and inexplicable perversity reminiscent of the depraved protagonist of Dostoevesky's *Notes from the Underground*: the desire to jostle the blind, puncture invalids' tires, and slap babies in the subway (91).

Clamence's creed, though usually dignified with the name existentialism, should more accurately be called nihilism. "Fundamentally, nothing mattered" (49). Human existence has no meaning and serves no purpose. Paris is inhabited by four to five million "silhouettes" (6). Collectively, people are little better than "human ants" (24), "locusts" (18), flesh-devouring piranha (7-8). Individually. man is a "primate" (4), an "ape" (3), "a salacious monkey" (102). Clamence is obsessed with human cruelty. He describes a hospitable pacifist disemboweled by some soldiers who accepted his hospitality (12). He cites a German officer who courteously asked an old woman to choose which of her two sons should be shot as a hostage (11). One of Clamence's friends who had succeeded in giving up smoking read in the paper one day about the explosion of the first H-bomb, and "hastened to a tobacco shop" (87). Don't count on your friends to telephone[2] to prevent your committing suicide or to mourn your passing should you succeed at the attempt. "Don't wait for the Last Judgment," Clamence advises. "It takes place every day" (111). Nor can our past teachers help us in our predicament because "their mouths [are] filled with earth" (32). Dead men can no longer see; "The earth is dark. . .the coffin thick, and the shroud opaque" (74). Death was faithful at Clamence's own bedside; he "used to get up with it every morning" (91). Chance is the only reasonable divinity (79). What might be called "the nihilistic slip" betrayed itself one day in Clamence's reply to a motorist thanking him for his help, "No one would have done as much"—when he obviously meant to say "anyone" (47).

Admittedly, it is difficult to distinguish between Clamence's creed and Clamence's character. But that very difficulty, I suspect, is Camus's point: The individual is an abstraction; the specificity of personhood dissolves into the vagueness of philosophical generalizations.

Two incidents in particular seem to have been instrumental in forming both Clamence's character and creed. The first is a laugh that broke out behind him at a climactic moment of self-satisfaction. The sound continued downstream for a long while. Later the same evening, it burst out once again underneath his window (29). The laughter continues to harass him throughout the novel (cf. 80 and 142), poetic justice in that Clamence boasts of himself possessing "a good, hearty laugh" (41). The second is

Clamence's failure to prevent a woman from jumping off a bridge to drown herself or, moments later, to rescue her from the water. This episode, described at the very center of the novel (69-71), is hinted at repeatedly beforehand (15, 36, 69) and continues to haunt Clamence (108) even on the last page of the novel (147). Its central location in the novel suggests its central role in the formation of Clamence's character and creed. Its capacity to haunt and harass the protagonist suggests the haunting and harassing quality of life. The ghosts of the past keep materializing.

Camus's skillful use of symbols reinforces the cynicism of the protagonist and the nihilism of his creed. The reoccurring laugh and the protagonist's failure to prevent a woman from drowning herself symbolize human indifference. Camus singles out the little-ease and spitting cell as symbols of human cruelty. The locale of the novel, Amsterdam—with its pile of ashes, gray dike, a "sea the color of a weak lye-solution" (72) overcast by a colorless space, doves flying over the water indistinguishable from snow flakes—is a microcosm of the universe. "Is it not universal obliteration, everlasting nothingness made visible?" (72). The Zuider Zee adjoining Amsterdam is a dead sea covered with fog. Boats traveling on it, having no landmark, cannot gauge their speed. They "are making progress and yet nothing is changing" (97)—a symbol of human history! The void left on the dirty wall of the *Mexico City* bar by the removal of the picture "The Adoration of the Lamb" suggests the absence of Christ from the world.

In this context the title of the novel becomes ambiguous. To a theologian *The Fall* calls to mind the fall of humankind into sin recorded in Genesis 3. But the title need not refer to that fall. Might it not suggest, more blasphemously, the failure of Christ and/or the church? Could it, perhaps, allude more specifically to the protagonist's fall: his failure to rescue the drowning woman? Or, conversely, to the occasional lapse from his agnostic/atheistic creed? Less imaginatively, the fall might merely refer to the literal fall of the woman into the water, the central episode of the novel.

Given so cynical and unethical a character as that of Clamence and a creed so devoid of hope and principle, what Gospel pattern can possibly be present in *The Fall?* What Gospel good can come out of this nihilistic Nazareth?

The simplest answer might be that no Gospel good can be derived from Camus's book at all and that none was intended.

Whatever Gospel references the novel contains (and, admittedly, there are many) are simply there to be attacked and ridiculed. The evidence for this view is easy to assemble. For a starter there's Clamence's blasphemous paraphrase of the opening words of the Lord's Prayer: "Our Father who art provisionally here" (136). After alluding to a number of Gospel promises, Clamence senses his companion's doubt, "You don't believe it?" He then adds, "Nor do I" (146). Certainly, the closing words of the novel resemble the reaction of a person damned to hell: full of regrets, yet unwilling to accept a second chance even though it should be provided. "O young woman, throw yourself into the water again so that I may a second time have the chance of saving both of us!. . . . what a risky suggestion. . . . The water's so cold!. . . . It's too late now. It will always be too late. Fortunately!" (147). In another passage Clamence denies Christ's deity: "He was not superhuman, you can take my word for it" (114). Worse yet, he even rejects Christ's innocence, affirming that Christ himself "knew he was not altogether innocent" (112). Even if he were not guilty of the crime for which he was executed, at the very least he "was at the source" of the "Slaughter of the Innocents" (the children massacred by Herod). "Why did they die if not because of him?" (112). Still worse, Clamence dethrones the Son of God and puts himself into his place. After noting certain parallels between himself and Christ, like Christ, being "of respectable but humble birth" (28) and feeling "like a king's son" (29)—Clamence later asserts that he is the Alpha and Omega: "I am the end and the beginning" (118). It is Clamence who presides at the Last Judgment (143).

Just as often it is Christ's church rather than our Lord which Clamence attacks. For the three years of Christ's earthly ministry Clamence credits his religion as "a huge laundering venture" (111). "It was a stroke of genius to tell us: 'You're not a very pretty sight. . . . Well, we won't go into the details! We'll just liquidate it all at once, on the cross!'" (114). But since then the situation has deteriorated. "Soap has been lacking, our faces are dirty" (111). "Too many people now climb onto the cross merely to be seen from a greater distance" (114). Unlike their master, Christ's followers "smite, they judge above all, they judge in his name" (115).

Given so obvious and so vitriolic an attack on Christ and the church, *The Fall* does not seem to qualify as a book that contains a

Gospel pattern (let alone a Gospel echo or fragment) either by design or by accident. The Gospel is present only as a target for Camus's antipathy. The only way the novel can even remotely support the Gospel thesis is that the negative presentation of the Gospel still shows the impact of the Gospel event on literature. One must come to terms with that event—even if one has to hiss at it. "What think ye of Christ?" The question cannot be ignored.

But the issue is not quite that simple. Curiously, one of the factors attracting Clamence to his unidentified addressee in *The Fall* was his familiarity with the Bible. "So you know the Scriptures? Decidedly, you interest me" (9). Grace is what people want, Clamence concedes, even if they don't believe in it (135). Clamence himself yearns for vicariousness as a way of life. "Who . . . will sleep on the floor for us?" Clamence asks as he pictures humankind condemned to a prison in which the hard floor is the only available space for sleeping (32)—a poignant wish he repeats late in the novel (145). Clamence speculates whether he would be capable of so generous a sacrifice. "I'd like to be and I shall be," he replies (32). "We shall all be capable of it one day, and that will be *salvation*," he continues (32; my emphasis). Maybe the similarity of Jean Clamence's initials to those of Jesus Christ[3] is not a blasphemous attempt to put himself in the place of God, but rather is intended to show Clamence's desire to live vicariously, to "sleep on the floor" in behalf of others. Clamence describes his failure to rescue the drowning woman as his "baptism," albeit the water is "bitter" and he is fearful of never escaping "this immense holy-water fount," a reference to the Zuider Zee (108-109). In passages cited earlier, Clamence seemed to admire the laundering aspects of Christ's religion and regarded Christ's liquidation of sin as a stroke of genius. Of Christ's cry of desolation on the cross, Clamence confessed, "That's why I love him, my friend who died without knowing" (114). Clamence admired Christ for not condemning the adulterous woman of John's gospel (115).[4] Best of all, Clamence (i. e., Camus, if I may commit "the personal heresy") understands the fullness of Christ's vicarious act on the cross, that he was not merely crucified there but that he was also forsaken (i. e., damned). "He was not upheld, he complained. . . . 'Why hast thou forsaken me?'" (113). The severance of the panel "The Just Judges" from the stolen painting "The Adoration of the Lamb" symbolizes that tension between God the Father's love for the Son and the Father's justice toward him, later described by Clamence as "justice being definitively separated from innocence" (130). The passage demonstrates a profound understanding of the cross-event.

At the very least, the foregoing evidence demonstrates that if Camus didn't accept the Gospel, he'd like to. If the Gospel isn't true in Camus's opinion, perhaps he wishes it were. Might Camus identify with the atheist he describes in the novel who, despite 'giving it to God in his books,' found himself praying every night (133-134); or with the militant freethinker who unconsciously raised his hands to heaven (134); or with Clamence, his protagonist, who perversely annoyed freethinkers with the forbidden expressions (in their circles), "Thank God" and "My God"? (93). Philip Thody in his book *Albert Camus, 1913-1960* regards *The Fall* as a poignant cry for salvation. C. Hobard Edgren in *Of Marble and Mud: Studies in Spiritual Values in Fiction* suggests as an alternate title for *The Fall* "Almost Persuaded," reflecting Agrippa's response to St. Paul's argumentation, "Almost thou persuadest me to be a Christian" (Acts 26:28, KJV).

I agree with Robert de Luppe's assessment in his book *Albert Camus* that the ultimate irony of *The Fall* is our inability to trust the narrator. But a yearning for the very Gospel he attacks is a possibility for Camus: "Methinks, [he] doth protest too much!"

Notes

1. Albert Camus, *The Fall*, tr., Justin O'Brien (Random House, New York, 1956), 48. All future page locations for citations from this book will be included in parentheses in the text of this chapter.
2. Even their act of telephoning is likened to "shooting a rifle" (32).
3. Other famous literary figures with initials resembling those of Jesus Christ are Joe Christmas (Faulkner), Juan Chicoy and Jim Casey (Steinbeck), and Jean Cheval (Greene).

   The initials J. B. (Jean-Baptiste) have suggested to some a comparison between Clamence and John the Baptist, a view reinforced by the references to a prophet crying in the wilderness and the decapitation in the novel (146-147).
4. The name Clamence itself reminds us of clemency, mercy.

Study Guide for *The Fall*

1. Why might *The Fall* be called a dramatic monologue? How does the genre of the book match the character of the protagonist?

2. What two incidents are referred to repeatedly in the novel? What is the stylistic function of these references? The structural function? The thematic function?

3. Note the virtues of Camus's style. What is ironic about the protagonist's comments on style at the top of page 6, the middle of page 69, and the bottom of page 85?

4. Highlight the many passages in the novel that accord with your experience of life and your knowledge of human nature.

5. Enumerate the most noticeable traits of the protagonist's character. Note how difficult it is to distinguish the specific individual named Jean-Baptiste Clamence from the abstraction called existentialism. What is the thematic significance of this difficulty? What similarities exist between the protagonist of this novel and the "hero" of Dostoevsky's *Notes from the Underground*?

6. What does Clamence mean by frequently calling himself "a judge-penitent"?

7. Itemize those observations that categorize *The Fall* as an existential and/or nihilistic novel. Note what might be called "the nihilistic slip" at the bottom of page 47. What difficulty does the presence of the existential/nihilistic creed in this novel pose for the thesis of this book?

8. Find symbols that concretize Camus's existential/nihilistic creed. For instance, why is Amsterdam chosen as the site for this novel? Why is the void left on the wall of the *Mexico City* because of a missing picture?

9. What is the significance of the following for the book's thesis: the frequent biblical allusions, the title of the novel, and the name of the protagonist? Point out ambiguities in the title and in the name of the protagonist.

10. Does *The Fall* contain a genuine or a distorted Gospel pattern? Find evidence for both of these possibilities.

11. Establish a connection between Acts 26:28 and a possible interpretation of the novel.

For Further Reading

Amoia, Alba. *Albert Camus*. New York: The Continuum Publishing Co., 1989.

Bree, Germanie. *Camus*. New Brunswick, New Jersey: Rutgers University Press, 1959.

Cruikshank, John. *Albert Camus and the Literature of Revolt*. London: Oxford University Press, 1959.

Edgren, C. Hobart. *Of Marble and Mud: Studies in Spiritual Values in Fiction*. New York, 1950.

Ellison, David R. *Understanding Albert Camus*. Columbia, South Carolina: University of South Carolina Press, 1990.

Hanna, Thomas. *The Thought and Art of Albert Camus*. Chicago: Henry Regnery Co., 1958.

Lazere, Donald. *The Unique Creation of Albert Camus*. New Haven, Connecticut: Yale University Press, 1973.

de Luppe, Robert. *Albert Camus* (tr. John Cumming & J. Hargreaves), New York: Funk & Wagnalls, 1966.

O'Brien, Conor Cruise. *Camus*. London: Wm. Collins Sons & Co., 1970.

Onesimus, Jean. *Albert Camus and Christianity* (tr. Emmett Parker). University of Alabama Press, 1970.

Peterson, Carol. *Albert Camus* (tr. Alexander Gode). New York: Frederick Ungar Publishing Co., 1969.

Rhein, Philip H. *Albert Camus*. Boston: Twayne Publishers Inc., 1969.

Scott, Nathan A. *Albert Camus*. Folcroft, Pennsylvania: The Folcroft Press Inc., 1962.

Spritzen, David. *Camus: A Critical Examination*. Philadelphia: Temple University Press, 1988.

Thody, Philip. *Albert Camus*, 1913-1960. New York: The Macmillan Co., 1961.

_____. *Modern Novelists: Albert Camus*. New York: St. Martin's Press, 1989.

_____. *A Study of His Work*. New York: Grove Press, Inc., 1957.

Willhoite, Jr., Fred W. *Beyond Nihilism: Albert Camus's Contribution to Political Thought*.

CHAPTER TWELVE

The Rime of the Ancient Mariner
by Samuel Taylor Coleridge

Coleridge's *The Rime of the Ancient Mariner* first appeared in 1798 in *Lyrical Ballads,* a publication jointly authored by William Wordwsorth and Samuel Taylor Coleridge. In fact, it is commonly believed that Wordsworth made some contributions to Coleridge's poem.[1]

The *Rime of the Ancient Mariner* is a ballad consisting of four-line stanzas of alternating iambic tetrameter and iambic trimeter, the trimeter lines rhyming. (See, for example, the second stanza of the poem.) Of course, as is true of all good poetry, there are exceptions to this prevailing pattern.

Notable among the many virtues of this poem is its structure. The ballad is a classic example of the frame or bookend technique. Brief descriptions of a wedding at the beginning of the poem and again at its end enclose the Mariner's lengthy but arresting tale, thereby bringing that tale into sharper focus and giving it more impact on the reader. But the frame is more than an enclosing device. It is also a foil. The prosaic descriptions of an everyday event, a wedding, are in sharp contrast to the colorful, imaginative tale of the Mariner's remarkable voyage. The happiness of the wedding brings into sharper relief the horror of the Mariner's experience. The frame is natural, realistic; the material framed is supernatural, unrealistic. But to a Romantic poet such as Coleridge, what we call supernatural or unrealistic is the ultimate reality. To the Romantics the world of the imagination was more real than our everyday, workaday world. This basic contrast of the poem between the prosaic and the imaginative, the natural and the supernatural, is again and again mirrored by little contrasts throughout the poem: wind versus calm, noise versus silence, heat versus cold, wet versus dry, sun versus moon, color versus pale, life versus death. Numerous repetitions unify the poem's materials: ice everywhere versus water everywhere; the ribs of the spectre ship versus the "ribbed sea-sand;" the disappearance of the kirk, hill, and lighthouse as the ship leaves the harbor and the appearance of the same items (only in realistic reverse order) when the ship returns to port; the Wedding Guest's beating his breast and expressing his fear of the Mariner; above all, a reference to the albatross at the end of each of the first six parts of this seven-part poem.

Like the Wedding Guest (the addressee of the Mariner's tale), with whom we perhaps share too prosaic a view of life, we get hooked on the Mariner's story and, like the Wedding Guest, learn and grow from the experience. Each of us, too, becomes "a sadder and a wiser man."[2]

What is the wisdom that we gain? What is it that we learn from the poem? There have been a number of interpretations, many of them basically secular in character.

The simplest is that the poem conveys no particular meaning or moral at all. It is just a story—and a very good one at that. Support for this view comes, unintentionally, from a certain Mrs. Barbauld who, at the time of the poem's publication, found fault with it because it lacked a clear moral. Coleridge may have welcomed this negative criticism since it is common knowledge that he detested overt moralizing. The woman's criticism may have been a compliment from his perspective.

Another simple interpretation does find a moral in the poem and that is, specifically, "Don't shoot an albatross," or, more generally, "Be kind to animals." But such an interpretation is not just simple; it risks being simplistic as well.

It was Robert Penn Warren who was the first to suggest more than a surface meaning to *The Rime of the Ancient Mariner*. Among the more sophisticated interpretations of the ballad is the view that the poem is a study in the nature of evil. Reminiscent of the disproportion between the accidental dropping of the handkerchief and the dire consequences that resulted in Shakespeare's *Othello* is the marked contrast in *The Rime of the Ancient Mariner* between the casual, arbitrary shooting of the albatross and the grave and unforeseen ills that result from it. Although the Mariner who shot the albatross lives on, his shipmates die. One explanation suggested for this "unfairness" in outcome is that the Mariner's evil was impulsive whereas the crew's evil was deliberate and voluntary, their evil consisting of their fickleness in praising the Mariner for his careless act so long as the voyage was going well but then faulting him when the weather turned bad. Really, no explanation is needed, since the life-in-death the Mariner endures seems more horrible than the death his companions experience. The poet suggests the Mariner's greater evil by associating him with the "thousand, thousand slimy things" that "lived on" (lines 238-239).

More positive and more in tune with contemporary critical fashion is the view that the poem is about alienation and reconciliation. In killing the friendly albatross that joined and accompanied the ship, the Mariner violated the host/guest relationship. As a result of separating himself from the companionship of the sociable bird, the Mariner is isolated from human companionship too when all his shipmates die. "Alone, alone, all, all alone / Alone on a wide wide sea" is how the poet describes the alienation of the Mariner (lines 232-233). The Mariner is alienated from God also, for he finds himself unable to pray (lines 244-247), and later in the poem the Mariner admits that the sea was so lonely "that God himself / Scarce seem'd there to be" (line 600). But when the Mariner finally blesses the creatures teeming in the sea, he suddenly finds himself able to pray, the albatross suspended from his neck as a memento of his crime falls off, he is able to sleep again, and he hears harmonious music—all evidence of his emerging reconciliation with nature, people, and God (lines 284-290, 350-366). His reconciliation nears completion at the end of the poem when the Mariner exults in human companionship:

> O sweeter than the marriage-feast,
> 'Tis sweeter far to me,
> To walk together to the kirk
> With a goodly company! — (lines 601-604).

Not mutually exclusive from the prior interpretation is the view that *The Rime of the Ancient Mariner* is a tribute to the power and value of love in human affairs. In the Mariner's own explicit words at the end of the poem, "He prayeth best, who loveth best / All things both great and small" (lines 614-615). God, for the Mariner, is the precedent for his view of love's power and value. "For the dear God who loveth us, He made and loveth all" (lines 616-617).

The last two interpretations above, though not necessarily Christian, can easily be incorporated into the Gospel interpretation that some have accorded this poem.[3]

The editor of the Avon edition of the poem, Walter S. Hallenborg, tempts us to a Gospel interpretation with two prefatory remarks to his analysis of the poem. First, "The poem consists of seven parts. There is a kind of supernatural significance to the number seven" (18). Later on the same page he comments, "The poem may be thought of as an allegory on the Christian faith." In a marginal comment on the poem itself, the editor speculates, "If the poet has created a symbolic hell, will he show us a means for gaining release from hell?" (i. e., the Gospel) (40). Coleridge's epitaph, written by himself in anticipation of his demise, also encourages this interpretative approach when it expresses Coleridge's prayer for eternal salvation in language echoing the experience of the Ancient Mariner:

> That he who many a year with toil of breath
> Found death in life, may here find life in death!
> Mercy for praise—to be forgiven for fame
> He asked, and hoped, through Christ. Do thou the same!

There is possible evidence in the poem itself. To begin with, the Christian context. The number seven is a prominent biblical number. Not only does the poem consist of seven parts, but twice in the poem there are overt references to the number seven: "Seven days, seven nights, I saw that curse" (line 261) and "Like one that hath been seven days drowned" (line 552). Both the ship and the voyage are common Christian symbols. Why, for example, does Coleridge capitalize the word "pilot" in the Mariner's remark, "But swift as dreams, myself I found / Within the Pilot's boat"? (lines 554-555). Wedding imagery, too, is frequent in biblical parables and biblical proclamation of the Gospel. The numerous references to God and Christian images in the poem are largely conventional, yet it is their frequency and their specificity that make the reader increasingly alert to their interpretative significance. Included in these references are an association of the Sun with "God's own head" (lines 97-98); a brief prayer to Mary (line 178); the power of the Spirit (though not capitalized) in steering the ship (lines 379-380); the love of the Spirit for creation, specifically the albatross (lines 402-405); the sign of the cross by the Hermit (line 575); and the repeated beating of his breast by the Wedding Guest (lines 31 and 37). Above all, there is a possible reference to the Trinity:

> The Pilot and the Pilot's boy,
> . . . .
> I saw a third—I heard his voice:
> It is the Hermit good!
> . . . .
> He'll shrieve my soul, he'll wash away
> The Albatross's blood." (lines 504-513)

Concerning the latter the editor comments in the margin, "The reader may be tempted to think of the Pilot, his son, and the Hermit as a kind of metaphorical trinity" (112).

The most compelling argument for a Gospel approach to the poem is the significant role played by the albatross. Like the phoenix, the albatross often functions in literature as a symbol for Christ. It is clearly so used by C. S. Lewis in *The Voyage of the "Dawn Treader"* as the ship and crew seek to escape the island of darkness. In *The Rime of the Ancient Mariner*, the albatross, like Christ, comes from above and is "hailed . . . in God's name" (lines 63-66). Like Christ, the albatross does good things and bestows blessings. Like Christ, the albatross dies by a kind of cross, a crossbow (lines 81-82). Like the cross of Christ, the albatross is worn around the Mariner's neck, though as a badge of shame rather than as a sign of allegiance: "Instead of the cross, the Albatross / About my neck was hung" (lines 141-142). The association between the albatross and Christ becomes almost unavoidable when a voice asks,

> . . .Is this the man?
> By him who died on cross,
> With his cruel bow he laid full low
> The harmless albatross. (lines 398-401)[4]

Like the Son of God, the albatross is murdered by one who "knows not what he does." The Mariner's cruel action is senseless and motiveless. Others die for the sin of one (original sin?). Yet these others participate in the Mariner's evil by their fickleness toward the Mariner himself, first praising him for his slaying of the albatross, then blaming him for it (actual sin?) Surely, their death brings to mind the biblical reminder that "the wages of sin is death" and that "in Adam all die."

> The souls did from their bodies fly—
> . . . .
> And every soul it passed me by,
> Like the whizz of my cross-bow! (lines 220-223).

The alienation of the Mariner from God and man, his inability to pray and sleep (already described above as part of a secular interpretation) can easily be incorporated into the Christian interpretation as symptoms of the curse of sin. And the rotten deep and slimy creatures crawling upon the slimy sea (lines 123-126), the dungeon grate of the skeleton ship flecking the Sun with bars and through which the Sun peers and burns (lines 177-180)[5] and the water burning an awful red (lines 270-271), and the taunting availability of water but "not any drop to drink" (lines 119-122) can easily account for the Avon editor's conclusion that Coleridge has provided in the poem "a symbolic hell." Most convincing to me is the name Coleridge assigns to one of the specters in the ghost ship, "Life-in-Death," and her description: ("Her skin was white as leprosy /. . . .Who thicks man's blood with cold" [lines 192-194]). Like this ghostly creature, the Mariner, too, is condemned to life-in-death, a synonym for the experience of consciousness in the eternal death to which the damned are condemned. Hell is life in death, having the same quantity of life as heaven provides but utterly devoid of its quality.

The reconciliation with God and man with which the Mariner is eventually blessed completes the possible Gospel pattern in *The Rime of the Ancient Mariner.* When the Mariner is empowered to bless the creatures in the sea swimming alongside the ship, the albatross drops from the Mariner's neck—not only signifying the fact of the Mariner's release from guilt and punishment but also the means for that release. That is, the albatross, like Christ, is "made sin for us" (lines 288-291). Now the Mariner is able to pray. Now he can fall asleep again. Now he hears music, a symbol of his being in harmony with God and God's world. The blessed rain that falls and slakes the Mariner's thirst (lines 300-304) may be viewed as a sort of Baptism or, at the very least, as Coleridge's use of the common biblical metaphor for Christ's salvation, water. One who drinks of that water "will never be thirsty" (cf. John 6). As already indicated, the Mariner now yearns for and enjoys the company of people; he finds it pleasant to join the "goodly company" enroute to the kirk (lines 603-604) and he loves "both man and bird and beast" (line 613).

Finally, like every Christian, the Mariner "cannot but speak of the things he has seen and heard." His heart burns within him (line 585), he feels compelled to tell the story (as the Wedding Guest learns to his initial discomfort), even though the telling pains the narrator as much as it satisfies him (lines 578-590). Most interestingly, the tale empowers the teller (line 587) as the Christian message does. The Wedding Guest is "stunned," "of sense forlorn," but he arises the next day "a sadder and wiser man" (lines 622-625). How reminiscent of the writer to the Hebrews words: "The Word of God is living and active, sharper than any two-edged sword, piercing until it divides soul from spirit" (Hebrews 4:12).

Like much great literature, *The Rime of the Ancient Mariner* is capable of varied interpretation. The wealth of evidence makes the Gospel interpretation, if not the only possible one, at least a viable and respectable one.

Notes

1. Wordsworth may have suggested to Coleridge the ideas of shooting the albatross and of dead sailors navigating the ship. Wordsworth may have even authored specific lines of the poem: the fourth stanza of Part I and the last two lines of the first stanza of Part IV.
2. Samuel Taylor Coleridge, *The Rime of the Ancient Mariner* (New York: Avon Books, 1967), line 624. Future line locations for citations from this poem will be included in parentheses in the text of this chapter.
3. This interpretaion, hinted at by Robert Penn Warren in "A Poem of Pure Imagination: An Experiment in Reading," is more explicit in R. L. Brett, *Reason and Imagination* and in Martin Gardner, *The Annotated Ancient Mariner.*
4. The editor of the Avon edition says, "Some have seen the bird as symbolizing Christ" (page 32).
5. Incidentally, in this gruesome description the Mariner inserts the desperate prayer, "Heaven's Mother send us grace!"

Study Guide for *The Rime of the Ancient Mariner*

1. What is the purpose of the marginal glosses that Coleridge added to a later edition of the poem?

2. Describe the genre, meter, and rhyme scheme of the poem.

3. What is referred to at the end of each of the first six parts of this seven-part poem? Find other instances of repeated ideas and repeated lines. How do these repetitions serve the poem?

4. What functions does the wedding setting perform? How might these functions affect the search for meaning in the poem?

5. What is the relationship of the many pairs of opposites in the poem to the basic structure of the poem?

6. Note the riot of color in the poem and comment on its possible function.

7. Is the Mariner the only one in the poem who is initiated, who changes and grows?

8. What is the relationship between the auditor of the Mariner's story and the reader of the poem?

9. What factors make the reader cautious about finding a specific meaning in the poem?

10. What might the poem tell us about the nature of evil? What evidence is there that the ballad is a story of alienation and reconciliation? What interpretation is explicitly offered in lines 610-617?

11. Determine and evaluate the evidence for a possible Gospel pattern in the poem.

For Further Reading

Barth, J. Robert. *Coleridge and Christian Doctrine.* Cambridge, Massachusetts: Harvard University Press, 1969.

_____. *Coleridge and the Power of Love.* Columbia, Missouri: University of Missouri Press, 1988.

_____. *The Symbolic Imagination: Coleridge & the Romantic Tradition.*, 2nd. ed. New York: Fordham University Press, 2001.

Beyer, W. W. *The Enchanted Forest.* Oxford: Basil Blackwell, 1963.

Boulger, James D. *Coleridge as Religious Thinker.* New Haven, Connecticut: Yale University Press, 1961 .

_____ (ed.). *Twentieth Century Interpretations of The Rime of the Ancient Mariner: A Collection of Critical Essays.* Englewood Cliffs, New Jersey: Princeton University Press, 1969.

Ciardi, J. *How Does A Poem Mean?* Boston: Houghton Mifflin, 1960.

Coburn, Kathleen (ed.). *Coleridge: A Collection of Critical Essays.* Englewood Cliffs, New Jersey: Princeton University Press, 1967.

Lockridge, Laurence S. *Coleridge the Moralist.* Ithaca, New York. Cornell University Press, 1977.

Lowes, J. L., *The Road to Xanadu: A Study in the Ways of Imagination.* Boston: Houghton Mifflin, 1960.

Newlyn, Lucy (ed.), *The Cambridge Companion to Coleridge.* Cambridge, England: Cambridge University Press, 2002.

Radley, Virginia L. *Samuel Taylor Coleridge.* New York: Twayne Publishers, Inc., 1996.

Richards, I. A. *Coleridge on Imaagination.* New York: Harcourt, Brace & Co., 1950.

Warren, R. P. *Selected Essays, a Poem of Pure Imagination: An Experiment in Reading.* New York: Random House, 1958.

Wendling, Ronald C. *Coleridge's Progress to Christianity: Experience and Authority in Religious Faith.* London: Associated University Presses, 1995.

Wheeler, K. M. *The Creative Mind in Coleridge's Poetry.* Cambridge, Massachusetts: Harvard University Press, 1981.

PART THREE

Unintentional Gospel Patterns in Literature

The criteria for the literary selections considered in Part Three are (1) that the author in each instance had no intention as far as we can tell of inserting any aspect of the Christian Gospel into the work under consideration and (2) that no published critic (to my knowledge) has discovered any such Gospel in the literary selection. Nevertheless, I contend that the Gospel is indeed present. If valid, my contention demonstrates the power of the Gospel event to impinge itself upon literature even when that impingement is neither planned nor generally detected. If invalid, my contention betrays how my commitment to the Gospel has colored my perception of those literary works considered.

In the first three selections analyzed in Part Three, T*he Picture of Dorian Gray, The Eternal Husband,* and *Holes,* I am serious about their inclusion of the Gospel. In the fourth selection, *The Adventures of Huckleberry Finn,* I am highly ambivalent, taking away with the right hand the position established by the left hand. In the fifth selection, *The Adventures of Tom Sawyer,* I will show how a case for its inclusion of the Gospel could be made, but then will deliberately knock down the house of cards I have built—for the express purpose of spoofing the thesis of this book. I think it a worthwhile thesis—in many instances. But it needs to be put into proper perspective. Any good theory, I fear, can be rendered ridiculous if applied to every situation. In the last selection, dealing with fairy tales, I will again return to the serious advancement of the thesis of this book.

CHAPTER THIRTEEN

The Picture of Dorian Gray
by Oscar Wilde

Since the interpretations of *The Picture of Dorian Gray* depend heavily upon the plot, a brief summary of that plot is in order. An artist named Basil Hallward paints a portrait of the handsome young Dorian Gray and gives it to him. One day Dorian rather casually expresses the wish that his picture could grow old and wrinkled and careworn while he himself might retain his vigor and youth and good looks. Lo and behold, that is exactly what happens! Dorian had forgotten about his careless wish until one night he looked at the portrait right after he had cruelly and snobbishly jilted Miss Sibyl Vane, causing her to commit suicide. To his surprise he noted a cruel sneer on the portrait that wasn't there initially. From then on it snowballed. Whatever crime Dorian committed, the ugly consequences were reflected in the portrait rather than in himself. When he finally committed murder, there was even blood on the picture. Eventually, the portrait became a hideous monstrosity, but Dorian himself remained young and handsome.

Late in the novel Dorian repents of his past behavior and resolves to reform. Expecting to see a corresponding improvement on the portrait, Dorian instead finds a look of cunning and hypocrisy not present before. In a fit of rage he stabs the portrait. There is a loud cry of pain and terror. When his domestics enter the room, they find the body of an old, wrinkled, withered man lying on the floor with a knife in his heart. Alongside the ugly corpse is the portrait of a handsome young man.

A number of factors discourage the reader from attempting to find any sort of moral in *The Picture of Dorian Gray,* let alone any trace of Gospel. The most obvious factor is the notorious life-style of the author himself until his deathbed conversion to Catholicism. As a college student Oscar Wilde reveled in shocking others by his words, actions, and bizarre dress. He was fat and indolent, fond of wealth and flattery. He was casual about plagiarizing. Accused of homosexual behavior, he was found guilty and sentenced to prison. If there is any validity to the contention that what one writes to some degree reflects one's life and beliefs, then a novel with an obvious moral or a lofty theme would be unexpected from the pen of Oscar Wilde.

Another factor is the character of Lord Wotton, second in prominence in the novel only to the protagonist, Dorian Gray. If not immoral, Lord Wotton is at the very least amoral. Witty, urbane, smart-alecky, cynical, unprincipled (at least in word, if not in action), Lord Wotton has all the charm of a naughty boy, a delightful person to have around in a crowd but one you would never want to draw as your college roommate. He has a penchant for epigrams, the most notorious of which are: "The only way to get rid of temptation is to yield to it." "Young men want to be faithful, and are not; old men want to be faithless, and cannot." "The man who would call a spade a spade should be compelled to use one."[1] As a matter of fact, Wotton is accused of cutting "life to pieces with [his] epigrams" (108) and of sacrificing "anybody . . . for the sake of an epigram" (224). So prone to the epigrammatic is Lord Wotton that it is difficult to distinguish his character from his sayings, who he is from what he says. Lord Wotton is epigram personified, suggesting by this characteristic a blaspehemous parallel to the Christian doctrine of the Word, which is both a person (Jesus Christ) and a book (the Scriptures). Add to all this the fact that Wilde portrays him winsomely and that many readers regard Wotton as the vehicle for Wilde's own views, and it becomes difficult to expect the novel in which Wotton dominates to be the vehicle for any particular theme of high moral quality.

The final factor is Wilde's creed of art for art's sake. Art need not convey a moral, it need only be beautiful. Art should not be didactic. This view of art is clear from the preface to the novel. "There is no such thing as a moral or an immoral book. Books are well written or badly written. That is all" (3). "No artist has ethical sympathies" (3). "All art is quite useless" (4). It is a philosophy of art supported by explicit statements in the body of the novel: "An artist should create beautiful things, but should put nothing of his own life into them" (16). "We are not sent into the world to air our moral prejudices" (83). "It is better to be beautiful than to be good" (213). "Art has no influence upon action. . . . It is superbly sterile" (239). With this creed, it is unlikely that Oscar Wilde would consciously write a novel designed to convey a moral or Gospel truth.

One common interpretation of *The Picture of Dorian Gray* is highly compatible with Wilde's creed of art for art's sake. The moral of Wilde's novel—if one dare to attribute a moral to it at all—is, in the view of many, the triumph of art. Art is more important than people, specifically of more value than the creator of a work of art or its subject. And art is more enduring than people. So long as Sibyl is artistic in her acting, Dorian loves her. But when she ceases to be an artist, Dorian (rightly, according to this view) spurns her. Fickleness toward Sibyl is justified by the protagonist's loyalty to art. In the words of Lord Wotton, it is better to grieve over the death of fictional creatures from the works of Shakespeare than to mourn the passing of Sibyl (113). When Sibyl died, "she passed again into the sphere of art" (121). Late in the novel Dorian, surveying the wreckage of his reputation, blames the portrait: "It was the portrait that had done everything" (243). This accusation, ironically, turns out to be a tribute to the power of art. Indeed, "the portrait . . . had done everything." When Basil Hallward reminds Dorian of Dorian's claim that he had destroyed the picture, Dorian replies, "I was wrong, It has destroyed me" (172). Wilde suggests that it was the portrait that prompted Dorian to murder Basil (173). The last paragraph of the novel depicts the victory, if you will, of the portrait. For when Dorian in a fit of rage tries to destroy the portrait with a knife, the outcome is the wizened corpse of himself and, hanging above him, the splendid portrait of a handsome young man. By the close of the novel both the artist and his subject are dead, but the portrait lives on. Thus the title of the novel is accurate. It accents not the *person* of Dorian Gray but the *picture* of Dorian Gray.

Another common interpretation of the novel is less heedful of Wilde's art for art's sake philosophy. In fact, it sees *The Picture of Dorian Gray* as unblushingly didactic and moral. According to this view, the novel is a sort of old-fashioned morality play, a struggle between good and evil, with the latter prevailing. Dorian, initially "unspotted from the world" (21), oscillates between his good and evil angels. Dorian is a Faust caught between Mephistopheles (Wotton) and the Chorus (Basil), the standard for distinguishing between right and wrong, and ultimately, like Faust, Dorian is damned. "Each of us has Heaven and Hell in him," Dorian cries to Basil (172), and eventually the Hell in him wins out. Dorian sells his soul in exchange for eternal youth. "They say he has sold himself to the devil for a pretty face," says a woman to James, Sibyl's brother (210). "What does it profit a man if he gain the whole world and lose his own soul?" When Dorian hears this Scripture quoted by Lord Wotton, he is suddenly jarred (236).

In this interpretation Lord Wotton is the evil angel,[2] the one who corrupts Dorian. Basil Hallward, the artist, aware of Lord Wotton's "bad influence over all his friends" (22), doesn't want Lord Wotton to meet Dorian. But when the contact is unavoidable, Basil pleads with Lord Wotton, "Don't spoil him. . . . Your influence would be bad" (18). No sooner said than done, for moments later Basil sees a look in the young lad's face that he had never seen there before (23). Dorian himself, upon meeting Wotton, becomes "dimly conscious that entirely fresh influences were at work within him" (24). Even Lord Wotton is amazed at the sudden impression his opening words had on Dorian. "He had merely shot an arrow into the air," and it seems to have hit its mark (25). Basil is deeply hurt when Dorian chooses to accompany Lord Wotton to the theater rather than dine with Basil at the artist's home (35). Soon afterward Dorian dismisses Basil as "a bit of a Philistine" and attributes this assessment to his acquaintance with Wotton (63). When Dorian expresses a certain sentiment at a dinner, his addressee replies, "Ah, that is one of Harry's views, isn't it?" (52). Dorian even acquires Wotton's manner of lighting a cigarette and flinging himself down on a couch (106). It is Wotton who lends Dorian the poisonous book that had so profoundly a corrupting influence on the protagonist. It is not for nothing that Lord Wotton's first name is Harry—calling to mind one of the titles for Satan himself, "the old Harry."

Striving to keep Dorian on the path of righteousness are his good angels, Basil Hallward and to a lesser degree Sibyl Vane. Even Dorian is aware of Basil's superiority to Lord Wotton. "I know that you are better than he is," he admits (122). "I don't think I would go to Harry if I were in trouble. I would sooner go to you, Basil," he continues (129). Besides, Dorian recognizes the potential of Basil to rescue him. "Yes, Basil could have saved him" (132). It is a role that Basil actively plays moments before Dorian murders him. "You have a wonderful influence. Let it be for good, not for evil," Basil advises Dorian (167). "Pray, Dorian, pray," Basil pleads when he sees the monstrosity his portrait of Dorian has become as a result of Dorian's corrupt living (173). But to no avail: Dorian stabs him to death.

In Sibyl Vane's case, her very name suggests her role as Dorian's good angel. "Sibyl" suggests "prophetess" or "oracle," and "Vane" suggests "direction" or "guidance." It is Basil who recommends her to Dorian. "The gods made Sibyl Vane for you," he tells Dorian. "Without her you would have been incomplete" (92). Dorian agrees. He describes her to his friends before the curtain rises on her acting, "You will see the girl . . . to whom I have given everything that is good in me" (92). Later, repenting of having jilted her, Dorian resolves to return to her as a source of a happy, beautiful, and pure life (103). After her suicide Dorian concedes, "There is nothing to keep me straight. She would have done that for me" (111).

Certainly, those who view the novel as a morality play have plenty of explicit evidence to support their interpretation, despite the fact that it flies in the face of Wilde's expressed contempt for didacticism in art.

The abundance of personifications in *The Picture of Dorian Gray* tempts some to view the book as allegorical. Abstractions such as love, wisdom, and memory (109), and soul and desire (112) are capitalized and assigned human traits. Dorian is named Prince Charming and is described as "this son of Love and Death" (43). Lord Harry Wotton is called Prince Paradox (213), and we have already seen that his first name, Harry, may be another name for the devil.

But, an allegory of what? The only answer I have found in Oscar Wilde criticism is that the novel is an allegory of conscience.

Admittedly, there is some evidence for this conclusion. After his initial reaction of horror at his first sight of the change wrought in his portrait by his jilting of Sibyl, Dorian determines, "The picture, changed or unchanged, would be to him the visible emblem of conscience" (103). A few pages later Dorian views the portrait Basil had painted of him as "a guide to him through life . . . what holiness is to some, and conscience to others, and the fear of God to us all" (107). To Dorian the portrait's censure and rebuke is even more effective than Basil's had been (133). When he sees the face of James Vane (Sibyl's avenger) peering at him through a window, Dorian is unsure whether what he saw was reality or illusion. But if it were only the latter, "How terrible it was to think that conscience could raise such fearful phantoms, and give them visible form"—just as the portrait had been doing (219-220). Frustrated and desperate at the end, Dorian decides to destroy the portrait—that is, his conscience—and he only destroys himself! One must heed his conscience, not ignore it, and certainly not attempt to destroy it. That is the moral of this allegorical interpretation.

It is this allegorical interpretation that led me to see the novel as allegorical in a different direction. T*he Picture of Dorian Gray* is—or can be viewed as—an allegory of vicariousness. Here too there is some evidence. Shortly after Sibyl's suicide as a result of Dorian's rejection of her, Dorian realizes that "the [changing] portrait was to bear the burden of his shame: that was all" (117). "What did it matter what happened to the coloured image on the canvas?" Dorian considers. "He would be safe. That was everything" (118). Sometimes Dorian would contemplate the deteriorating portrait that in his words "had to bear the burden that should have been his own" (155). The most significant evidence is this passage: "What the worm was to the corpse, his sins would be to the painted image on the canvas. They would mar its beauty, and eat away its grace. They would defile it, and make it shameful. And yet the thing would still live on. It would be always alive" (132). All the Christian reader has to do is regard the portrait of Dorian Gray as a symbol of Christ's assuming our sins and suffering their consequence, and a Gospel pattern emerges!

Specifically, Jesus Christ is to us as the portrait was to Dorian Gray. He grows old with our sins, so to speak, while we remain young and innocent; that is, Christ has been made our sin and our curse for sin (1 Corinthians 5:21 and Galatians 3:13). Whatever wrong we have done, still do, and will do, Christ has suffered the ugly consequences of it on the cross, while we get off scot-free. He became vile, a worm and no man, a reproach unto people and an abhorring unto God, while we are regarded as children of the kingdom. This vicariousness, this substitutionary act on the part of Christ, is the very core of the Christian religion.

One can push the similarity between Wilde's novel and the Christian Gospel even farther. As described earlier, Dorian at the end of the novel finally stabbed the portrait in a fit of rage. There was a loud cry of pain and terror, and when his domestics entered the room, they found the portrait of a handsome youth and the body of an old, wrinkled, withered man lying on the floor with a knife in his heart. In rejecting Christ you become your old, hideous, sinful self again, destined for that place prepared for the devil and his angels. Like all good things the Christian Gospel is so devastatingly simple. We lay our sins on Jesus. That's it. That's all there is to it. We can either take it or leave it—preferably take it, and enjoy the eternal life that goes with accepting Christ as our substitute, as our sin and our curse for sin. Although Oscar Wilde might reject the suggestion, *The Picture of Dorian Gray* can help us to regard the innocent but accursed Jesus on the cross as the portrait, so to speak, of our sinful nature and of its inevitable consequence—and of our blessed escape from that dread possibility.

Notes

1. Oscar Wilde, *The Picture of Dorian Gray* (London and New York: Penguin Books, 1985), 23, 35, and 213. All future page locations for citations from this book will be included in parentheses in the text of this chapter.
2. Some readers have noticed that Dorian eventually outdoes his mentor in respect to evil. In this instance the temptee turns out to be worse than the tempter, an outcome that may call into question the accuracy of dubbing Lord Wotton a devil or evil angel. For all his irreverence and flippancy, Wotton's bark is worse than his bite. No less a person than Basil admits of Wotton, "You never say a moral thing, and you never do a wrong thing" (8-9). In the light of this aspect of Lord Wotton's character, there may be more truth in rather describing the relationship between Wotton and Dorian as that of hypothesis to documentation. What Wotton suggests in theory as evil, Dorian puts into practice. Early on Wotton said to Dorian, "I represent to you all the sins you have never had the courage to commit" (89). Turns out that Wotton was wrong: Dorian does have the courage—indeed!

Study Guide for *The Picture of Dorian Gray*

1. How does the preface foreshadow the style of the novel? The philosophy of the novel? Does the novel contradict the philosophy of art advanced in both the preface and the body of the book?

2. How does Wilde arouse our interest in both the person and the portrait of Dorian Gray?

3. Note how carefully Wilde develops the plot in the opening chapters.

4. How is the outcome of the story cleverly and pleasingly foreshadowed early in the book?

5. What are Lord Wotton's functions in the novel? How does Wilde use this character to suspend our disbelief? Itemize Lord Wotton's most noticeable traits.

6. Note the many epigrams in *The Picture of Dorian Gray*. Is their frequent presence a strength or weakness of the novel? Can the remarks about epigrams on pages 46, 108, and 224 be given broader application than Wilde intended?

7. What is the most prominent image Wilde uses? How is it useful?

8. Who are Dorian's good angels?

9. What function does Dorian ultimately serve in respect to Lord Wotton?

10. How does the role of Dorian's portrait change in the closing pages? In what sense does it emerge as the real hero of the novel? What is the interpretative significance of this triumph? How is the portrait connected with the double motif in literature?

11. Why isn't Wilde more specific about the many crimes attributed to Dorian?

12. What, if any, is the moral of the novel? Why is it ironic that a meaning can be found in the story?

13. Does the novel have allegorical possiblities? Gospel possibilities?

For Further Reading

Ellmann, Richard (ed.). *Oscar Wilde: A Collection of Critical Essays*. Englewood Cliffs, New Jersey: Princeton Hall, Inc., 1969.

Hyde, H. Montgomery. *Oscar Wilde: The Aftermath*. New York: Farrar, Straus and Company, 1963.

Jullian, Philippe. *Oscar Wilde* (tr. Violet Wyndham). New York: The Viking Press, 1969.

Pearson, Hesketh. *Oscar Wilde: His Life and Wit*. New York: Grosset & Dunlap, 1946.

Raby, Peter (ed.). *The Cambridge Companion to Oscar Wilde*. Cambridge, England: Cambridge University Press, 1997.

Roditi, Edouard. *Oscar Wilde*. Norfolk, Connecticut: New Directions Books, 1947.

Sandulescu, C. George (ed.). *Rediscovering Oscar Wilde.* Gerrards Cross, England: Colin Smythe Ltd., 1994.

San Juan, Jr., Epifanio. *The Art of Oscar Wilde.* Princeton, New Jersey: Princeton University Press, 1967.

Willoughby, Guy. *Art and Christhood: The Aesthetics of Oscar Wilde.* London: Associated University Presses, 1993.

Winwar, Frances. *Oscar Wilde and the Yellow 'Nineties.'* New York, 1940.

CHAPTER FOURTEEN

The Eternal Husband
by Fyodor Dostoevsky

Fyodor Dostoevsky's *The Eternal Husband* is a novelette with three goals. That is both the book's strength and its weakness. The three goals are not only achieved but also remarkably executed. That is the book's strength. Each goal could have constituted a book in itself. Trouble is, there are three goals. Unless skillfully integrated, a three-goal book is not as likely to be as effective as a one-goal book. And Doestoevsky's three goals are not well integrated. In fact, they are incompatible. That is the book's weakness.

These three goals are (1) to show how a wronged man gets revenge on his abuser; (2) to demonstrate how certain personality types cannot change their nature, try how they will; (3) to trace how a wrongdoer atones for his misdeeds through the shedding of blood.

It is the third goal that may contain a Gospel pattern or echo, if any Gospel is present at all in the book. But it is difficult to restrict my analysis to that third goal, for all three goals interact on one another. That interaction has a bearing on both the presence and the limitations of the Gospel I see in this short novel.

So I begin with the first objective of the novel: to show how a wronged man gets revenge on his abuser. For some time Velchaninov, the protagonist, has been periodically encountering on the streets a man with crape on his hat, a man vaguely familiar. One night Velchaninov has a troubling dream about a crowd collecting in his room to accuse him of some crime and of a man, again vaguely familiar, joining the crowd ostensibly to give compelling evidence of that crime and whom Velchaninov beats repeatedly because of his stubborn silence. The doorbell rings and awakens Velchaninov. He rushes to the door, but no one is there. So Velchaninov concludes that the doorbell's ringing was just part of the dream. He furthermore concludes that "all this business with the crape gentleman is a dream too."[1]

But then, in typical Dostoevskian fashion, dream and reality telescope. Looking out his bedroom window, Velchaninov sees the man of his dream staring at his house. Suddenly, he approaches the house, comes up the stairs, and tries the door that Velchaninov had just hooked. Impulsively, Velchaninov unfastens the hook and lets him in.

The moment the man with the crape on his hat sits down and introduces himself, Velchaninov recognizes him as Pavel Pavlovitch Trusotsky, an acquaintance with whose wife Velchaninov had a secret affair nearly a decade before. Under the guise of obsequiousness and buffoonery, Pavel begins a cat and mouse game reminiscent of Porfiry's questioning of Raskolnikov in *Crime and Punishment* and, in modern times, of the psychological harassment Columbo accords criminals in the television drama bearing his name. Here is where Dostoevsky's art comes to the fore. As Pavel gradually reveals a knowledge of Velchaninov's affair with his wife, since deceased, the reader sweats along with Velchaninov. How much does Pavel know and, if he knows, what will he do about it? How will he achieve his revenge?

Some of the high spots in Pavel's cat and mouse game consist of double-entendres. He claims that he and Velchaninov were "*intimately* acquainted" (540), that Velchaninov was "a *real* friend of the family" (546), "an *ardent* man" (576) offering Pavel a "priceless bond of friendship of which the dear departed was the precious *link*" (545). Pavel claims to be attending the funeral of a certain Bagautov who had "bestowed his friendship . . . *exactly* as you did" (547). He introduces his nine-year-old daughter to Velchaninov as "*our* Liza, *our* daughter Liza" (558). (Is the pronoun a royal we? Or is it inclusive?) Pavel enumerates the eight months it took for Liza to be born after Velchaninov's departure! Finally, with his fingers he makes the sign of the cuckold horns on his forehead in Velchaninov's presence and alludes to a revelatory letter his wife had left behind at the time of her death.[2]

Then comes an abrupt change in the relationship between Pavel and Velchaninov, a change baffling to first time readers of *The Eternal Husband.* Just when they are anticipating some uniquely horrifying vengeance on Velchaninov, Pavel becomes a weakling, a milquetoast (as the "trus" part of his last name suggests), the butt of jokes and tricks, a man trampled on by society. (I will account for the mystery of this change when I deal with the second goal of the novel.) The change becomes most apparent when Pavel invites Velchaninov to meet a young girl he is planning to marry and her family, the Zahlebinins. Pavel proves to be awkward and clumsy in his courtship, and the girl's family join her in making a fool of Pavel. Eventually, he loses the girl to a rival. Pavel's attempt to murder Velchaninov when he stays overnight with him is a miserable failure. Two years later Velchaninov runs across Pavel at a train station, married again to a woman who lords it over him, flirts with other men, and is accompanied by an irresponsible relative obviously sponging on Pavel. When Pavel's wife invites Velchaninov to stop by their house, he declines the invitation (much to Pavel's relief) and condescendingly offers a parting handshake to the man he wronged. The handshake is spurned; in fact, Pavel pulls his own hand back. Velchaninov is so crushed by the snub from a social inferior that he loses his enthusiasm for another affair with a nearby lady he had hoped to initiate. This is Pavel's revenge, a strange revenge indeed, neither the kind of revenge Pavel had planned or the reader had expected—but a revenge nonetheless.

This peculiar—and to the reader, unsatisfying—kind of revenge can be accounted for by Dostoevsky's second goal, namely, to demonstrate how certain personality types cannot change their nature, try how they will. Dostoevsky defines three personality types: the infernal woman, the predatory type, and the eternal husband. The infernal woman is beautiful, domineering, and flirtatious, "passionate, cruel, and sensual" (551). She lords it over whatever man she marries and carries on affairs with other men with nary a pang of introvertish guilt. "She is one of those women . . . born to be unfaithful wives . . . to the end they feel themselves absolutely right and, of course, entirely innocent" (552). In this novel both of Pavel's wives are "the infernal woman" type. In *The Brothers Karamazov* it is Grushenka. In Dostoevesky's own life it was Paulina Suslova.

The predatory type is the male counterpart to the infernal woman, the catalyst and/or object of her flirtatiousness. Master of small talk, self-confident, poised, and suave, the predatory type knows what to say and how to act in every social situation, especially romantic encounters. He is witty and charming, a ladies' man. Though polite, he never fawns over people or kowtows to them. He neither gives quarter nor expects any. Though Dostoevsky does not use the term, the predatory type could be called "the eternal lover" in contrast to what Dostoevsky calls "the eternal husband."[3] Velchaninov qualifies as the predatory type when he conquers the numerous females in the Zahlebinin household to which Pavel invites him and when he rescues Pavel's newlywed wife from an embarrassing brawl at a train station late in the novel.

Then there is the eternal husband: meek, obsequious, awkward, plagued with feelings of inferiority. No matter whom he marries he will be henpecked and always faithful to a faithless wife. "The eternal cuckold" could be a fitting synonym for the eternal husband. "Such a man is born and grows up only to be a husband . . . promptly transformed into a supplement of his wife . . . . The chief sign of such a husband is a certain decoration. He can no more escape wearing horns than the sun can help shining" (552).

It is Pavel, obviously, who is the eternal husband. Like the proverbial leopard, he cannot change his spots, do what he will. Pavel certainly tries to do so after the death of his first wife when he finds that she had committed adultery with both Bagautov and Velchaninov. He tries to be the predatory type. He attempts revenge in the classic tradition. For a while he succeeds. But ultimately he fails, at least failing to achieve the kind of revenge he hoped for and which the reader expects. Pavel reverts to type. Starting with his unsuccessful courtship of the young girl in the Zahlebinin family and climaxing in his marriage to another infernal woman, Pavel remains what he is destined to be, the eternal husband. That is the meaning of the title to the novel.

Once we realize this aspect of Pavel's character, we begin to understand the abrupt and otherwise inexplicable change in his behavior in the middle of the novel: from spine-tingling harassment of an intended victim for revenge in the first part to pitiful helplessness and buffoonery in the second part. He is, like it or not, the eternal husband. That realization removes the mystery and explains the puzzle.

But it is here that we encounter the first of the novel's thematic incompatibilities. Had it been Dostoevsky's only goal to show how an eternal husband type attempts revenge and then fails because his character type is determined, the reader might be satisfied. But, as we have already seen, Pavel gets his revenge—not the way he planned, not the way the reader expected, and not the way revenge is usually defined—but revenge, nonetheless, when he spurns Valchaninov's proffered handshake at the end. Trouble is, Dostoevsky, it seems, can't have it both ways. He cannot hope to write a revenge novel with a protagonist incapable of revenge. It is the familiar contradictory assumptions fallacy in a new form.

Thematic incompatibility becomes a more serious weakness, though, when we examine Dostoevsky's third goal, that of tracing how a wrongdoer "atones" for his misdeeds through the shedding of blood. Velchaninov is the predatory type. His character trait is every bit as unalterable as that of the eternal husband or the infernal woman. Yet it is he whom Dostoevsky chooses as a man to be redeemed and improved through suffering and the shedding of his blood. Again, it appears, Dostoevsky can't have it both ways.

From the opening page of the novel Velchaninov is a troubled man. Crimes that he had once cavalierly committed suddenly come to mind. Ghosts of the past, successfully dismissed to his thinking, reappear to haunt him. He recalls a couple of unpaid debts. He remembers squandering two fortunes. He recollects joining a group poking fun at an innocent clerk and then getting him drunk as an added joke. He recalls slandering a schoolmaster's wife, getting a young working girl pregnant and then abandoning both her and the child, shooting a young lad's leg off in a duel. Surprised that he is worrying about what he calls "higher ideas of which he would never have thought twice in earlier days" (525), Velchaninov semi-facetiously quips, "Why, one would think some one up aloft were anxious for the reformation of my morals, and were sending me these cursed reminiscences and 'tears of repentance'" (528). Symbolic of Velchaninov's depravity-caused suffering is a re-occuring and growing chest pain caused by an abscess. (See pages 598, 601, 640, 641, 642.)

The climactic memento of his sinful past occurs when Pavel comes onto the scene, like conscience personified, to harass Velchaninov with his knowledge of Velchaninov's secret affair with his wife, now deceased. In the course of their relationship it becomes gradually clear to Velchaninov that, despite his own superior gifts and personality, the clearly inferior Pavel is in fact the better man. Whatever faults Pavel had—and they were indeed both numerous and obvious—Velchaninov had in large part been responsible for by his cuckolding the man. Despite Pavel's drunkenness and buffoonery, despite his abuse of the daughter Liza, it grows upon Velchaninov that he is worse than Pavel. "It is you [Velchaninov] call me a scoundrel, *you* call *me*?" retorts Pavel (590, Dostoevsky's emphasis). It is he himself to his surprise, not Pavel, whom Liza calls "wicked, wicked, wicked, wicked!" (565). It dawns on Velchaninov that it is he who might be responsible for Pavel's abuse of Liza (599). And when Pavel nurses Velchaninov during a life-threatening attack of chest pain, Velchaninov admits, "You are better than I am! I understand it all, all. . . . Thank you" (645).

Shortly after Liza's untimely death it occurs to Velchaninov that loving and caring for his daughter might have "expiated" and made up for his "old putrid and useless life" (599). But that opportunity was gone. Some time later Pavel reminds Velchaninov of settling their account, a reminder that at the time serves only to anger the latter (628). But then comes Chapter 15, entitled "The Account Is Settled." In this chapter Pavel stays overnight with Velchaninov nursing him with hot plates when the pain in his chest worsens. But when Velchaninov falls asleep, Pavel tries to kill him with a razor, the result of the doubleness so common in Dostoevsky's works, specifically in Pavel's case, the tension between his desire to be the predatory type and the reality of his being the eternal husband. Predictably, Pavel fails. Velchaninov, awakened by the same nightmare he had experienced before Pavel's nocturnal visit to his lodging early in the novel, overpowers Pavel. But in the struggle Pavel does succeed in severely cutting the palm and fingers of Velchaninov's left hand. Almost immediately the pain in his chest, symbolic of his depravity, disappears (648). In the subsequent chapter, entitled "Analysis," Velchaninov feels relief. "Something was over, was settled," he notices, "as though that blood from his cut fingers could 'settle his account'" (649). When the doctor who binds his wounds assures him that there would be no particularly disagreeable results, Velchaninov "began to assure him that they had already had the most agreeable results" (650). Indeed, the account had been settled. Dostoevsky is suggesting that the cut had been redemptive, that the shedding of blood had atoned for Velchaninov's crimes. That is why Velchaninov at the end of the novel, when Pavel spurns his proffered handshake, calls attention to the scar on his hand and insists, "If I—I hold out this hand to you . . . you certainly might take it!" (664). Consistent with Dostoevsky's view expressed in many of his works, Velchaninov is convinced that suffering and bloodshed have redemptive and sanctifying value.

But here again Dostoevsky's trumpet blows an uncertain sound. For he has another goal to accomplish at this point: Pavel's achievement of some kind of modified revenge. Thus the socially inferior Pavel, despite his failure at traditional vengeance, succeeds in insulting and cutting the debonair man of the world, Velchaninov. But that emphasis undercuts the very truth about suffering and bloodshed that Dostoevsky has been trying to establish. Further, Pavel's success at revenge dilutes Dostoevsky's accent on the inability of the eternal husband to alter his chemistry. Still more perplexing, Velchaninov, despite his atoning, redemptive, and sanctifying razor cut, is not an improved man at the end of the novel. He flirts with Pavel's wife and, prior to that, had been on his way to see a lady acquaintance for less than ethical purposes. True, he abandons the intended visit—Pavel's "revenge" had taken the wind out of his sails—but the change of plans does not reflect any repentance on Velchaninov's part. "And how he regretted it afterwards!" are the closing words of the novel (665).

Although in the closing pages Dostoevsky takes away with his one hand the atoning value of suffering and bloodshed he has been establishing with his other hand, it is in his flawed effort to achieve the latter goal that, I believe, the Gospel emerges. Suffering and the shedding of one's own blood are redemptive. This is a common theme in many of Dostoevsky's works, especially *Crime and Punishment*, *The Brothers Karamazov*, and *The Idiot*. In those books there is clear mention of Christ's suffering and of Christ's bloodshed on the cross. That kind of explicit reference is absent from *The Eternal Husband*. To connect Dostoevsky's accent on the atoning and redemptive value of suffering and the shedding of blood in this novel with that of Christ can arise only from the principle of interpreting one work by an author in the light of other works he has written. Though I am convinced it is legitimate to do that, we are still faced with the ambivalence in Dostoevsky's concept of suffering, existing in this novel as well as in his other novels where he explicitly speaks of Christ. Does suffering redeem *per se*, or because it leads to Christ, who redeems? Does the shedding of blood atone for sins *per se*, or because it reminds us of the shed blood of Christ, which does the atoning?

Maybe we are drawing too fine a point. Really, could we even ask these questions had Christ not suffered and shed his blood on the cross? Could we even make the distinctions just described in the absence of the Gospel event? Could one even think of asserting the heretical doctrine that human suffering and the shedding of one's own blood are in themselves redemptive apart from the orthodox doctrine that it is Christ's suffering and Christ's shedding of blood that save us from our sins? Without truth there can be no heresy to deviate from that truth. Counterfeits are meaningless in the absence of the genuine article. Whether orthodox or heretical, Dostoevesky's very attempt at a doctrine of suffering in *The Eternal Husband* demonstrates the impact of the Gospel!

I fear I have done Dostoevsky's novel an injustice. I agree with those critics who maintain that in this novel Dostoevsky has bitten off more than he can chew, that he has pursued the achievement of goals that are mutually exclusive. In this respect, the novel fails. But if the novel is a failure, it is the most delightful failure I have ever encountered. Each goal is a worthwhile pursuit. And Dostoevsky pursues each one with utmost narrative skill and philosophical insight. *The Eternal Husband* is an attractively weird book, refreshingly original in design and execution. It has charm, an inexplicable charm like Coleridge's "Kubla Khan" or Kafka's *Metamorphosis*. If this novel is a house divided against itself, it is, nonetheless, a charming house in which to dwell. The realm of literature would be much the worse without the existence of this book.

Notes

1. Fyodor Dostoevsky, *The Eternal Husband*, tr. Constance Garnett, in *Great Short Works of Fyodor Dostoevsky* (New York: Harper & Row, 1968), 538. All future page locations for citations from this novel will be included in parentheses in the text of this chapter.
2. The emphasis in each of the citations in this paragraph is mine.
3. Detailed descriptions of the predatory type can be found on pages 589, 617, 635, and 662.

Study Guide for *The Eternal Husband*

1. What is the primary cause of Velchaninov's suffering at the outset of the story? Demonstrate Velchaninov's depravity. What is the significance of the frequent references in the novel to the pain in Velchaninov's chest? To what extent is Velchaninov responsible for Pavel's depravity? Which character is worse in Dostoevsky's judgment? (In this connection, what is the significance of the fact that Pavel refuses to shake hands with Velchaninov at the end of the novel?) Do Velchaninov's sufferings have any value? What role does the razor cut play in Velchaninov's suffering? (In this connection, note the title of the chapter in which the razor cut incident occurs.) When does the pain in Velchaninov's chest disappear? Does any Gospel pattern emerge from the answers to the preceding questions?

2. What are the functions of Velchaninov's two dreams? Is there any evidence for one critic's view that the novel is an allegory of a burdened conscience?

3. Note the definition of "the infernal woman" on pages 551-552, of "the eternal husband" on page 552, and of "the predatory type" on page 589.

4. Document in detail Pavel Trusotzky's cat and mouse treatment of Velchaninov.

5. Establish a connection between Pavel's anecdote on pages 589-590 and the meaning of the novel.

6. What change takes place in the relationship between Pavel and Velchaninov at the Zahlebinin house? Did you expect this change? Is it really a change? Why did Pavel invite Velchaninov to see his future bride? Connect all this with the title of the novel.

7. Relate Pavel's paradoxical treatment of Velchaninov to the definitions of "the predatory type" and "the eternal husband" and to Dostoevsky's concept of the double.

8. How is the last chapter related to the meaning of the novel?

9. Note the foil relationship between Velchaninov's connection with the Trusotzkys and his connection with the Pogoryeltzevs.

10. Demonstrate from Velchaninov's reaction to Pavel's tormenting that Dostoevsky deserves to be called a writer of psychological novels.

11. Note the prominence of the element of the grotesque in this novel.

12. In view of the major emphases of the novel, is there any validity to the contention that Dostoevsky's novel is "a house divided against itself"?

For Further Reading

Amoia, Alba. *Feodor Dostoevsky*. New York: The Continuum Publishing Co., 1993.

Bregor, Louis. *Dostoevsky: The Author as Psychoanalyst*. New York: New York University Press, 1989.

Cox, Roger L. *Between Earth and Heaven: Shakespeare, Dostoevsky, and the Meaning of Christian Tragedy*. New York, Chicago, San Francisco, 1969.

Edgren, C. Hobart. *Of Marble and Mud: Studies in Spiritual Values in Fiction*. New York, 1959.

Fuelop-Miller, Rene. *Fyodor Dostoevsky: Insight, Faith, and Prophecy* (tr. Richard and Clara Winston). New York: Charles Scribners Sons, 1950.

Gide, Andre. *Dostoevsky* (tr. Arnold Bennett). New York: Alfred A. Knopf, 1926.

The Huttarian Brethren (ed). *The Gospel in Dostoyevsky*. Ulster Park, New York: Plough Publishing House, 1988.

Magarshack, David. *Dostoevsky*. New York: Harcourt, Brace & World, Inc., 1961.

Mathewson, Rufus. *The Positive Hero in Russian Literature*. New York, 1958.

Mochulsky, Konstantin. *Dostoevsky: His Life and Work* (tr. Michael A. Minihan). Princeton, New Jersey: Princeton University Press, 1967.

Simmons, Ernest J. *Dostoevski: The Making of a Novelist*. New York: Oxford University Press, 1940.

CHAPTER FIFTEEN

Holes
by Louis Sachar

In 1998 Louis Sachar, a writer of popular children's stories, authored *Holes*, a book targeted primarily at older children but also amenable to adult tastes. The publication proved immensely successful. Readers soon recognized the book as deserving of the nearly dozen awards it had won, among them the Newbery Medal and the National Book Award for Young People's Literature. Recently, the novel was even made into a critically acclaimed movie by the same name.

Holes is an exciting adventure story. It conforms to C. S. Lewis's literary criterion that "to interest is the first duty of art." The plot is unique. A young lad named Stanley Yelnats is wrongly convicted on the basis of circumstantial evidence of a theft he didn't commit and is sentenced to hard labor in a camp in western Texas designed to reform bad boys. The specific hard labor to which Stanley and his fellow prisoners are assigned is for each of them each day to dig a hole five feet deep and five feet wide. Ostensibly, the activity is intended to build muscle and character. But a chance discovery while digging leads Stanley to conclude that the warden (a cruel woman named Ms. Walker) has a motive for the excavation other than the alleged reformation of the diggers: the hope of finding a box containing a considerable sum of money stolen many years before by a notorious female bank robber and rumored to be buried in or near the area of the prison work camp.

One day Stanley's best friend among the inmates, a quiet boy nicknamed Zero, cruelly abused, deserts camp. No effort is made to recapture him because the prison administrators, realizing that the escapee has no place to go in the surrounding desert, are confident that thirst and hunger will soon drive him back to the camp. When Zero doesn't return as expected, friendship and conscience impel Stanley to desert camp too in the hope of finding the lad before he dies of thirst and starvation. Finding Zero barely alive, Stanley carries his friend up a peculiar shaped mountain in the distance to which both of them are mysteriously attracted. To their pleasant surprise, they find at its top both water and onion plants to sustain them until they regain their strength. During their recovery Zero gradually divulges to Stanley that, although imprisoned for another theft, it was actually he, Zero, who had also committed the theft for which Stanley was condemned and sentenced.

Hoping to discover the alleged buried treasure themselves, the two boys return to the prison camp at night and furtively dig deeper in a hole where Stanley had once found a lipstick tube bearing the same initials as those of the name of the notorious outlaw. Sure enough, they find the box containing the money. But at the very moment of triumph they are discovered by the warden and her associates. After a series of crises in the ensuing stand-off (caused largely by an abundance of venomous yellow-spotted lizards in the vicinity), Stanley is eventually freed by the fortuitous arrival of his family lawyer and the attorney general of Texas with the good news that he has been cleared of the crime for which he had been imprisoned. Eventually, the work camp is closed because of its many irregularities, and the two boys live happily off the considerable sum of money they had unearthed.

Skillfully interwoven into this plot are two subplots, both of them stories from the distant past. The one is the story of Elya Yelnats, Stanley's great-great-grandfather. To beat out a rival for the affection of a girl friend, Elya had sought the advice of a local seer, a gypsy-like woman. For her help he had promised to carry the seer, an invalid, up a mountain to drink there from a magical stream. Inadvertently, Elya forgets to keep his promise, and he and his descendants are cursed for generations to come. This curse, we are told, accounts for the phenomenal tough luck that all Yelnats experience, so often being (as was Stanley) in the wrong place at the wrong time. The other subplot is the story of an attractive schoolteacher, Kate Barlow, who becomes a notorious outlaw in response to cruel mistreatment from the townspeople she served. She robs numerous banks and at the time of her death frustrates her pursuers by burying the loot somewhere in the dried up lake bed on which the prison work camp many years later was located. Both of these subplots impact the main plot, suggesting one of the novel's themes: the influence of the past on the present.

All three of the novel's plots, the main story and two subsidiary stories, are narrated in a charming, readable style; with delightfully short chapters and short paragraphs sprinkled with numerous short sentences. Take this excerpt from the opening chapter, for instance:

> Here's a good rule to remember about rattlesnakes and scorpions: If you don't bother them, they won't bother you.
> Usually.
> Being bitten by a scorpion or even a rattlesnake is not the worst thing that can happen to you. You won't die.
> Usually.
> . . . .
> But you don't want to be bitten by a yellow-spotted lizard. That's the worst thing that can happen to you. You will die a slow and pinful death.
> Always.[1]

Note how the arrangement of the three one-word paragraphs (usually . . . usually . . . always) adds to the effectiveness of this excerpt. It even has visual impact.

In the excerpt just cited the wry humor is a prominent feature throughout the book of the author's style. It deserves special mention, especially because of its appeal to younger readers. What boy won't identify with the hapless Zero who, when asked what he means by claiming he could have been "a ward of the state" replies, "I don't know. But I didn't like the sound of it"? (183). Who doesn't chuckle over the author's gratuitous reminder concerning Elya, who lived many, many years before Stanley came into the world, that "he didn't know he was Stanley's great-great-grandfather"? (28). What reader could fail to enjoy the pun at the end of the novel when the author, unable or unwilling to tie up all the loose ends, urges the reader, "You will have to fill in the *holes* yourself"? (231; my emphasis).

The presence of refrains, almost always the earmark of a good children's book, is another notable aspect of Louis Sachar's style: The warden's habitual statement, "Excuse me!" is always a warning of impending doom to the addressee, never the sign of courtesy it ought to be. Mr. Sir's sadistic reminder to the boys again and again that the site of their hard labor "is not a Girl Scout's camp." Sam's continual assurance to the schoolteacher, "I can fix it," whether that promise applies to the disrepair in her schoolroom or in her love life.

Even the art of suggesting a truth rather than explicitly stating it, usually the staple of more mature literature, surfaces in *Holes*. We realize that the girl Elya has been courting is shallow and insincere without the author supplying either of these spoon-feeding words. How so? Because when her father asks her to choose between the two rival suitors standing before her, she looks at Elya and asks, "You're Elya, right?" (34). Both Elya and the reader sense at this point impending defeat for this lover. We infer that Kate Barlow, the beautiful schoolteacher, is wary of her reputation and of her chastity when we're told of the adult males, instructed along with the children in her schoolroom, "All they ever got was an education" (102). We suspect that even a sophisticated person like the town doctor may have had a superstitious faith in the alleged curative powers of applications of Sam's widely acclaimed onion juice when we're told, "Doc Hawthorn was almost completely bald, and in the morning his head often smelled like onions" (109).

For good measure there's even a palindrome in the novel. The name of the hero, Stanley Yelnats, is spelled the same both backward and forward.

Much of the appeal of *Holes* derives from its numerous ironies. Remember my mention of Mr. Sir's sarcastic refrain about the prison site that it "is not a Girl Scout's camp"? Guess what happens to the institution when the state of Texas closes it? It becomes a Girl Scout camp! Early in the novel a bully dumps Stanley's notebook into a toilet bowl. In fact, it was the search for and retrieval of his notebook that caused Stanley to miss his bus and be compelled to walk home, a walk during which Stanley was once again in the wrong place at the wrong time: A pair of stolen sneakers fell on him from an overpass and he was accused of the theft. But that's not the end of the episode. In the closing pages of the novel we discover that the prank that implicated Stanley with the law provides him the alibi needed to clear him of the crime. It turns out that the very time the sneakers were stolen was the same time Stanley was retrieving his notebook. Delicious irony! The most significant irony in the novel develops when the time Stanley invested in teaching the illiterate Zero to read pays off eventually in Zero's being able to read the name "Yelnats" (the last name also of Stanley's ancestors) on the just unearthed box of treasure, thereby establishing the legitimacy of Stanley's claim to the treasure over that of the warden. The chickens come home to roost in a surprisingly satisfactory way!

Symbols abound. The rattlesnake tattoo on Mr. Sir's arm that wriggles when he writes suggests that the man himself is a snake of sorts. The nickname "Zero" betrays society's mistaken evaluation of the lad. The numerous holes dug by the prisoners symbolize the absence of societal values and the emptiness of the future in store for the diggers—a mere hole in the ground. The numerous items unearthed by the diggers suggest the truth that "nothing stays buried forever, especially the truth."[2] The central symbol of the novel, I believe, is the peculiar shaped mountain—resembling God's fist and God's thumb—that plays so vital a role in saving the lives of Stanley and Zero. (More about this later.)

If there is any weakness in the novel, it is in the area of characterization. The warden, Mr. Sir, and Mom are hardly three dimensional. They are caricatures. But given the fairy tale aura of the story, these Dickens-like exaggerations are forgivable. They are no more in need of realistic portrayal than the Troll under the bridge in *The Three Billy Goats Gruff*. Their evil is a given; it needs no motivation or development.

The book's numerous literary merits are in themselves enough to make *Holes* worthy of the honors it has won and of the reading delight it provides. But it is the contention of this chapter that there is a bonus in the novel—frequent echoes of the biblical account of human sin and divine grace.

In his customary wry manner Louis Sachar talks a number of times in *Holes* about the Yelnats family curse, initiated by ancestor Elya's failure to keep his promise to the gypsy-like seer he consulted for advice. That curse continued through subsequent generations. In fact, the offended seer had warned at the time that Elya's descendants "would be doomed for all of eternity"

(31). Stanley's great-grandfather, for example, had been robbed of his fortune by the outlaw Kissin' Kate Barlow. Stanley's father has consistently failed in his efforts to find a way of recycling discarded sneakers. Stanley himself has a knack of always being in the wrong place at the wrong time. The classic instance of this phenomenon is Stanley's proximity to the overpass from which the stolen sneakers fell on Stanley and for which theft Stanley is then accused by a passing patrolman. One of the refrains in the novel is the family's habit of always blaming their misfortunes on Stanley's "no-good-dirty-rotten-pig-stealing-great-great-grandfather" (7, 8, 25, 57). Yet at least one time, when he crashed a truck he had just "borrowed," Stanley recognizes that he himself, not his ancestor, is at fault. "He couldn't blame his no-good-dirty-rotten-pig-stealing-great-great-grandfather this time. This time it was his own fault, one hundred percent" (148). Might we have here a semi-facetious representation of our systematic categories of original and actual sins?

More audibly echoed in the novel is the remedy for the family curse, especially the vicariousness that informs the main plot. Stanley Yelnats is accused of a crime Zero had committed, and for a time he bears the punishment for that crime, digging holes in a barren, parched, sun-baked, lizard-infested desert that could well serve as a symbol of hell itself. When Zero deserts camp, Stanley goes in search of him, and when he finds him, sick and weakened from thirst and hunger, Stanley carries Zero up the mountain, where both are restored to health. By having taught Zero to read earlier in their relationship and by sharing his treasure with Zero at the end of the novel, Stanley liberates his companion from societal and financial bondage. Even when Stanley is freed from the prison, he refuses to leave without Zero. Ultimately, Zero is freed from prison too, cleared of the crimes he actually had committed as if they had never occurred because (1) his files cannot be located (222) and (2) the lawyer pretends not to have heard Zero's confession of having committed the theft for which Stanley had been accused and condemned (225).

Stanley's major acts of vicariousness are foreshadowed early in the novel by a minor instance of vicariousness when Stanley takes the guff and endures the penalties for another lad's theft of Mr. Sir's sunflower seeds on which the latter habitually chewed to cure a smoking habit.

Symbolic of Stanley's vicariousness having removed the family curse is the fact that rain falls on the prison camp locale for the first time in a century (225) and that Stanley's father successfully invents a cure for foot odor the very day after Stanley carries Zero up the mountain (229).

To be sure, Stanley is an imperfect "Christ figure" if he is that at all. But do types ever measure up to the perfection of the Antitype to which they point, even in the Scriptures (e. g., Moses, Joseph, David)? Stanley is only a more glaring instance of the rule. Nor is the effect of Stanley's vicariousness as universal as that of his biblical counterpart. After all, only Zero and other family members benefit from Stanley's noble deeds. But all this is simply an acknowledgement that a type isn't the antitype, that an echo isn't the original sound, and that an imitation isn't the real thing.

More subtle but even more exciting in its Gospel overtones is the mountain where Stanley and Zero take refuge. It gives them direction, preventing them from getting lost in the desert (153). It exercises a mysterious attraction on those approaching it: "[Stanley] kept walking toward it, although he didn't know why" (153). Even though appearing impossible to climb (171), the mountain seems to supply the strength to do so; "[Stanley's] strength . . . seemed to come from the outside as well . . . . it was as if the rock had absorbed his energy and now acted like a kind of giant magnet pulling him toward it" (170). The mountain is a place of refuge, not only for Stanley and Zero but even for Stanley's great-grandfather (93, 128, 143). Stanley and Zero rest in the shade it provides (180, 189). Above all, the mountain supplies the boys the food and water they need to stay alive. All of these—direction, shade, food, water—are prominent Gospel metaphors in the Bible.

The most intriguing aspect of the mountain is its peculiar shape. It looks like God's fist with God's thumb protruding. Is this shape metonymy for "the hand of God," another frequent Gospel metaphor? At one point lightning seems to emanate from God's thumb (129; Law?), but when they reach the mountain the boys discover the thumb to be a mysterious provider of water (185; Gospel?). Twice God's thumb is closely associated with the sun, in the one case pointing to it (164), in the other case appearing to balance it (166). Could Sachar be punning on the words "sun" and "son" (God's Son?)? "'Twere to consider too curiously, to consider so," Shakespeare's Horatio might caution us (Hamlet, V, i, 198).

As is the case with the Gospel events, there is the temptation to challenge the reality of the mountain, to dismiss it as "foolishness" (1 Corinthians 1:18), as "another kind of mirage" (153), "like chasing the moon" (153, 161). Finally, in the context of the events associated with the mountain resembling God's thumb, Stanley and Zero often exchange a "thumbs-up" sign in moments of crisis and triumph (159, 160, 161, 162, 165, 168, 169, 210, 219, 220). Could this suggest a parallel to the sign of the cross in Christian practice?

Subtle and unobtrusive as these echoes of the biblical account of sin and grace are, it is their abundance in *Holes* that ultimately removed my initial fear that I was forcing them onto the story rather than deriving them from it, committing eisegesis rather than exercising exegesis. There are simply too many Gospel allusions in the novel to dismiss them as accidental. I am convinced that the materials described above are in the thing beheld, and not just in the eye of the beholder. Although no reviews of either the novel or the movie, to my knowledge, have noted its Gospel overtones, it is curious that a few of them spoke of *Holes* as "a modern fable" or "parable" or suggested that it communicates "in a sophisticated way" a "subtle moral."

Unfortunately, I know too little about the author's life and his other works (at this juncture) to determine whether the Gospel aspects of the novel were deliberately inserted or whether the author's genius, as is sometimes the case in literature, says more than it is aware. I suspect the insertions were intentional, but it is also possible that my conclusions are enough to make Louis Sachar turn over in one of the holes with which he has peppered his novel! Even if the Gospel overtones were deliberate and conscious on Sachar's part, it does not follow that he intended them for Gospel purposes. He may simply have regarded the biblical account of sin and grace as a sort of good story or tradition or mythology to be exploited, like the Oedipus myth or the King Arthur legend, for literary purposes. If such were the author's purpose, it need not prohibit the Christian reader of *Holes* from recognizing in this same material the truth of the Christian revelation itself with all of its salvific and sanctifying potential. It wouldn't be the first time that a reader has derived more from a work of art than the author intended.

More serious than violating the author's intention, I believe, is violating the spirit or tone of the novel. *Holes* is primarily an adventure story written in a mildly humorous vein. It is designed to entertain especially younger readers. In his legitimate search for a moral or lesson (above all, a Gospel pattern), the reader musn't make the mistake of chewing lemon meringue pie as if it were a porterhouse steak. Treating a work of such delightful lightness too seriously is to sin against Alexander Pope's famous dictum to interpret a work of art "in the spirit the author writ" [sic]. We must be careful not to assign more freight to a literary genre than it is intended to carry. To see a lesson or moral in a work of art must always be in keeping with the tone of the medium conveying that art. While adventure and humor may carry a serious message, we musn't eliminate adventure and humor in the act of decanting that message. In the fare that Sachar has provided in *Holes*, the Gospel is a possible dessert, but it is not the main course. In other words, I wouldn't want this analysis of *Holes* to turn a delightful adventure story into a Sunday school lesson or a Gospel tract. *Holes* is not a sermon. It is a charming adventure story—with the possible bonus of artistically reflecting certain aspects of the biblical account of sin and grace. And for that bonus the reader can be happy even as he revels also in the other joys the story provides.

When the sneakers fell onto Stanley from the overpass, he viewed them as "a gift from God" (24). He thought that somehow his dad could use them in his lifelong dream to discover a way to recycle old sneakers. In the light of what immediately follows, Stanley's arrest and imprisonment, Stanley's initial assessment of the sneakers as a gift from God appears to be myopic. Yet, ironically, his assessment is ultimately correct. Given the removal of the family curse and the improved fortunes of Zero, Stanley, Stanley's family, and others as a sequel to the accident of the sneakers, it develops that the shoes were "a gift from God" at that. Like plot, like book. It is my conviction that the novel itself is—or can be—a gift from God.

Notes

1. Louis Sachar, *Holes* (New York: Dell Yearling, Random House, 2003), 4. All future page locations for citations from this book will be included in parentheses in the text of this chapter.
2. Monique Vescia, *Scholastic Book Files: A Reading Guide to Holes by Louis Sachar* (Scholastic Inc., 2003), 35.

Study Guide for *Holes*

1. Read the opening sentence and page 4 for a quick introduction to the attractiveness and effectiveness of Sachar's style.

2. Find instances of Sachar's ability to suggest a truth without stating it explicitly.

3. What elements of Sachar's style appeal particularly to the juvenile reader?

4. How do Mr. Pedanski's counseling cliches characterize the speaker? How do they help the juvenile reader to identify with the boys in the detention camp?

5. Find instances of attractive ambiguity in Sachar's choice of words.

6. Describe the connection between Sachar's use of irony and poetic justice.

7. What is unique about the name of the protagonist?

8. Find examples of repeated sayings and repeated actions in the novel. What is the connection between refrain and genre? Between refrain and characterization? Between refrain and theme?

9. Identify prominent symbols in the novel.

10. What is the justification for Sachar's use of caricature in the characterization of the warden, Mr. Sir, and Mr. Mom?

11. Describe the main plot and the suplots of *Holes*. What are the key ingredients in the development of the main plot? How does the author connect the three plots through intersection and parallelism? What is the thematic significance of these plot connections? How does the thematic significance provide a transition to the theological possibilities of the novel?

12. What biblical doctrine might be suggested by the frequent refrain about Stanley's "no-good-dirty-rotten-pig-stealing-great-great-grandfather"? See particularly pages 8, 31, and 57. What biblical doctrine is suggested by Stanley's admission concerning the car theft and accident on page 148?

13. Note numerous similarities between the imagery of *Holes* and the imagery of the Old Testament.

14. How does the pattern of vicariousness inform the main plot? What other incidents in the novel mirror this vicariousness?

15. Why does the mountain that plays so prominent a role in the novel tempt the reader to see a Gospel pattern in the book? What does the mountain do for people? What does it look like? How do Stanley and Zero signal its impact on their lives?

16. Is it possible that the author inserted Gospel imagery into his book for other than Gospel purposes? If so, is it valid for the reader to infer Gospel purposes from these Gospel images?

17. Is a Gospel pattern compatible with the tone of the novel?

18. Were the sneakers that fell onto Stanley's head "a gift of God" as Stanley initially viewed them on page 24? (See also page 187.)

For Further Reading

Vescia, Monique. *Scholastic Book Files: A Reading Guide to Holes by Louis Sachar:* (Scholastic Inc., 2003).

CHAPTER SIXTEEN

The Adventures of Huckleberry Finn
by Mark Twain

Reader stance toward *Huckleberry Finn* has changed considerably in my lifetime. I remember as a teen-ager taking the book off a shelf in a St. Louis bookstore for probable purchase and being admonished by my English teacher (retired from the classroom but now employed in the bookstore) to select something more serious and significant. *Huckleberry Finn* was then regarded as little more than a boy's adventure story, entertaining perhaps, but not worthy to be placed alongside books by Charles Dickens, Henry James, Leo Tolstoy and other classics. Even the appearance of the book (then published by Grosset and Dunlap) evidenced its status in the critical world: large print and colorful jacket and inside cover designs picturing boys in strawhats and wielding simple fishing tackle. If the academic world had any reservation about the novel—besides its lack of seriousness—it was that exposure to its bad grammar might prove contagious to the youthful reader.

If *Huckleberry Finn* was taken too lightly then, it is, in my opinion, taken too seriously nowadays. Today its adventure and humor are largely ignored. It is, rather, viewed as a serious social and political document speaking profoundly to the concerns of late twentieth and early twenty-first century readers. If the critical world today has any reservations about the novel, it is concerning its alleged crude and intrusive humor and its politically incorrect language about race.

I provide this brief overview of the evolution of reader stance toward *Huckleberry Finn* not because of its historical interest but because of its bearing on the validity of many modern interpretations of the novel as well as on the likelihood of Gospel elements surfacing in the book.

Because *Huckleberry Finn* has been deemed worthy in recent times of sophisticated academic and critical notice, the novel has been accorded a number of mature-sounding interpretations, some of them, unfortunately, riddled with modern code words and literary psychobabble. Certain patterns (e. g., initiation, the quest, the search for identity or authenticity) fashionable in modern literature and in current literary criticism have been, rightly or wrongly, discovered also in *Huckleberry Finn*; and in many cases the alleged presence of these patterns has been proclaimed the mark of the book's greatness.

It is difficult to determine whether these patterns are actually present in *Huckleberry Finn* and even more difficult to determine whether Mark Twain intended their inclusion. Certainly, if one approaches the novel with the presupposition that these patterns are present—or ought to be—it is easy to discover supporting evidence in each instance. The problem in these pattern interpretations is not the lack of evidence but, rather, the validity of that evidence in the context of the tone or spirit of the novel, specifically, its episodic adventures, practical jokes, hilarious humor, colorful dialect, and legendary superstitions.

Take the pattern of initiation, for example, a modern favorite. Huck Finn, a mere lad, is successively initiated into the phenomena of child abuse from an alcoholic father, practical jokes that go too far and hurt people, slavery and its attendant evils, the nature of freedom, the complexity of truth, the inevitability of maturity, the folly of feuding, con artists, phony religion, conscience pangs, and conflicting loyalties, just to name a few. To see *Huckleberry Finn* as a quest novel is even easier. Obviously, both Jim and Huck are on a quest for freedom, the former from slavery and the latter from an oppressive parent and stifling civilization. Thus they proceed down the Mississippi River (or the river of life) in pursuit of their respective goals. When we come to the pattern of the search for identity or authenticity, there is even specific and explicit evidence if one ignores the context for that evidence. Not comprehending whom Aunt Sally has mistaken him for, Huck reacts, "I had my mind on the children all the time; I wanted to get them out to one side and pump them a little, and find out who I was."[1] Moments later, when he overhears that Aunt Sally takes him to be Tom Sawyer, Huck rejoices, "It was like being born again, I was so glad to find out who I was" (223). If the reader suspects levels of meaning in these remarks, it seems quite reasonable to regard them as Huck Finn's search for an authentic identity, especially in the light of the numerous disguises, both physical and moral, that he assumes in the course of the novel.

But can any of these interpretations be what *Huckleberry Finn* is about? Seriously? Really? Come now! Granted, these themes may be present, but only incidentally, at best secondarily. This is true even if the evidence for these interpretations is objectively present in the novel and properly understood, not the outcome of a predisposition so strong that it invents or distorts evidence that it sees. Initiation into life experiences, the quest for meaning or freedom, the search for an authentic identity—so rich is Twain's understanding of life and human nature that these sparks too may fly from the anvil of his authorship, but they most certainly are not the thrust of *Huckleberry Finn*. To claim otherwise is to load the genre of the novel with more freight than it is intended to bear. To claim otherwise is to violate Alexander Pope's hermeneutical dictum that a work of art must always be interpreted in the spirit in which the author wrote. And in that light, initiation, quest, and identity interpretations simply don't cut it.

I am, of course, aware that humor can often be a vehicle for serious meaning. But humor to the degree it is present in *Huckleberry Finn*? And there's more than humor. There's folklore. There's superstition—a veritable encyclopedia of it. There's adventure—gobs of it. There are all the twists and turns, eccentricities and paradoxes of cussed but lovable human nature. There is the clear warning from the author himself, the "Notice" prefacing the book: "Persons attempting to find a motive in this narrative will be prosecuted; persons attempting to find a moral in it will be banished; persons attempting to find a plot in it will be shot." There is simply too much sheer fun in the novel for the reader to treat it with overweening seriousness. *Huckleberry Finn* is pudding, not hard tack—delightful pudding and rich in texture to be sure, but pudding nonetheless. We are not meant to break our teeth on it. It is my conviction that *Huckleberry Finn* is a superbly styled, carefully crafted, and highly entertaining book sharply delineating human nature and revealing all the richness of life. Only secondarily, it is probing, sometimes incompletely and unsatisfactorily but always with sensitivity, a variety of social and ethical issues.

One of the unfortunate consequences of an overly sophisticated approach to *Huckleberry Finn* is modern critical rejection of the novel's ending, the hilariously convoluted rescue of Jim from the cabin in which he is imprisoned as planned and carried out by Tom Sawyer and Huck Finn—a delightful parody of melodramatic rescues and escapes in swashbuckling romantic novels such as Alexander Dumas's *The Man in the Iron Mask* and *The Count of Monte Cristo*. "What a shame," say the critics, "that a Huck Finn who is so close to maturity, who has found his authentic identity, and who has acquired a proper perspective on the nature of slavery, of truth, of life itself, should relapse by becoming party to so insensitive a practical joke on a slave companion he has learned to respect and love!" Of course, this ending to the book is out of sync with patterns of initiation, quest, and search for authentic identity. But Mark Twain never intended such patterns—at least not primarily. To fault him for this conclusion of his novel is to fault him for a kind of novel he never meant to write! With this hilarious ending to the book, Twain was simply trying to restore the comic spirit with which the novel began. No less a person than T. S. Eliot has defended the novel's ending, and I heartily join him in his defense. The ending belongs! It is a major factor in the book's elevation to classical status.

Another unfortunate outcome of overweening seriousness toward *Huckleberry Finn* is the current charge of racism leveled against the book and its author—even to the absurd extent of occasionally banning this book from school libraries and classroom syllabi. Granted, there are stereotypes, dialects, even the offensive "n" word that jar on modern ears (including my own). But Twain was a friend of African Americans (the appropriate designation for the race of which he could not have been aware) and an opponent of slavery. His portrait of Jim, the runaway slave, is a masterpiece of sensitivity in the context of the times in which it was written. Again and again he portrays Jim as a hero, a man of winsome emotional depth, of superior common sense, and of incorruptible integrity. True, Jim has laughable (but lovable) eccentricities. But so does everyone else in the novel. True, he is the target of crude jokes. But so is most everyone else in Twain's writings. Though Twain had not risen (in fact, could not rise) to the level of racial tolerance we have achieved—or claim to have achieved—he was a man light years ahead of his time in towering above widespread racial prejudice. We cannot evaluate a nineteenth-century man exclusively by twenty-first century standards.

It may appear that I have wandered from the subject of this book, the issue of Gospel in literature. Not really. The above considerations are relevant to that issue. In two ways: The first is that an attempt to see a Gospel pattern in *Huckleberry Finn* is no worse (and no better, either) than to see patterns of initiation, quest, or the search for identity in the book. And the second is that the arguments enumerated above against the search for those patterns apply equally well to any attempt to see a Gospel pattern in *Huckleberry Finn*.

In the context, then, of both this justification for the attempt and this caution against it, I proceed to the evidence for some sort of Gospel impact on the Twain classic.

To begin with, there is unquestionably a theological context for the adventures of Tom, Huck, and Jim, much of it too irreverent to take seriously. The novel is permeated with the question "What is truth?" although it is never framed in these words of the biblical Pontius Pilate. Repeatedly, Huck lies. He lies to Jim about his role in Jim's rattlesnake bite (53). He disguises himself as a girl when he visits a woman to pump her for information and lies to her about his background. Even when she catches him at his lies, he continues to lie in his true identity as a boy (61). He lies to the hare-lip about his residence in England and confirms it with an oath when the hare-lip accidentally administers that oath on a dictionary rather than on a Bible (174). He lies to the Duke and Dauphin about the whereabouts of Peter's gold. He uncorks a string of lies to cover for Mary's absence to protect her from the Duke and Dauphin (191-194). He lies frequently to Aunt Sally in the closing chapters. Nearly as often Huck ponders the advantages and disadvantages of the practice of lying. Even from his utilitarian perspective, certain lies are less justified than others, particularly if they're mean and hurtful. One of the most moving moments in the novel is when Huck realizes that one of his lies to Jim was degrading to his friend, and he apologizes for it (85-86). There are even times when Huck is tempted to tell the truth and, in fact, risks the truth on one occasion, when he lets Mary know that the Duke and Dauphin are trying to cheat her of her inheritance (186). Others lie too, Tom Sawyer *par excellens*, the Duke and Dauphin and Pap habitually, and even Jim (but in his case for a good reason, to help Huck).

There are other theological considerations. Does prayer work? (12 and 27). Does Christian stewardship work? (47). Was the world created? Or did it just happen? (118). There are frequent references to the role of Providence (e. g., 219), the seriousness of most of them undone by Huck's theological coinage "preforeordestination" (109). Twain presents the ironic contrast of a sermon on brotherly love preached to the feuding Grangerfords and Shepherdsons with guns on their laps (109). On the same page Twain quips that hogs attend church more voluntarily than people do. Huck draws distinctions between stealing and what he calls "borrowing" (241-242). And Huck's tension over the conflict between the horrors of slavery and the property rights of slave owners, above all his bout with conscience pangs over turning Jim in as a runaway slave, rise above the customary humor and flippancy with which Twain presents most theological and ethical issues. At this point the tone of the novel turns uncharacteristically serious.

In this theological context there appear superficial Gospel patterns. There is the pattern of vicariousness: Huck is willing to suffer the dire consequences of helping a runaway slave achieve freedom; Jim risks his chance for liberty by emerging from his hiding place to help a doctor treat Tom's gunshot wound. It is a pattern "reinforced" by specific references to the cross (both of them too incidental to constitute serious reinforcement). The cross is the badge of Tom's robber gang (7), and Pap wore a cross in his left boot-heel "made with big nails, to keep off the devil" (16). There is the pattern of baptism and rebirth—that is, if the reader dare view Huck's experience on the waters of the Mississippi as a baptism of sorts and his humorous reaction to discovering his identity as Tom Sawyer at Aunt Sally's as a rebirth of sorts: "It was like being born again" (223). There is the pattern of death and resurrection: flippantly in the description of the amputee who, as a result of "mortification," "died in the hope of the glorious resurrection" (221); a bit more seriously when Tom suspects Huck (allegedly drowned) of being a ghost and Huck replies in words echoing our Lord's resurrection appearance, "You come in here and feel of me if you don't believe me" (224).

The only possible Gospel pattern that has any merit in my opinion is that of vicarious damnation,[2] primarily because it occurs in a serious context. Huck is tormented between returning Jim to his owner (at that time considered the ethical thing to do in terms of property rights) and helping Jim escape to freedom (with which Huck feels more comfortable). The struggle is not portrayed in Mark Twain's customary humorous and irreverent manner. Huck experiences genuine agony and finally resolves to do what was then considered the wrong thing: to persist in helping Jim escape. "I was a-trembling," he says, "because I'd got to decide, forever, between two things. . . I studied a minute, sort of holding my breath, and then says to myself: 'All right, then, *I'll go to hell*—and tore it [the letter reporting the runaway's locale] up" (214, my emphasis). Like Christ, Huck is willing to suffer damnation on behalf of another's freedom. In biblical terms, he is willing to "be made sin" and to "be made the curse for sin" in Jim's behalf. And Huck's decision poses the central irony of the novel: Huck does right at the very moment he thinks he is doing wrong!

Of the few candidates for Gospel patterns in *Huckleberry Finn*, this is the only one I am tempted to view seriously. But the weight of the evidence to the contrary in the novel helps me to overcome even this temptation. As already argued, the tone of the novel—at least elsewhere—overwhelmingly militates against so somber a conclusion about a book that is primarily written for adventure, entertainment, and insight into human nature. Mark Twain himself had no use for organized religion and perhaps none for the Christian faith itself. There is nothing in the Mark Twain canon elsewhere to justify the finding of a Gospel pattern in this particular novel. Nor was it the fashion of the times, as it is today, to insert "Christ imagery" into a book for whatever purpose, theological or literary.

Notes

1. Mark Twain, *The Adventures of Huckleberry Finn* (New York: Bantam Books, 1981), 221. All future page locations for citations from this book will be included in parentheses in the text of this chapter.
2. Gospel patterns reflecting Christ's death in our behalf are frequent in literature, but patterns reflecting his suffering of hell in our behalf are rare. One author who presents the pattern of vicarious damnation clearly and knowledgeably is Graham Greene, specifically in *The Power and the Glory* and *The Heart of the Matter.*

Study Guide for *The Adventures of Huckleberry Finn*

1. How does contemporary treatment of *The Adventures of Huckleberry Finn* differ from that accorded it by previous generations? Is the novel an entertaining story or a serious social document? What is "the proper approach" to the reading of the book? What bearing does the author's prefatory "Notice" have on this question? How are the tone and content of the opening paragraph related to this question?

2. How does the opening paragraph of the novel intone one of the major concerns of the book? How is this concern portrayed in the character of the protagonist? How is it portrayed in the character of others in the novel? Does the novel resolve the issue it raises?

3. How does the point of view of *The Adventures of Huckleberry Finn* differ from that of its predecessor, *The Adventures of Tom Sawyer*? What are the advantages of this shift in point of view?

4. What does the title of the novel suggest about the structure of the novel? What factors justify such a structure? What factors, nevertheless, give the novel a degree of unity?

5. Identify prominent symbols in the novel.

6. What are the principal features of Mark Twain's style?

7. Identify the various phenomena satirized by Twain's hilarious humor. Note the occasional caustic strain in his humor. In what respect is the changing quality of the humor a microcosm of the novel itself?

8. Why might the novel be regarded as an encyclopedia of superstitions? How does the inclusion of these superstitions in the novel affect its tone and its interpretation (especially the issue of truth)?

9. What is paradoxical about Twain's characterization of Jim and Huck? In what respect is their characterization consistent with the novel itself?

10. Note how occasionally the author recommends a certain course of action by decrying it or by affirming its opposite. What might be a personal reason for doing this? What might be a literary reason for doing this?

11. Why might *The Adventures of Huckleberry Finn* be called a novel of initiation? A quest novel? A search for identity? How does the presence of these

possibilities affect contemporary reaction to the novel? What are the strengths and weaknesses of contemporary reaction to *The Adventures of Huckleberry Finn*?

12. Is *The Adventures of Huckleberry Finn* a better novel than *The Adventures of Tom Sawyer*?

13. Evaluate the end of the novel (pages 218-293). Is it thematically and artistically defensible?

14. Is there a Gospel pattern in *The Adventures of Huckleberry Finn*? For example, are there instances of vicariousness in the novel? Does the novel contain a "baptism and rebirth motif"? A "death and resurrection motif"? What unique Gospel possibility is suggested by Chapter 31? Evaluate the possibility of a Gospel pattern in terms of the novel's tone, in terms of the Mark Twain canon, in terms of what we know about Mark Twain's stance toward the Christian religion, in terms of literary fashion in Twain's time.

For Further Reading

Bellamy, Gladys Carmen. *Mark Twain As a Literary Artist*. Norman, Oklahoma: University of Oklahoma Press, 1950.

Bloom, Harold (ed.). *Mark Twain: Modern Critical Views*. New York: Chelsea House Publishers, 1986.

Covici, Jr., Pascal. *Mark Twain's Humor: The Image of a World*. Dallas: Southern Methodist University Press, 1962.

Cox, James M. *Mark Twain: The Fate of Humor*. Princeton, New Jersey: Princeton University Press, 1966.

Gerber, John C. *Mark Twain*. Boston: Twayne Publishers, 1988.

Lowry, Richard S. *"Littery Man": Mark Twain and Modern Authorship*. Oxford, England and New York: Oxford University Press, 1996.

Lynn, Kenneth S. *Mark Twain and Southwestern Humor*. Boston: Little, Brown and Co., 1959.

Mandia, Patricia M. *Comedic Pathos: Black Humor in Twain's Fiction*. Jefferson, North Carolina: McFarland & Co., Inc., Publishers, 1991.

Rogers, Franklin R. *Mark Twain's Burlesque Patterns as Seen in the Novels and Narratives 1855-1885*. Dallas: Southern Methodist University Press, 1960.

Smith, Henry Nash (ed.). *Mark Twain: A Collection of Critical Essays*. Englewood Cliffs, New Jersey: Prentice-Hall, Inc., 1963.

———. *Mark Twain: The Development of a Writer*. Cambridge, Massachusetts: The Belknap Press of Harvard University Press, 1962.

Stone, Albert E. Jr. *The Innocent Eye: Childhood in Mark Twain's Imagination*. New Haven, Connecticut: Yale University Press, 1961.

Wagenknecht, Edward. *Mark Twain: The Man and His Work* (3rd ed.). Norman, Oklahoma: University of Oklahoma Press, 1961.

Wiggins, Robert A. *Mark Twain: Jackleg Novelist*. Seattle: University of Washington Press, 1964.

CHAPTER SEVENTEEN

The Adventures of Tom Sawyer
by Mark Twain

If our consideration of *The Adventures of Huckleberry Finn* makes us hesitate to find Gospel in a work of literature simply because that work contains objective evidence for its presence, our study of *The Adventures of Tom Sawyer* will help us realize the folly of seeing Gospel in a work of literature merely because of the existence of objective evidence for its inclusion. To be sure, the presence of objective evidence for Gospel inclusion is a necessary cause for the recognition of a Gospel pattern or Gospel echo. But it is not a sufficient cause. There are other factors to be considered, such as the tone of the novel, its genre, our knowledge of the author's life and views, comparison with other works by the same author, etc. The purpose of the previous chapter and of this one is not to undo the thesis about the impact of the Gospel on literature. I have convinced myself—and, I hope, the reader also—that this thesis is a valid one, that the Gospel is present in works of literature more often and more abundantly than we think. But the purpose of this chapter and the previous one is to put that thesis in perspective; to realize that good as the thesis may be, we can end up with too much of a good thing. The Freudians, by pushing their approach too far, have, in my opinion, already had a negative impact on contemporary understanding and evaluation of literature. It is my purpose to keep theologians from making the same mistake.

Mark Twain himself seems to caution us against any overweeningly serious approach to the interpretation of *The Adventures of Tom Sawyer*. The title, *The Adventures of Tom Sawyer,* calls attention to a content designed for children. The word "adventures" is to a youthful reader what catnip is to a cat. Besides, the word "adventures" underscores the episodic nature of the book—a phenomenon with which the young reader is always more comfortable than the adult reader, who has come to regard the unity of a work as a *sine qua non* for its excellence.

But that word "adventures" is part of the title also for *The Adventures of Huckleberry Finn*, and, as we have seen, its inclusion there has not prevented readers from chewing its light fare as if it were a ten-course meal at a highbrow restaurant. So Mark Twain provides other warnings. In the preface to *The Adventures of Tom Sawyer* the author reminds the reader that the book "is intended mainly for the entertainment of boys and girls." The author hopes, of course, that men and women will not on that account shun the book, for (Twain continues) "part of my plan has been to try pleasantly to remind adults of what they once were themselves, and of how they felt and thought and talked, and what queer enterprises they sometimes engaged in." Consistent with this expressed approach to the novel is an early passage in the opening chapter appended to a detailed description of Tom's whistling technique: "The reader probably remembers how to do it if he has ever been a boy."[1] That, it appears, is the prerequisite for a proper reading of *The Adventures of Tom Sawyer*: if you're not a child presently, you need to have been one at some time! Or to paraphrase the Scriptures, "Let this mind be in you which is also in a child."

For the most part, readers of *The Adventures of Tom Sawyer* and literary critics have respected the author's stated wish about a proper approach to this novel. That widespread heed to Twain's caution has had two results, one bad and one good. The bad one is that *The Adventures of Tom Sawyer* is generally considered to be far inferior to *The Adventures of Huckleberry Finn*. I agree that it is inferior—if for no other reason than that the third person point of view in *The Adventures of Tom Sawyer* is nowhere near so effective as the first person point of view in *The Adventures of Huckleberry Finn*, a point of view that makes reader identification with protagonist (and author) much more likely. But far inferior? No! Both books are superbly styled and even surprisingly well-organized despite their episodic content. Both are chockful of humor. Both help the reader to better understand himself and others;

the novel is peppered with insights into human nature. To say that *The Adventures of Tom Sawyer* is "inferior" to *The Adventures of Huckleberry Finn* is to introduce a word applicable to neither. It would be more appropriate to say that *The Adventures of Tom Sawyer* is less "excellent" than *The Adventures of Huckleberry Finn*.

The good result of respect for Mark Twain's instruction on how to approach *The Adventures of Tom Sawyer* is that the novel has been largely spared overly sophisticated interpretations not congruent with the lighthearted tone or spirit of the novel. One seldom hears it called a quest novel or a novel of initiation.[2] There is no jargon about the search for identity or authentic selfhood in the critical essays on the book. At most, critics have seen in the novel a satire on the tradition in literature of the good boy ending up successful and happy and the bad boy ending up with the failure and misery he deserves. Twain stands the typical American Horatio Alger ideal on its head.[3] At worst, Tom has been criticized for betraying his anti-establishment code at the end of the novel by insisting that Huck conform to social conventions and criteria of respectability if he hopes to join Tom's highbrow band of robbers. On account of Tom's betrayal Twain himself has been criticized for compromising with the very WASP mentality he has been satirizing.

When it comes to the impact of the Gospel on *The Adventures of Tom Sawyer*, I don't believe the issue would have occurred to me if it had not been for a couple of passing remarks I encountered in literary criticism. The first one I ran across years ago in Northrup Frye's *Anatomy of Criticism*. Mr. Frye pointed to Tom and Becky's tragic entrance into the cave and their celebrated emergence from it as an instance of the death and resurrection motif in literature. Frye coupled this example with Jonah's being swallowed by a big fish and later extricated from it as another instance of the same motif. But the critic did not make a case for either claim; it was merely an observation. More recently I recall reading in Kenneth Lynn's *Mark Twain and Southwestern Humor* that the three days Tom and Becky spent in the cave were significant, but Lynn did not expand on his suggestion. It was perhaps because of their hints that I reluctantly decided to "play the game" and look for evidence of Gospel in *The Adventures of Tom Sawyer*. And, just as reluctantly, I must admit that the evidence is technically present. Not only were Tom and Becky in the cave three days as Christ was in the grave a similar period of time, but their being lost in the cave and then being delivered from it could serve as a metaphorical representation of Christ's literal emtombment and resurrection. Certainly, it is interesting that Twain chanced upon the number "three," three days, not two or four. But there is more evidence for the death and resurrection motif than that hinted by Frye and Lynn. Early in the novel while reveling in a humorous martyr complex as a result of rejected puppy love for Becky, Tom wishes, "Ah, if he could only die *temporarily*" (60, Twain's emphasis). That is the very hope Christianity proclaims, that physical death is temporary! Tom and his companions, thought to be drowned, show up alive at their own funeral, a funeral at which the text for the sermon was, "I am the resurrection and the life" (118). Could this be more fodder for the death and resurrection motif? Returning to the cave incident, we might add that while trapped in its interior, Becky dreamed of a beautiful country and assured Tom, "I reckon we are going there" (195). Could this beautiful country be heaven? And when the two children emerged from the cave alive, the report of their deliverance, like the news of Christ's resurrection, was considered a wild tale at first (201).

Less obvious, I suspect, is a pattern of vicariousness. But a central episode of the novel is Tom's taking upon himself the blame and punishment for Becky's "sin" of tearing a picture in her schoolteacher's book. And Tom's noble deed effects repentance in Becky, even as Christ's vicarious death on the cross is the power for repentance in the Christian's experience (135). As in *The Adventures of Huckleberry Finn,* there are even specific references in *The Adventures of Tom Sawyer* to the cross, references more tempting to see levels of meaning in than those in the sequel. The treasure that Injun Joe buried is "*under* the cross" in the cave (210, Twain's emphasis) and moments before Huck had said, "It is luck for us that cross is" (209).

When one assembles the evidence, the whole seems much greater than any of its individual parts. The evidence, in totality at least, seems impressive. But I have to keep reminding myself that to see anything more than coincidence in the evidence is to violate the child-like spirit and the humorous, adventurous tone of the novel. Besides, everything we know about Twain's stance toward Christianity and about the context of his other works militates against seeing Gospel footprints in the fertile soil of Twain's writing. To see Gospel patterns in *The Adventures of Tom Sawyer* strikes me to be as foolish as seeing Squinty's adventures in *Squinty, the Comical Pig* (a book I remember enjoying as a child) as evidence of the initiation pattern! To paraphrase the Scriptures once again, what fellowship does the pattern of initiation have with the simple joy of a delightful children's book! Who would think of letting this toad into a child's imaginative garden!

Notes

1. Mark Twain, *The Adventures of Tom Sawyer* (New York: Penguin Books, 1986), 11. All future page locations for citations from this book are included in parentheses in the text of this chapter.
2. One exception is the interesting critical analysis of the novel provided by Albert E. Stone, Jr. in *The Innocent Eye: Childhood in Mark Twain's Imagination.*
3. See Blair's essay in Henry Nash Smith (ed.), *Mark Twain: A Collection of Critical Essays* and Kenneth S. Lynn, *Mark Twain and Southwestern Humor.*

Study Guide for *The Adventures of Tom Sawyer*

1. In view of the last paragaraph of the preface and the parenthetical remark at the top of page 11, what appears to be the proper approach to this novel? What are the implications of this approach for the Gospel in literature thesis?

2. What kind of structure does the novel's title suggest? What two prominent threads serve to tie together many of the episodes in the story? What is the relationship in the novel between character and plot? Find occasional cause and effect connections between some of the novel's episodes. Find instances of author intrusion and editorializing.

3. What are the principal virtues of Mark Twain's style? Note among other things his capacity for apt metaphor.

4. Evaluate Mark Twain as a humorist.

5. Note the surprising amount of "human nature passages" in what purports to be a mere adventure novel or funny story.

6. Demonstrate Mark Twain's ability in characterization. What characters are obviously in sharp contrast to each other? What is the technical name for such a relationship? In view of what happens to the allegedly "good" and allegedly "bad" characters in the novel, how might *The Adventures of Tom Sawyer* be regarded as a satire?

7. Is Tom's advice to Huck at the end of the book out of character? Is *The Adventures of Tom Sawyer* thematically "a house divided against itself"?

8. Is there a Gospel pattern in *The Adventures of Tom Sawyer*? For example, does the novel contain a "death and resurrection motif"? Are there instances of "grace" and "vicariousness"? What use does the novel make of the "cross"? Evaluate the possibility of a Gospel pattern in terms of the novel's tone? In terms of the Mark Twain canon? In terms of what we know about Mark Twain's stance toward the Christian religion? In terms of the literary fashion of his time?

For Further Reading

Bellamy, Gladys Carmen. *Mark Twain As a Literary Artist.* Norman, Oklahoma: University of Oklahoma Press, 1950.

Bloom, Harold (ed.). *Mark Twain: Modern Critical Views.* New York: Chelsea House Publishers, 1986.

Covici, Jr., Pascal. *Mark Twain's Humor: The Image of a World.* Dallas: Southern Methodist University Press, 1962.

Cox, James M. *Mark Twain: The Fate of Humor.* Princeton, New Jersey: Princeton University Press, 1966.

Gerber, John C. *Mark Twain.* Boston: Twayne Publishers, 1988.

Lowry, Richard S. *"Littery Man": Mark Twain and Modern Authorship.* Oxford, England and New York: Oxford University Press, 1996.

Lynn, Kenneth S. *Mark Twain and Southwestern Humor.* Boston: Little, Brown and Co., 1959.

Rogers, Franklin R. *Mark Twain's Burlesque Patterns as Seen in the Novels and Narratives 1855-1885.* Dallas: Southern Methodist University Press, 1960.

Smith, Henry Nash (ed.). *Mark Twain: A Collection of Critical Essays.* Englewood Cliffs, New Jersey: Prentice-Hall, Inc., 1963.

_____. *Mark Twain: The Development of a Writer.* Cambridge, Massachusetts: The Belknap Press of Harvard University Press, 1962.

Stone, Albert E. Jr. *The Innocent Eye: Childhood in Mark Twain's Imagination.* New Haven, Connecticut: Yale University Press, 1961.

Wagenknecht, Edward. *Mark Twain: The Man and His Work* (3rd ed.). Norman, Oklahoma: University of Oklahoma Press, 1961.

Wiggins, Robert A. *Mark Twain: Jackleg Novelist.* Seattle: University of Washington Press, 1964.

CHAPTER EIGHTEEN

Fairy Tales, An Analysis and Two Examples

Since the thesis of this book originated from my experience years ago with fairy tales, it is appropriate that I end this book with an analysis of the fairy tale genre as a vehicle for the Gospel.

Let me admit up front that there is no objective evidence for a Gospel pattern in any fairy tale I have read. What is seen is wholly in the eye of the beholder. Yet the recognition of the Gospel in the fairy tale genre is not entirely an exercise of the reader's imagination. Certain frequently repeated characteristics of the fairy tales act as catalysts upon the Christian reader, triggering a reasonable suspicion that "there may be Gospel at that in them thar fairy tales."[1] Although none of these characteristics by itself is particularly convincing, it is the frequency of each characteristic (e. g., "living happily ever after") and the totality of these characteristics that make the reader strongly suspicious of the probability that fairy tales somehow reflect—or at the very least distort—certain facets of the Christian Gospel. The fairy tales, in my opinion, are the principal evidence for my belief that the central event of history—the Gospel event of the Son of God's incarnation, life, death, damnation, and resurrection for our salvation—has had so profound an impact on our world that it has spilled beyond the bounds specifically chosen by God to contain it and convey it, namely, Scripture. Many aspects of the Gospel, such as the Son of God becoming man, the Creator sacrificing himself for the creature, the God-man dying and rising again, are in varying degrees of accuracy and completeness foreshadowed or reflected in nature, in items of human manufacture, in pagan religious beliefs and practices, in mythology, in music, in art, and in literature.

I would like to illustrate this capacity of the fairy tale with two sermons, the first on Sleeping Beauty, the second on Jack and the Beanstalk.[2] But, first of all, an apology and, secondly, a caution.

The apology concerns the methodology employed in these two sermons. It is brazenly allegorical. That is, numerous aspects of the fairy tale in each instance are assigned spiritual equivalencies. Allegorizing is a sort of *persona non grata* nowadays, both in the realm of literature and of homiletics. Some readers or listeners may be turned off by the very attempt. Yet might there not be precedent, at least for the format if not the methodology,[3] in our Lord's parables? He used stories, fictional ones at that and surprisingly earthy, as vehicles for divine truth. Why, then, may we not also use fictional stories—among them fairy tales—as conveyors for devine truth? There seems to be but a whisker's difference between the two genres, parables and fairy tales. Bizarre as the sermonic use of the fairy tale genre may initially seem, the practice is actually surprisingly conservative. It reverses the current trend: Instead of finding myth in the Gospel, it finds the Gospel in myth. Instead of demythologizing the Gospel, it "de-Gospelizes" the myth!

The caution is this: Whatever Gospel ore we mine from the fairy tale, the fairy tale must remain a fairy tale. The fairy tale is a story meant to charm and delight, thrill and excite; it is not a Sunday school lesson. The Gospel message may be legitimately derived from or associated with the fairy tale medium, but the medium must somehow survive the attempt. The fairy tale medium deserves to exist in its own right, especially for children, regardless of its potential to support the thesis of this book.

SLEEPING BEAUTY

Like so many myths, legends, nursery rimes, and fairy tales, the story of Rose-Bud or Sleeping Beauty is a reflection of, or at worst a distortion of, Christian truth. There are many variations of the tale, but the basic ingredients are these: A beautiful princess is born; a bad fairy, disgruntled at not being invited to her christening dinner, prophesies that on her fifteenth birthday the princess will prick her finger on a spinning wheel and die; another fairy, of a somewhat better disposition, softens the blow by reducing the tragedy to a hundred years sleep; despite the parents' precautions to remove all spinning wheels from the kingdom, the princess encounters one in a tower room on her fifteenth birthday; instead of making a hasty retreat as a princess with any common sense would have done, she touches it, pricks her finger, and not only falls into a deep sleep herself but causes everyone else, people and animals, in her vicinity to do so also; along comes a prince after a century, wanders into the thicket-enshrouded, dust-covered castle, sees the beautiful princess, and finds her so irresistible that he kisses her; she wakes up and so does everyone else; the prince marries the girl; the story ends with the usual refrain about living happily ever after.

For Sleeping Beauty substitute Adam and Eve. For the bad fairy substitute Satan. For the spinning wheel substitute the tree of the knowledge of good and evil. Despite God's precautions Adam and Eve eat of the forbidden tree, an action every bit as incredibly stupid as Sleeping Beauty's approaching the spinning wheel in the tower room. The curse ensues: death. Not only are Adam and Eve victimized by it, but also, through their foolish sin, they cause everyone else to be victimized by the curse. For the castle-wide trance substitute original sin; "by one man sin entered into the world, and death by sin." But along comes Christ; the Prince of peace enters our sin-enshrouded, iniquity-covered world, where he experiences life, damnation, death, and resurrection, and by so doing awakens us and all other people. For the kiss substitute the atonement that Christ achieved on the cross. We become the brides of Christ and live happily ever after, both of these familiar truths of the Bible.

Now there are two applications of this story that occur to me. The one is quite obvious, and that is in the area of bodily death. Originally part of the curse of sin, bodily death has been reduced by Christ from an eternal nightmare to a temporary sleep. No one really knows what death is like. Those who have experienced it empirically have never described it to us. I take that back: One of them has, Christ. He died, and he came back. And he tells us that death is a sleep; "she is not dead, but sleeping," he said of Jairus's dead daughter. If death is sleep, it certainly is a very sound sleep, and surely the sleeping quarters leave much to be desired. At the same time we cannot dismiss the analogy because it is not presented as an analogy. If death resembles anything, it resembles sleep. I conclude from Jesus' words that death is more like sleep than anything else in our experience. So, what follows? Where there is sleep there is awakening. We arise from our grave as we arise from our bed. God's pleasant alarm goes off on Judgment Day. Our bodies awaken, we consummate our wedding with the Bridegroom, Christ, and we live happily ever after—literally.

The second application is not so obvious. It is in the area of spiritual death. The fall into sin, induced by our first parents and continued by ourselves, need not bring upon us a permanent judgment. With God's help we can arise from it. Even as God through Christ awakens us on Judgment Day from the grave, so God through Christ arouses us from death in trespasses and sins (today if you wish). If I can say it without committing the heresy of implying dormant goodness and denying total depravity, each of us is a sleeping beauty. With God's help through Christ we can awaken to a life of attractive goodness and beautiful virtue. Look at the challenge of the Scriptures: "Awake, thou that sleepest, and arise from the dead, and Christ shall give thee light." Good can be beautiful. As Paul told the Philippians, "Whatever is true, whatever is honorable, whatever is just, whatever is pure, whatever is pleasing, whatever is commendable, if there is any excellence and if is anything worthy of praise, think about these things." Virtue is beauty, and may we awaken to this heaven on earth as well as look forward to awakening in heaven itself some day.

You may have been tricked into reading this sermon by wondering what possible connection there could be between a familiar fairy tale and the familiar Gospel. I hope you have seen the connection. But you have also caught me exploring the themes of "justification" (in the first application of Sleeping Beauty) and "sanctification" (in the second application). Maybe these theological concepts aren't so stuffy, after all.

JACK AND THE BEANSTALK

One of the many paradoxes of the Christian religion is that it is both sensible and foolish. The psalmist, you may remember, called that person a fool who said in his heart, "There is no God." In a later psalm he explained why: because "the heavens declare the glory of God; and the firmament showeth his handiwork." Some of us when we were children were taught a number of proofs for the existence of God, the created world being one of the principal ones. "For every house is builded by some man; but he that built all things is God" was the biblical support for this approach. In fact, we were told that one of the things that distinguished the Christian religion from all other religions in the world was that it was historical, that it was a religion of hard facts and verifiable events. The Christian religion was not merely teaching and philosophy and precept and ethic; it was, above all, about a God who entered history, who was born and who lived and who died and who rose again, all of these being hard, solid facts as capable of empirical verification as any other historical event of equal antiquity. We found ourselves agreeing with St. Paul when he told King Agrippa that "this was not done in a corner."

Yet there is the other side of Christianity too, the foolish side. God entered our world in weakness rather than in strength—as a baby. Our vulgar idiom "born in a barn" captures all the insult and humiliation of his birth; there being no room for him in the inn, he was born among animals. Some humble shepherds were the first to know about this birth. Why start with them? A number of his friends and relatives thought he was "beside himself" ("crazy" would be our word for it today). The first official act of his public ministry was a temptation from the devil out in a barren wilderness. Some start! He turned the other cheek, walked the extra mile, blessed those who persecuted him. True, He performed some mighty miracles, but he was reluctant to have people know about them. When Pontius Pilate met this innocuous teacher, he snickered at his claims about truth and kingship.

The climax in foolishness came when he was put to death. He was crucified, you know. The cross didn't just kill—it humiliated. It added insult to injury. Just to make sure he and his followers got the point, he was executed, for good measure, in the company of two gangsters. That people should someday put crosses in places of worship and wear crosses as ornaments or jewelry was as impossible for the people who witnessed Christ's death to imagine as it would be for you and me to imagine that someday in the future people would place miniature gallows in churches or devoutly wear them suspended around their necks.

Anyhow, in the midst of all this foolishness, one of the gangsters did what appeared to be a foolish thing. He turned to Jesus and said, "Lord, remember me when you come into your kingdom." "What faith!" we exclaim. But what foolishness too! True, this gangster may have seen a lot of Jesus during the trial and during the trip to Calvary. He had noted a marked difference in this man's conduct, that when Jesus was reviled he didn't revile back. He had probably heard Jesus say those remarkable words, "Father, forgive them; for they do not know what they are doing." I suppose the thief had witnessed much of this, and it had made a deep impression on him. But still, look at what he was doing. He was putting his future into the hands of a person about to die just as he was. He was trusting in a man obviously at the mercy of the crowds, the crowds who were daring Jesus to step down from the cross and prove that he was the Son of God. He was counting on one forsaken by God and man alike. The thief on the cross didn't have the resurrection of Jesus to bolster his faith as we have. And yet he went to him as the Son of God, who could give him eternal life. Here was the cross in all its "foolishness," and yet here was a man who believed! In response to his irrational response to a seemingly hopeless situation Jesus replies, "Today you will be with me in paradise."

St. Paul captured this paradoxical aspect of Christianity when he wrote to his Corinthian readers, "For the message about the cross is foolishness to those who are perishing, but to us who are being saved it is the power of God. . . .But we proclaim Christ crucified, a stumbling block to Jews and foolishness to Gentiles, but to those who are the called, both Jews and Greeks, Christ the power of God and the wisdom of God. For God's foolishness is wiser than human wisdom, and God's weakness is stronger than human strength."

Jack and the Beanstalk has captured this unique "foolish–sensible" characteristic of Christianity too. Jack, you remember, did a lot of foolish things, chief of which was selling the family cow for a handful of colored beans. Yet this turned out to be the wisest investment he ever made. For those beans, thrown in disgust out the window, became a towering beanstalk by which Jack scaled the heights and captured all sorts of valuable treasures, a hen that laid golden eggs, a harp that played beautiful music upon command, and numerous money bags. Most of all, that beanstalk turned out to be not only the means by which Jack was periodically rescued but also the instrument by which the Giant was killed.

On the face of it, the cross of Christ appears to be little more than a handful of beans, a nonsensical thing to invest in. But it has turned out to be like Jack's beanstalk. The foolishness of God has proved to be the wisdom of God, and the weakness of God has proved to be the power of God. That disgraceful instrument of execution has become "the tree of the cross" by which we have recovered all sorts of spiritual blessings: forgiveness of sins, peace of mind, eternal life, the power to do good, the capacity to be happy, purpose in everyday living, peace with our fellow human beings—just to mention a few. Whatever the peril in life, the cross is always our route to safety. Most of all, it has proved the undoing of that Giant Satan.

There is an element of poetic justice in the fact that a tree, "the tree of the cross," should prove Satan's downfall. Because, you'll remember, it all began with a tree, the tree of the knowledge of good and evil in the Garden of Eden, the fruit of the tree Satan persuaded Adam and Eve to eat, thereby precipitating sin into the world. Satan struck through a tree, and God countered with a tree." A familiar Lenten collect has captured this element of poetic justice in God's plan of salvation: "Who on the tree of the cross did give salvation unto mankind that, whence death arose, thence Life also might rise again; and that he who by a tree once overcame [Satan] might likewise by a tree be overcome, through Christ our Lord."

We humans, I guess, have always aspired to the heights. There are legitimate and illegitimate ways of attaining our aspirations. The endeavor to be "as gods" by scaling the tree of the knowledge of good and evil and eating its fruit represents one illegitimate way. Building the Tower of Babel represents another. But Jacob dreamed of a legitimate way, of a ladder reaching from earth to heaven and from heaven to earth and enabling us to communicate with God. Jacob's dream came true when Christ provided the tree of the cross. It destroyed Satan for us. And it opened up heaven for us, enabling us to communicate with God, making available to us all the treasures of Paradise. Jack and the

Beanstalk with its foolish colored beans transformed into a mighty beanstalk reminds us of this aspect of the Christian Gospel. Let us have the courage, the folly if you will, to invest in this foolishness. Our Lord once told this parable: "The kingdom of heaven is like unto a merchant man, seeking goodly pearls: Who, when he had found one pearl of great price, went and sold all that he had, and bought it." Let us be like that merchant. Or, in terms of the fairy tale, let us be like Jack in Jack and the Beanstalk.

Notes

1. See the first page of the Introduction to this book for a summary of these characteristics.
2. I have in my files sermons on the following additional fairy tales: Beauty and the Beast, Puss in Boots, The Little Red Hen, The Three Billy Goats Gruff, Rumpelstiltskin, Hansel and Gretel, Peter Rabbit, The Three Little Pigs, The Princess and the Pea, The Brave Little Tailor, Little Red Riding Hood, Cinderella, The Three Bears, and The Gingerbread Man.
3. Yet look at our Lord's allegorical methodology in one of these parables, that of The Weeds Among the Wheat in Matthew 13:24-30, 36-43.

Appendix

The central event of history called the Gospel event (the Son of God's incarnation, life, death, and resurrection for our salvation) has had such a profound impact on our world that it has spilled beyond the bounds chosen by God to convey it, namely the Holy Scriptures. As we have seen, that Gospel event has so influenced our culture so as to appear in non-biblical literature.

There are many other areas in our world impacted by the Gospel event. Echoes of it are a reality with which we live and which are obvious to those who "have eyes with which to see." An ordinary example is the division of our calendar into B. C. and A. D. Certainly, our mode of reckoning time (although of Christian origin and not exercised by every culture) is a powerful tribute to the impact of the birth of Jesus on human history. This phenomenal event has initiated and perpetuated a widespread practice of designating time.

Some lesser known areas of our world impacted by the Gospel event are presented and illustrated below.

The Gospel in Nature

The Seed Analogy

An interesting Gospel echo is the everyday process of plant growth, in which even the Bible itself sees analogy to human death and resurrection. In his famous resurrection chapter (1 Corinthians 15) Paul says (v. 36): "Fool, what you sow does not come to life unless it dies." Accustomed as we are to this everyday process of sowing and growing, isn't it actually amazing? Who would ever think that the way to produce new life would be to bury a seed in the ground, out of sight, and more or less forget about it? To all appearances that should be the end of the seed. But, surprisingly, it experiences a resurrection. Even though the seed decays, a little plant soon springs up, and a new and glorious life is begun. The point Paul makes is this: In the case of plant life, burial and decomposition precede the new life; they are prerequisites for it. In addition, the new life follows such burial and decomposition. In other words, if there's death, there's also resurrection.

St. Paul's illustration is rather fitting because what we do to a dead person is very much like what we do to a seed. We plant the corpse in the ground; we bury it out of sight and in the course of time forget about it. Eventually, it decays. But all this, strange as it may seem, is only a prerequisite for the new life. Who would ever think that the way to the heavenly life should be by means of confinement and nauseating decay in a six-foot deep plot of ground in a cemetery? To all appearances that's the end of it all. Yet the day will come when the body will rise and live more gloriously and abundantly than ever before. The resurrection follows the burial and decomposition. That's the way it works with a seed. That's the way it works with the human body.

The seed analogy, however, not only foreshadows; it reflects. It points not only to our future hope but also to the past event on which that hope rests. I refer to that climactic Gospel event, Christ's resurrection, that "first fruits" which is the promise of our own resurrection. Certainly, no seed ever fell into so cold and dark a soil as when the Son of God was removed from a Roman cross and placed into the tomb of Joseph of Arimathaea. Jesus is the prime exhibit of St. Paul's argument from the seed analogy. In fact, Jesus applied this analogy to his person and to his mission in John 12:24: "Unless a grain of wheat falls into the earth and dies, it remains just a single grain; but if it dies, it bears much fruit." Jesus was literally buried! He literally rose again! And the everyday process of sowing and growing is a reflection of this Gospel event so basic to our Christian hope.

The Caterpillar-Butterfly Clichè

Another phenomenon, so commonly regarded as a reflection of the death and resurrection aspect of the Gospel that it has become a cliché, is the process by which a caterpillar becomes a butterfly. The caterpillar's entrance into the dull and dreaded cocoon stage—dull and dreaded at least from a human perspective—is strikingly parallel to the Christian's confinement in a casket. But just as from the cocoon there emerges an exquisite, radiant butterfly, so from the casket there will emerge on Judgment Day that same Christian, only with a glorified body, better than ever before.

The Womb-Tomb Analogy

Similarly suggestive of death and resurrection is the origin of human and animal life in the womb—a crude, stifling, death-like phenomenon that is hardly more pleasant to think about than being buried in a cemetery. (Is it mere coincidence that in the English language "womb" rhymes with "tomb"?) None of us, now that we are enjoying life on earth, would regard that nine-month period as the whole meaning of life beyond which there is nothing more. By now we know better.

But suppose that during our prenatal life we had the capacity to think, to hope (or not hope). Further suppose that while in our mother's womb we got word that another life lay before us, a life that might last the incredibly long time of eighty or ninety years. The new world we would someday enter would contain light in which we could see things and vast reaches of space in which we could move around. It would contain towering skyscrapers, majestic mountains, queer-looking quadrupeds called animals, large plants called trees, four-wheeled vehicles moving at shocking speeds. Someday, we are assured, we would be able to do such impossible (and unimaginable) things as walk and talk. What's more, we wouldn't be alone in this world. There would be millions of other creatures similar to ourselves (and where could there possibly be room for them all?). Strangest of all would be the mode of entering this new world, a rather perilous process called birth, involving pain, danger, doctors, and hospitals, a process we would never guess could thrust us into such a beautiful life as we live at present.

What reaction might an unborn child have toward this talk of another and more abundant life (assuming that an unborn child can have reactions)? Despite the fact that the child couldn't possibly understand what earthly life would be like, he could still believe in it and look forward to it. Doing so would make his nine-month existence much more pleasant. Or he could be a realist, a cynic, and assume that the darkness and cramped quarters he lives in are the whole meaning of life and that beyond the dreaded process called birth there is no more. "All this talk about another life is wishful thinking, and one might better make the most of what one has."

Then comes the day—the day of birth. It turns out true, after all, ecstatically true. There is another life. You can live eighty or ninety years. There are such things as light and space and skyscrapers and mountains and animals and plants and fast-moving vehicles. You can walk and talk. And this dreaded process called birth, in spite of appearances, turns out, after all, to be the gateway to this new and wonderful world.

The possible Gospel parallel is obvious. Our present life is not the climax of life. It is but a stage in our journey. In relation to the heavenly life, we might speak of it as a prenatal stage. We have it on good word—God's Word—that there is another life, another world, ahead of us called heaven. In it we shall live unbelievably long—forever. It is a world without the limitations of space and time. Angels will share its mansions with us. We shall behold the face of God. In fact, we shall be like God. All the ills and inconveniences of this present life, chief of which is sin, will have vanished. Strangest of all, the mode of entering this world is a dreaded and painful process called death, a process involving undertakers, caskets, tombstones, and bodily decay, a process we would never guess could thrust us into such a beautiful life as the heavenly existence is.

Obviously, we cannot conceive of this life, no more than an unborn child can imagine life on earth. But we can believe in it and hope for it. We can join the apostle John in saying, "Beloved, we are God's children now; what we will be has not yet been revealed. What we do know is this: when he is revealed, we will be like him, for we will see him as he is" (1 John 3:2).

Nature's Principle of Vicariousness

I turn now from the death and resurrection Gospel pattern in nature to the Gospel pattern of vicariousness in nature. No one has put it better than C. S. Lewis in his classic work *Miracles: A Preliminary Study*. "Self sufficiency, living on one's own resources, is a thing impossible in [nature's] realm. Everything is indebted to everything else, sacrificed to everything else, dependent on everything else"[1] Lewis immediately concedes that the principle of vicariousness is not always necessarily good. Although the bees and the flowers live on one another in a manner acceptable to us, we may not approve of the way in which the hawk lives on the chicken. We frown on the parasite that sustains its life at the expense of its host's life. But we have no qualms about the unborn child that feeds on its mother. Even in social life vicariousness can provide a climate for exploitation and oppression. But, simultaneously, vicariousness also provides opportunity for kindness and gratitude. Vicariousness is "a fountain both of love and hatred, both of misery and happiness. When we have understood this we shall no longer think that the depraved examples of Vicariousness in Nature forbid us to suppose that the principle itself is of divine origin."[2]

The Gospel in Paganism

Pagan religious beliefs and practices, according to C. S. Lewis, can also echo—although often in a distorted way—aspects of the Gospel. At one point in *Miracles* Lewis takes up the issue of the considerable similarities between the Corn-King of paganism and the Christ of Christianity. Those similarities are no accident, he contends. After pointing out that the Corn-King is derived from the facts of nature and the facts of nature, in turn, derived from the Creator, Lewis asserts more specifically, "The Death and Rebirth pattern is in [nature] because it was first in Him."[3] Granted these similarities between paganism and Christianity, why then are both the Old and New Testaments of Scripture so silent about the elements of nature-religion? Lewis's answer: Because in these testaments "nature's original is manifesting itself."[4] Lewis continues, "Where the real God is present the shadows of that God do not appear; that which the shadows resembled does. The Hebrews throughout their history were being constantly headed off from the worship of Nature-gods; not because the Nature-gods were in all respects unlike the God of Nature but because, at best, they were merely like, and it was the destiny of that nation to be turned away from likenesses to the thing itself."[5] The frequency of counterfeits in pagan religions does not argue that everything, either in paganism or in Christianity, is counterfeit. The very word "counterfeit" has no meaning, in fact, unless there exists the real thing, the genuine article, for which the counterfeit is being a counterfeit.

The Gospel in Human Constructs

Curiously, there are even recent items of human manufacture that possibly reflect certain aspects of the Gospel. One such is the invention of the rocket. It could be argued that the modern day rocket is useful for other than scientific and military purposes in that it illustrates a profound Gospel truth. Many rockets go through multiple stages. At some point after the initial lift-off, the rocket, amoeba-like, divides. The one part may be left behind to disintegrate, while the other part enters a new trajectory and begins a new phase. This process may occur again at a later point. In some respects the Christian life resembles a multiple-phase rocket: The first phase is from conception to birth; the second phase is from birth to death; the third phase is from death into eternity. And just as there is a critical point in the progress of a rocket at which a certain phenomenon needs to occur if the rocket is to complete its mission successfully, so there is a critical point in the life of a human being at which a certain phenomenon needs to occur in order to attain the goal. At some time in the second phase (and the earlier the better), a human being needs to experience the phenomenon we call conversion. Having been born already, one needs to be "born again" (the urgent language in which John 3:3 [KJV] describes this critical stage. Having gotten bodily life, one needs to receive spiritual life as well, else the whole process sputters and fizzles out into eternal death. The success of the second and third phases depends one hundred percent upon the person at some point receiving Christ as Savior.

We Christians are now in the second phase of our multiple-phase existence. Each of us, by God's grace, has successfully undergone the critical phenomenon called conversion. "Beloved, we are of God's children now" (1 John 3:2). The thing to keep in mind, though, is that it is only the second phase. Another phase, the final one, still lies ahead. Glorious and significant as is this present phase, from womb to tomb, there is an even more glorious and significant phase ahead, a phase that staggers the imagination and with which nothing in this present mode of existence is worthy to be compared. I refer, of course, to heaven. Best of all, no part is left behind to disintegrate. The body, the capsule of the second phase, is recovered and restored. There is a resurrection.

Notes

1. C. S. Lewis, *Miracles: A Preliminary Study* (New York: The Macmillan Co., 1947), p.143.
2. Ibid.
3. Ibid, p. 140.
4. Ibid.
5. Ibid.

Francis C. Rossow

Dr. Francis C. Rossow has served as professor of practical theology at Concordia Seminary, St. Louis, Missouri, from 1976 until the present. Previously he was on the faculty of Concordia Senior College, Fort Wayne, Indiana, as professor of English and acting dean (1975-76). Ordained in North Dakota in 1948, he served as a parish pastor until 1959.

Dr. Rossow received his Litt.D. from Christ College, Irvine, California; his M.A. from Michigan State University, East Lansing, Michigan; his M.Div and B.A. from Concordia Seminary, St. Louis, Missouri.

He is the author of *Preaching the Creative Gospel Creatively* and *Gospel Handles: Finding New Connections in Biblical Texts*, as well as numerous articles and reviews. He edited *Lectionary Preaching Resources*, published by Concordia Publishing House.

Rossow has five adult children. He is married to Marilyn Rose Rossow.

www.ingramcontent.com/pod-product-compliance
Lightning Source LLC
Chambersburg PA
CBHW050317120526
44592CB00014B/1948